Sheffield Hallam University
Learning and Information Services
Adsetts Centre, City Campus
Sheffield S1 1WB

102 142 118 9

SHEFFIELD ... WITHDRAWN FROM STOCK

D0352768

Co... ...on
...gn

Fairchild Books
An imprint of Bloomsbury Publishing Plc

50 Bedford Square   1385 Broadway
London   New York
WC1B 3DP   NY 10018
UK   USA

www.bloomsbury.com

**FAIRCHILD BOOKS, BLOOMSBURY and the Diana
logo are trademarks of Bloomsbury Publishing Plc**

First published 2015

© Bloomsbury Publishing Plc, 2015

All rights reserved. No part of this publication
may be reproduced or transmitted in any form or
by any means, electronic or mechanical, including
photocopying, recording, or any information storage
or retrieval system, without prior permission in
writing from the publishers.

Derek Yates and Jessie Price have asserted their
rights under the Copyright, Designs and Patents Act,
1988, to be identified as authors of this work.

No responsibility for loss caused to any individual
or organization acting on or refraining from action
as a result of the material in this publication can
be accepted by Bloomsbury or the author.

British Library Cataloguing-in-Publication Data
A catalogue record for this book is available from
the British Library.

ISBN: PB: 978-1-4725-3440-8
ePDF: 978-1-4725-3167-4

Library of Congress Cataloging-in-Publication Data
Yates, Derek.
Communication Design/Derek Yates and Jessie Price
Pages cm.—(Required Reading Range)
Includes bibliographic references and index.
ISBN 978-1-4725-3440-8 (paperback)
1. Visual communication. 2. Graphic arts. I. Price,
Jessie (Graphic artist)
II. Title. P93.5.Y38 2015 74.6—dc23
2012045678

Design by Zoë Bather
Printed and bound in China

Design

Insights from the Creative Industries

Derek Yates & Jessie Price

Fairchild Books
An imprint of Bloomsbury Publishing Plc

B L O O M S B U R Y
LONDON · NEW DELHI · NEW YORK · SYDNEY

Navigation

Advocacy

Critique

Appendix

This is a book ab

make a differen

We don't do marketing or campaign —the best marketing is great user experience.
Mills, co-founder, ustwo

The UK design industry has grown since 2005, despite the recession. There are 232,000 designers, 29% more than in 2005 and earnings have increased by £3.4 billion.
The Design Council

50% of new jobs in the UK economy in 15 years time will be in the creative sector.
Christopher Frayling, quoting the UK Treasury

It is not about marketing, advertising, graphic, interaction, or even digital design—it's about all of these disciplines and the spaces that connect them. It's about a new generation of collaborative designers that are creating visual experiences that connect across media channels.

In a highly competitive global market, consumers are bombarded with messages. Producers, and indeed even governments, struggle to differentiate themselves within this barrage. At the same time, economists have realized that association and instinctive perception can radically alter the real-world value of a product or service. In today's markets perceived value provides a much more meaningful measure of what something is worth than the inherent values

derived from tangible evidence such as labor, engineering, or raw materials. In short, the way people feel about a product or service is what really influences what they are prepared to pay for it.

Within the complexity of this landscape, traditional techniques for shaping perception are being re-assessed. Established models for advertising and marketing are questioned, and there is a realization that we need to find new ways to engage an audience. We can no longer instruct and expect to be obeyed. Increasingly sophisticated consumers distrust obvious attempts to persuade, and a sales pitch is often rejected without consideration. In this world, an audience requires you to provide evidence of a claim,

can validate far more successfully than a broadcasted message.

Brands build interconnected strategies that explain values and provide proof that what they mean runs deeper than the tagline. In this way, a trust is built between brand and consumer that will influence future preferences. The success of brands like Apple and Nike is built on more than clever advertising—it comes from the coordination of marketing alongside great design. Designers are able to underpin a brand's communication with consumer experiences that demonstrate its values in tangible terms. They create compelling content and tell visual stories that bring a brand to life. Their ability to orchestrate experiences that enable

ut designers who

Don't blast messages—create compelling content!
Günther Schumacher, president and chief operating officer of OgilvyOne Worldwide

in the world.

Investing in design represents a 26% better return than banking and a 20% improvement over investing in computing.
The Singapore Trade Organization

There is a "black hole" or "cliff" that looms large for every design student.
Fred Deakin, co-founder of Airside

them a place at the top table in the businesses they work with. Not only can design provide the key to the creation of a successful brand, in the public sector it is seen as having the power to positively influence behavior. In May 2012, American business magazine *Forbes*, hailed a new "Era of Design" in which "design-oriented businesses are winning." Evidence from across the sector suggests that we are in a creative boom, especially in the UK, where the industry has grown by almost a third between 2005 and 2012.

These opportunities require designers with new skills. The ability to analyze, understand, clarify, and define is as important as the ability to visually style and aesthetically judge. These designers need to be able to collaborate across disciplines and not be restricted to particular

medias. By working in both the digital and physical environments, they are able to create narratives that frame zeitgeist and initiate culture. Maybe more importantly, in a world of dwindling natural resources, designers can influence attitudes that might help us value what we have and use it more wisely.

Unfortunately education has struggled to keep pace with these developments, and the new skill sets required are not always being addressed in a formal context. As a result, in the UK, while graduate unemployment increases, successful creative agencies are unable to fill vacancies. This situation has led some designers to question the economic sustainability of a subject like graphic design; others, such as Fred Deakin speaking at AltShift in April 2013,

talk of the "'black hole' or 'cliff' that looms large for every design student."

Communication Design: Insights from the Creative Industries aims to help graduates avoid this black hole by bridging the gap between education and emerging practices. In doing so it hopes to provide students and practitioners with the information they need to understand the new skill sets required. Organized into themes of Brand, Experience, Conversation, Participation, Navigation, Advocacy, and Critique, it explores the core principles that are shaping contemporary practice. Alongside case studies of game-changing projects, it uses analysis of the historical context and interviews with key thinkers and practitioners to provide a relevant and contemporary guide to the creative employment landscape.

Brand

Businesses have always used visual identities to differentiate themselves. Up until the beginning of the 20th century, artists were employed to create graphic representations of products or the people and processes that made them. These images were shaped by heritage and tradition rather than by creative decision making. In the 1920s, a new generation influenced by the Bauhaus sought to underpin their craft with thought and analysis. As a result, commercial artists began to communicate more abstract, intangible qualities. Slowly the discipline of design took shape, and visionaries such as Walter Landor began to realize its commercial potential. In 1941, he founded global brand consultancy Landor Associates, stating that "products are made in the factory, but brands are made in the mind." In the years that followed, brand identity became big business.

The influx of artists and designers from central Europe to the United States after World War II brought with them ideas that enabled a younger generation of creative talent to make a valuable contribution to the rapidly developing economy. Designers such as Paul Rand and Saul Bass created visual identities that defined how businesses were perceived, and as a result, were able to bring design into the boardroom. This was the age of corporate identity and businesses aspired to an image of authoritative efficiency, with designers using the template of European modernism to create clean, geometric visual identities that were systematically applied.

Today, brands are much more complex, and as a result, identities can no longer be defined through production-line consistency. The 21st-century business seeks to communicate an air of open humanity. It seeks trust by talking in a language that is relaxed, informal, and inclusive, but at the same time wants to bring its products and services to life as powerful, emotion-driven embodiments of desire. It uses design as a primary tool in the creation of these perceptions. As a result branding is one of the most rapidly expanding areas of the creative economy.

Systems

Corporate identities were applied using systems that enabled adaptations for different uses within a business.

A Trademark is a picture. It is a symbol, a sign, an emblem, an escutcheon, an image. A symbol of a corporation, a sign of the quality, a blend of form and content. Trademarks are animate, inanimate, organic, geometric. They are letters, ideograms, monograms, colours, things. They indicate, not represent but suggest, and are stated with brevity and wit.
Paul Rand

Visual identities help define a commercial proposition. After World War II, this practice evolved into a service industry. Modernist ideas influenced the design of "corporate identities" design, and businesses began to use abstraction to communicate their intangible values. Professionalism, efficiency, and trust were promoted through geometric symbols that allowed growing corporations to appear trustworthy and authoritative. This process is described by Michael Bierut in his brilliant "Helvetica period!" speech from the recent movie about the typeface. He tells the story of how in the 1960s U.S. businesses were persuaded to "scrape the crud" from their "dusty" and "homemade" identities to reveal an image of shining corporate modernity through the use of geometric logos and typefaces like Helvetica. This came to be known as "corporate identity design."

The best corporate identities were applied using systems that enabled adaptations for different uses within a business. At IBM, Paul Rand examined the creation of a trademark that could be applied according to a range of specifications to suit different purposes. He even created the iconic *Eye Bee M* rebus to demonstrate the flexibility of the mark. It is widely recognized that Rand made a massive contribution to persuading business that design was something that was worth investing in, and doing so, he created some of the world's most memorable trademarks, including Westinghouse, NeXT, Enron, and UPS.

Meanwhile, in Europe in 1963, graphic designers Ben Bos, Wim Crouwel, and Benno Wissing and product designer Friso Kramer established an agency that extended this approach across disciplines. This agency was called Total Design, and as a multidisciplinary design company, it was able to coordinate the implementation of an identity to every aspect of a business from the design of stationery, through to uniforms, vehicles, architecture, and interiors. Their systems offered professional consistency without being dull and uniform and were implemented using complex guideline documents. Total Design became the quality standard for corporate identity through the 1970s and into the 1980s. During this period, a system with a logo at its heart and supported by color and typeface specification became the accepted norm, but as we moved into the 1990s, businesses required a higher degree of flexibility. Guidelines became toolkits, and systems became more complex.

London-based agency Wolff Olins pioneered a more dynamic and adaptive approach for what was now called "brand" rather than "corporate identity." This approach can be seen in their work for the Tate, a family of successful art museums in the UK, where according to the Wolff Olins website, they "created a range of logos that move in and out of focus, suggesting the dynamic nature (of the institution)—always changing but always recognizable." This approach had more longevity because it provided options for adaptation and renewal. At the same time, another London-based studio, North, was creating identity systems for national institutions such as the RAC, the Barbican Centre, and the UK Land Registry that balanced commercial functionality with seductive contemporary styling. Intelligently applying the rigor of Swiss modernism

3

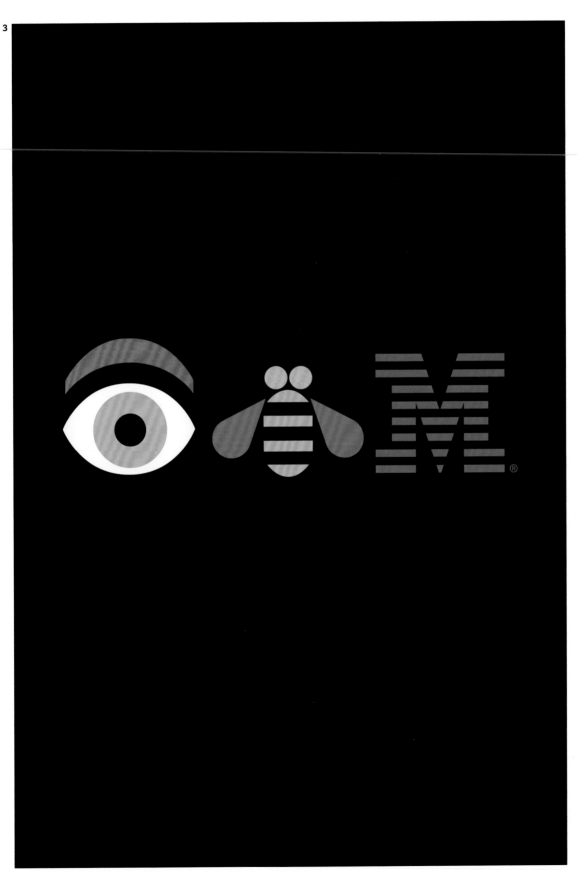

1 & 2. Visual identities like this one by Moving Brands for online graphic novel publishers Madefire help define a commercial proposition.

3. Paul Rand's iconic *Eye Bee M* is an example of his desire to evolve flexible, dynamic corporate identities.

4

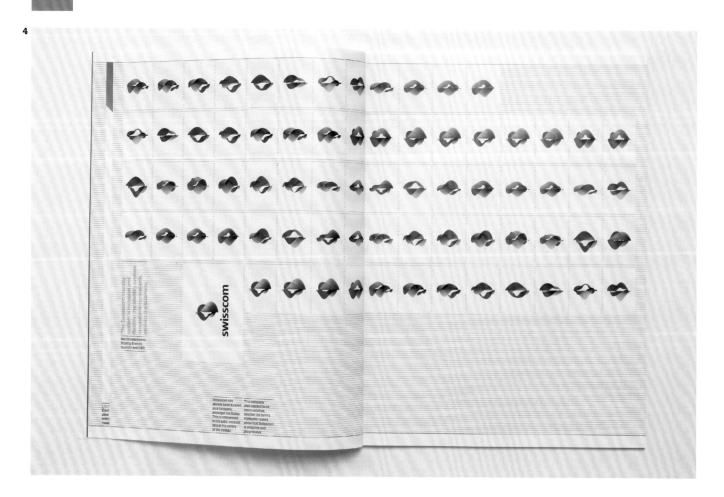

5

4 & 5. Today, identity systems like this one created for telecom giant Swisscom by Moving Brands need to evolve across multiple media touch points.

6. This Wolff Olins identity for the Tate family of museums in the UK was designed to be always "changing but always recognizable."

7. Part of the Moving Brands identity system for CX.

6

7

Most brands remained fixated on yesterday's problem—consistent reproduction across media. But today a brand must be alive to change, just like the people it wants to connect with and the business it is part of.
Moving Brands

to the complexity of a contemporary organization, they provided inspiration for a plethora of identities that were created during the UK's post-millennium boom.

Developments in new technology at this time meant that any identity system would need to incorporate motion-based options. So in 2001, North worked with a newly established digital studio to help them create graphic mark that was based on pulsing fiber-optic cables. This studio was called Moving Brands, and as its website states, it was set up to provide "creativity for a moving world." This strategy recognized that brands exist in a rapidly changing technology-driven environment. Moving Brands initially organized its work into four areas: motion, static, sonic, and responsive. Its work for technology-oriented brands such as Swisscom and CX demonstrates how to create brands that adapt and change according to context and media.

Consistently managing brand identities in this environment requires the utilization of a broader range of consistent variables within complex and fluid systems. Designers need to work with code as much as they work with typography. The power and flexibility of this approach can be seen in the identity that experimental technology studio Green Eyle recently designed for the MIT Media Lab. The media lab is renowned for its innovative interdisciplinary research, and Green Eyle set out to create an identity that reflected this reputation. To do this, the team produced a series of algorithms that enabled each student, teacher, or member of staff to generate their own unique rendition of a new logo. They could then create their own custom-made identity. Using code this system cleverly allows for richly individualized outcomes that are still consistent to an overall visual identity. As consumer culture develops, we will continue to demand that brands provide us with made-to-order options, so it seems likely that adaptive code-based identity systems will become more and more prevalent.

We believe that design should be about honesty— not about creating a veneer.

In Conversation

with Mason Wells,
founding partner,
Bibliothèque Design

Bibliothèque is one of the UK's most respected creative agencies. Founded in 2005 by Wells, Tim Beard, and Jonathon Jeffrey, it has been featured on the front of Creative Review magazine and has been commissioned by cultural institutions such as the Victoria & Albert Museum, the Barbican, and the British Council.

bibliothequedesign.com

Bibliothèque is one of the UK's most respected creative agencies. Founded in 2005 by Wells, Tim Beard, and Jonathon Jeffrey, the company has been featured on the front of *Creative Review* magazine and has been commissioned by cultural institutions such as the Victoria & Albert Museum, the Barbican, and the British Council.

Wells started his career at Cartlidge Levene, a studio known for sparing use of beautifully crafted sans serif typography and points of reference that include conceptual artists such as Laurence Weiner and Barnett Newman. He later joined former employees of Cartlidge Levene Sean Perkins and Simon Browning at North, which they had set up in 1995. In its early years, North began to apply a European sensibility to design for businesses increasingly aware of the importance of their visual perception.

One of the early projects that Wells worked on was an identity for the Royal Automobile Club (RAC). Looking back, he notes how up until this point, aside from Sean Perkins, the designers' experience within identity design was quite limited. They saw the RAC job as an opportunity to create something groundbreaking in this area. There was definitely an element of learning on the job and Wells talks about how the challenge of doing things for the first time gave them a real focus. What they eventually produced was an identity that positioned the RAC as an forward-thinking and technically efficient organization.

"The core element of the brief was about looking to the future—celebrating their heritage but looking forward to the next 100 years of motoring. At the time I had read a poignant comment by Peter Saville that spoke about the futuristic intent of the NASA logo (designed in 1975 by Richard Danne and Bruce Blackburn)—this really resonated with me as we worked on the identity."

Wells describes referring to identity programes from BMW and Lufthansa when creating the RAC guidelines—admiring their rational organization and systematic technical rigor. This almost scientific approach to identity (as the Germans refer to it, "Erscheinungsbild," or "appearance") had evolved from institutions like the HfG Ulm in Germany but had never really been appreciated in the UK. These reference points seemed to have inspired an incisive attention to detail in the way that North went on to specify its identity guidelines and are still present in the work at Bibliothèque. "We all spend time detailing things that often go unnoticed—as designers we have an obligation to do this."

The severity of North's early work starts to soften in the identity the agency produced for Telewest in 2002. The system is built from a mark that is an abstraction of fiber-optic technology and uses a Dalton Maag–designed rounded typeface to communicate a friendlier, more welcoming attitude. North also developed the fiber optic idea into motion-based assets to take advantage of developments in new technology.

Wells talks about how a new world of graphic expressions was opening up for brand identity at this time and how these opportunities have allowed Bibliothèque to apply the rigor of its design methodology to a much wider range of applications. This is particularly evident in Bibiothèque's spatial design work. Starting with small "below the line" projects with Adidas before progressing to a series of internationally acclaimed exhibitions, the studio has been able to build a substantial portfolio of three-dimensional spaces. From Dieter Rams at the Design Museum to Cold War Modern at the V&A and Le Corbusier at the Barbican, Bibliothèque creates spaces that are an expression of content with a ruthless eye for detail.

The agency's ability to develop core communication concepts across mediums and disciplines can be seen in projects like its presentation and promotion of the 2010 D&AD Awards ceremony and dinner. Working from a central idea that celebrated the decisive nature of judging—a yes or no answer—the team created marketing, environmental, and ambient executions that each gave the idea a new twist. The campaign culminated in a collaboration with pioneering technologists the Rumpus Room that allowed them to take the concept from a static typographic expression into an immersive video installation playing out across five stadium-sized screens in the Roundhouse in Camden, London.

Bibliothèque is also using new technologies in order to create more playful and immersive identities. A good example of this can be seen in the naming and visual identity for a new telecom brand providing high-speed Internet access to emerging markets—Ollo—which features a logo that can evolve and be adapted by the user through a touch screen.

Wells and Bibliothèque believe in design as a set of principles that have honesty and integrity at their heart. They are interested in producing work that has longevity and is conceptually appropriate. As Wells points out, "Of course we know people have a different relationship with brands now—and identities have evolved accordingly, but at the same time you cannot sweep 70 years of

design evolution under the carpet. Instead we should harness and build upon what we have learned from the past. Our preference is to foster long-term relationships with our clients as opposed to leaving a set of guidelines and walking away. That way the work evolves in tandem with changes in people's behavior and technology. We work with several organizations in this way." He creates a distinction between marketing and campaign-led graphic design and work that defines ideas and helps people gain understanding. He feels that there is still a place for businesses to communicate an ideology—to stand for something—and that design has a role in helping them do this.

There is idealism in what Bibliothèque stands for. They have principles and care about doing things in the right way. As Wells says, "In this studio we believe that timeless things matter, we are not interested in throwaway. We do not believe in transience. Things matter more when they are constructed correctly and with meaning."

It can be amazingly liberating to be systematic—to have a set of restrictions and to make them work for you.
Mason Wells

1–4. Examples from the Ollo identity guidelines.

5. The Ollo multi-touch responsive logo in action.

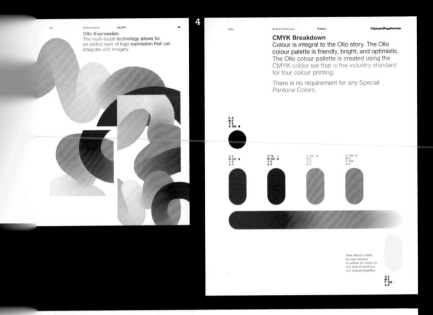

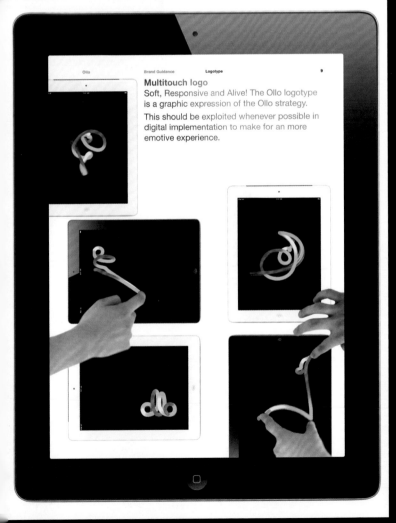

Case Study: Ollo

Bibliothèque named and created the visual identity and strategy for a new telecom brand providing high-speed Internet access to emerging markets. The concept for the brand Ollo defines a line of communication connecting communities. The logo is the first to exploit the new multitouch hardware of smartphones and tablets. It utilizes custom software to allow manipulation of the logo to become a creative tool in building its visual language.

"We wanted to put stake in the ground here and do something that nobody else has done. We wanted to do a logo that would really take advantage of the touch screen. A logo that could be genuinely manipulated but still be recognizable and hold true to the core values of the identity."

The responsive logo was not a requirement of the job, but Bibiothèque invested in the development of the technology that powered it so that they could demonstrate its potential to the client. "At the presentation, the client actually experienced it [the way] we wanted the end user to experience it."

This project demonstrates that although Bibliothèque has a connection with the heritage of graphic design, it does not mean it is looking back into the past. At the core of the modernist principles Bibliothèque admires is a desire to utilize new technology to redefine your world—this desire can be seen very clearly in a project like Ollo.

bibliothequedesign.com/projects/branding/ollo/

Strategy

As the nature of brands has changed within our economy, a designer's ability to analyze, understand, and clarify has become ever more important.

What we once charged for, we now give away and what we once gave away, we now charge for.
James Bull, co-founder of Moving Brands

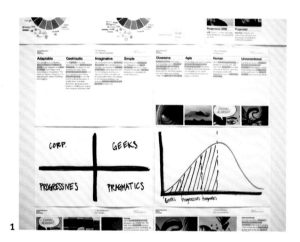

1

1. An example of the process that studios such as Moving Brands use to clarify, name, and define.

The success of a piece of communication has always been dependent on a connection between content, form, audience, and context—what the message is, who it's aimed at, what it looks like, and how and where it's communicated. In recent years, the balance between these elements has shifted. Communication designers have traditionally offered style and packaging solutions for brands and products. However, as the nature of brands has changed within our economy, a designer's ability to analyze and understand has become ever more important. Dutch editor and design critic, Max Bruinsma pointed out as far back as 1997 in his article for *Eye 25*, "Learning to Read and Write Images," that "analyzing and criticizing form with respect to content becomes all the more urgent at a time when forms and contents and media seem to be floating around in a primordial soup of possible contexts and meanings." Bruinsma calls for designers to be involved in the "whole trajectory of a communication product."

Desktop publishing means that the tools of graphic design styling are available to everyone: as a result it no longer has the same financial value. At the AltShift design conference in 2012, Russell Holmes, creative strategy partner at London-based studio ico, pointed out, "The challenge now is to create compelling communication in a world where anyone can design." In this world, the thinking behind a communication outcome is much more significant to the income of a creative agency, and designers are often employed to help a client understand what sort of design they need, rather than style what they think they want. Processes of definition, clarification, and naming are fundamental to a designer's craft and are today every bit as important as layout, typography, and art direction.

The process that underpins a design solution is now much more important, and contemporary creative agencies structure this process very deliberately to incorporate the input of the client. Russell Holmes describes how ico

SEARCH: Max Bruinsma "Learning to Read and Write Images"; James Bull/ Moving Brands; ico Design Benugo; Bear Design Foxtons; Russell Holmes ico Design; Steven Heller "What Do We Call Ourselves?"

2

2–4. ico's redefinition of Benugo's visual identity is designed to reflect insights that were gained through client research. As a result, posters and signage enhance the customer experience and explain key elements of the business proposition.

worked with the management and staff of high-street food brand Benugo when redefining its visual identity.

"We went round to all their locations; we talked to managers, we talked to baristas; we talked to people behind the till; we talked to all the key stakeholders around the business, including the board, and interviewed them individually. We asked lots of questions: about how the visual brand worked, what they thought they could do better and things that were already working really well. Also the way that they interacted with customers, what it was about the stores that appealed and what about the stores could work better, etc., etc. . . . At the end of this process we put everything together and went though it all and our findings helped us frame our creative response.

The important thing is that the team isn't just the creative agency—it's also the key stakeholders. There needs to be buy-in from those guys, they need to say yes, we believe that this is right for us."

Detailed analysis and inquiry enable a designer to organize and clarify a complex business or communication problem and to put together a proposition that can then be articulated in ways that will elicit empathy and understanding in the consumer. This is where the real economic value of contemporary communication design lies and as a result both evidencing creative thinking and explaining its significance are now vital to an agency's survival. As James Bull, founder of Moving Brands, said in a recent lecture, "We are what we document. If you didn't document it, you might as well have not done it."

3

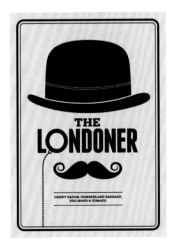

4

Case Study:
Bear—the Foxtons Mini

The importance of the thinking behind the making can be clearly seen in the contribution that London-based creative agency Bear has made in helping Foxtons become London's leading property agents. Bear was initially brought in to brand Foxtons' fleet cars, but creative director Roberto D'Andria soon realized that their decisions could have a deeper significance.

In a conversation with the author from the summer of 2013, D'Andria noted, "Looking at their marketing strategy, we saw that they described themselves as 'London's estate agents' and we suggested that they allow us to help them become 'THE estate agent for Londoners', by using this as the key proposition for all of their communication materials."

From this central concept, Bear put together a rationale for using the recently relaunched Mini Cooper as the Foxtons fleet car to take advantage of its iconic link to London. As a result it created the Team Foxtons Mini, with numbered cars and custom liveries designed to reflect the personalities of the areas around individual Foxtons' offices. The success of this approach led to Bear being appointed as Foxtons' sole creative agency in 2001. Since then, Bear's ideas have helped elevate Foxtons from also-rans to best of breed. The business was sold for £390 million in 2007 and continues to dominate the London property market.

D'Andria believes that "the only way for a small independent agency (or any agency for that matter) to survive in today's economic climate is to establish ongoing relationships with their clients." These relationships

develop out of an ability to understand and provide insight into the nature of the client's business. D'Andria also points out that if an agency ties itself to a particular visual style, specific processes, or a narrow range of production techniques, it will be limiting their potential commissions.

Bear works with a range of specialists to implement each individual client's vision and will utilize any appropriate output—from high-end fashion photography, to motion-captured animation, or letterpress typography. The most recent Foxtons' Mini is a confident and playful comment on the transparency of its client's business transactions and features an X-ray of a whole car with the driver in it. This provided a huge production conundrum—one that could only be solved by taking a Mini apart section by section and individually X-raying each piece in photographer Nick Veasey's concrete bunker. The outcome was Foxtons' most popular Mini and their continued belief in Bear's creative vision.

bearlondon.com/work/foxtons-brand

1. Foxtons' use of design, particularly in relation to the customer experience, has made them London's leading property agents.

2–4. Examples of the individual Team Foxton liveries applied to individual Minis.

5. The X-ray Mini as it appeared on the street.

6–8. The original Nick Veasey x-rays.

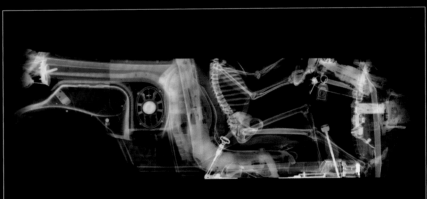

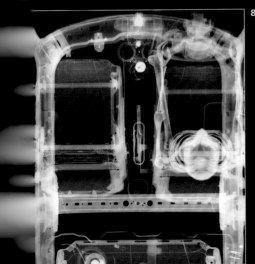

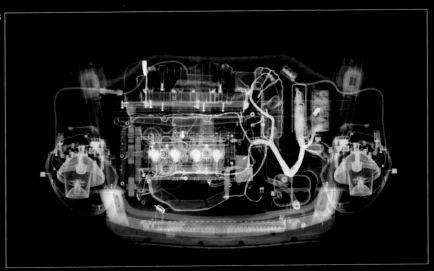

A lot of design is about problem solving, but it's more interesting to create opportunities.

In Conversation

with Mat Heinl, CEO, Moving Brands

Moving Brands is an independent global creative company. It work in partnership with some of the best companies in the world, defining and articulating their stories, building systems, and designing and producing emotive experiences. Moving Brands' clients include Nokia, Swisscom, Hitachi, Infosys, and Hewlett Packard.

movingbrands.com

Moving Brands is defined by a set of core thoughts and attitudes. Mat Heinl began our conversation by trying to define them. The first is the power of a team.

"We are in a team business: as a result everybody who works for us needs to be able to understand this. Our business is inherently multidisciplinary, inherently complex, and inherently involves lots of people who are not from the design industry. . . . We need people [who] are able to move from an individual mentality to a group mentality. Our business is built around the capabilities of the team. And it is the different qualities of each member of the team that come together to solve a problem."

Heinl highlights a desire to build narratives around the brands Moving Brands work with. This interest in storytelling can be traced back to the filmmaking backgrounds of the company's original founders. There is also what he calls a "slightly obsessive desire" to exploit the latest technology. From the beginning they have had an insatiable curiosity to find out how things work and how to use them to do new things.

Moving Brands is "not wedded to accepted norms"—it is actually suspicious of these norms. Its project teams have no desire "to be framed by their capabilities" and instead see each task as an opportunity to extend these capabilities. "We try to look at a [project] brief a bit differently and drill down into what the client is really trying to achieve, then having established this—we bring the talent we have in the studio to bear in the delivery of this objective."

Heinl has a deeply held belief in the importance of quality. Several times in our conversation, he talked about not letting something leave the studio until it had reached a certain standard. Many other digital agencies talk about a minimum viable product and seeking to perfect in the marketplace, but Moving Brands has a visual rigor that we might trace back to its early collaborations with print-led studios like North and Bibliothèque. Heinl points out that "there is an

honor in going for perfection. This is inherent in the characters within our studio. There is a sense of wanting to get something right and being prepared to stay until it is."

This is not altruism but business sense. Moving Brands offers a premium service, and the quality of its work enables them to market itself as doing so. As with any digital agency, Moving Brands also recognizes the need "to ship," to get work out and perfect through user input, but at the point that this process starts, the standard is probably is a little higher than at some other digital agencies.

As a start-up studio, Moving Brands defined its practice in different types of experience: static, moving, responsive, and sonic. This helped create a proposition that related to a new way of thinking about brands. Now this experiential approach is inherent to how everyone has to think. These ideas now no longer differentiate them in the marketplace. Using experiential technology simply helps you create identities that are fit for purpose.

Heinl says, "Media-responsive systems are now simply more cost-effective because they have a longer life. Sooner or later a system will need to address a range of new touch points and this is something that has always been part of the Moving Brands offer. It has value in terms of the economics of profit and loss. So while we might get excited about it the visual richness that these options add—to a businessman they just make sound economic sense."

This ability to look at a project from a business perspective is something that is built into the way Moving Brands works. Every project employs both a business and a creative lead with input at every stage of a project. Heinl stresses the need for a balanced perspective to avoid only looking through a design lens. "A lot of agencies try to design their way through every problem—but a lot of problems have nothing to do with design; they are to do with commerce, with people's careers or the power relationships within an organization. These factors might be what created the need for the project in the first place and we try to be sensitive to this fact."

Every project begins with a proactive conversation with the client. "The point of the brief is not to say thank you very much and then go away into a pit, make something amazing, and hand it back to them. The point is to ask why the brief was written in the first place."

As do many agencies, Moving Brands structures the design process in stages:

1. Assess
2. Define
3. Create
4. Thrive

Initially, this process works like a waterfall, with insights at the assessment stage leading exploration at the definition stage. However, once they have moved into the definition stage, the whole process becomes more agile and the team then uses its expertise to move back and forward through the process, creating prototypes that are tested with the user.

As well as solving problems, the team is looking for creative opportunities. "A lot of design is about problem solving, but more interesting for me is opportunity creation," Heinl says. By this he means identifying the things a company can do to extend its business, such as developing new products and services. "Let's look at creating the thing that does that thing.

"People think we are in the business of changing perception, but the design industry is about so much more that. It's about making things safer, making things cheaper, or just simply making things work better."

Moving Brands defines the success of a project by how "correct" it is to what a client is trying to achieve. This idea of correctness is not just about function, satisfaction, or service—it's also about feeling right for the brand, i.e., its character, attitude, and principles. Heinl deliberately uses the word "correct" instead of "appropriate." Correct is stronger and more incisive and as a result feels much closer to what Moving Brands stands for.

This approach makes Moving Brands' work extremely hard to pigeonhole. "If somebody sees that you have done a really high-tech responsive environment for somebody like Infosys and they also see that you've created a really traditional brand for Norton & Sons and both are completely correct—then this is really exciting."

The openness and complexity of Moving Brands' approach provides a very particular set of challenges and a special type of a designer. Its leaders have set up a culture of high achievement—of people who relish a new challenge with every project. As Heinl points out, "To work at Moving Brands you need to give a shit; you need to work hard and you need to give of yourself. There is no sitting around and being quiet if you've got an opinion—you need to state it at any level. You need to be prepared to stand apart and have your own position."

Case Study: iO

iO is an example of "a thing that does that thing."

Moving Brands has engineered a long-term partnership with the telecommunications giant SwissCom after designing its corporate identity in 2007. From the start, Moving Brands sought to move beyond the traditional branding agency model of guideline creation for third-party implementation. Instead, its leaders and team members see themselves as stewards in an ongoing and evolving interpretation of their original brand definition. iO is the latest step in this process.

It started with a piece of in-house software that Moving Brands identified as having commercial potential. Recognizing a creative opportunity, it worked with Swisscom to develop and evolve it into the SwissCom brand. It is a great example of what Mat Heinl sees as a key area of future development—the symbiotic evolution of products alongside the brands that created them. iO Illustrates the studio's desire to connect brand identity and product development to help evolve an ecosystem of touch points that seamlessly define a brand experience.

In the short term, iO is an application that delivers free calls, chats, and messages to SwissCom customers, but it is envisioned that, with Moving Brands' help, it will become much more. It is engaged with both product and brand development—shaping what iO does and helping it feed into the definition (and re-definition) of the visual identity through a website, brand films, photographic treatment, guidelines, messaging, and launch campaigns.

movingbrands.com/work/keeping-your-world-simple-secure-and-close

3

Examples of adding brightness

Button within iPhone application
highlighting on press

4

5

1. Poster describing the iO identity guidelines.

2. Initial ideas for the iO mark.

3–5. Wire frames and other visuals designed to define the iO user experience.

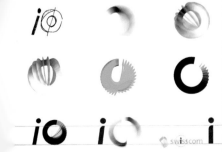

Ecosystems

Coherence is now more important than consistency.

Until the late 1970s, businesses sought trust through authority, and their identities reflected this attitude. They used serious typography and abstract symbols to communicate neutrality and corporate efficiency. Then came MTV—an identity that was not only irreverent but alive—changing and adapting according to context. Designer Frank Olinski and the team at Manhattan Design refused to provide guidelines for color or background for their distinctive logotype; instead they allowed animators and designers to re-interpret it according to context. Suddenly a brand could have a complex multifaceted personality.

The growth of the Internet provided opportunities for brands to enter into a conversation with their audience and the dot.com start-ups of the late 1990s were ideally placed to explore identities that responded to this opportunity. The best known example is probably the search engine Google, which, after its launch in 1998, created multiple logo iterations called "Google Doodles" that respond to the date and time they are displayed. Technology offered opportunities for brands to be more adaptive, and more established brands such as Sony also took advantage of this opportunity. In 2000, working with Tomato, it created the "connected identity" enabling users to download a custom identity from an ever-evolving set of graphic variables.

Technology provided new ways of presenting the identity of a company, but ideas were developing that went beyond presentation and examined how the perception of a business might be influenced by experience. In 2003, Wally Olins, one of the founders of UK brand consultants Wolff Olins, published *On Brand*, setting out the ground rules for what was now called "branding" rather than "corporate identity." Olins's approach was sociological and anthropological as well as commercial, and he stressed the need for business to understand all of the different factors that influence its perception. At the same time, Mark Gobé (who had famously said in the 1980s, "People love brands, but brands don't love people back.") published *Emotional Branding*, in which he called for brands to understand marketing through the eyes of an audience and communicate with them on an emotional level. For both Olins and Gobé, design had a fundamental role in this new world of brand creation, and over the next decade they used it to establish a wealth of new economic opportunities for their agencies Wolff Olins and Emotional Branding LLC.

The logic of corporate identity arranges visual elements within a system of specifications and guidelines that aim to provide consistent reproduction across different media. Branding is more human and aims to communicate complex attitudes or values through a series of coherently designed touch points. New technology enables the creation of an endless array of brand-related experiences, and linking these experiences together requires complex strategic thinking. The traditional mechanism for this is a logo, but some industry figures have questioned our continued reliance on this approach. According to Simon Manchipp (see pp. 31–33), designers and clients love logos, but consumers want something more dynamic. He advocates the creation of a "brand

SEARCH: Red Bull brand; Google doodles; Mark Gobé "Emotional branding"; Adrian Ho Zeus Jones; Gary Holt O2; Frank Olinski/ MTV; Wally Olins "On Brand"; Wolff Olins; Simon Manchipp; Design Studio/ Nokia/ Uusi; Simon Waterfall

3

4

A strong brand is not just a visual identity, it is the credo of the company.
Russell Holmes, strategy director, ico Design

1 & 2. Google presents an ever-changing interpretation of its logotype. These doodles reflect the nature of their business and enable the identity to remain fresh and alive when viewed millions of times a day in almost every country in the world.

3–5. Examples of the O2 visual identity in use and evolving through combinations of water, bubbles, the night sky, and neon tubes.

5

6–8. The Red Bull brand is brought to life by the participants in the activities it sponsors.

6. The French B-Boys—Chakal, Tim, and Francklyn— "representing" the day before Red Bull BC One Western European Final at Piazza Plebiscito, Naples, Italy, 2013.

8. The winner from the Summer X Games Los Angeles, 2013, Tyson Bowerbank.

world" and points to the success of brands like O2 as proof. Since its transformation from BT Cellnet in 2002, O2 has built a complex visual landscape from a very simple idea— essentially bubbles in water. This idea has inspired the evolution of a surreal world of photography, sound, color, and movement. If you removed the O2 logo, we would still connect to the brand.

Along with many industry thinkers, Russell Holmes, creative strategy partner at London-based studio ico, believes that these ideas are giving brands a new place within contemporary culture. As he noted in a conversation with the author, "In the 1970s and '80s, designers were largely packagers of culture. They came in at the end and applied a badge. Now brands create popular culture, and they employ designers to be part of this process." This culture will develop out of and be defined by a set of principles and values rather than a set of identity guidelines. Elements of an identity will give clues to its source, but the form will be far more open to an interpretation of the personality of the brand. Brands are able to develop ecosystems where partners with similar values link their activities to feed from the same culture.

As a result, how each brand communicates its values is extremely important, as is the part creative agencies play in helping them do this. They are employed to create internal as well as external communication that bring the values of a brand to life. Sometimes this might include the creation of documentary films

6

or publications that help align the brand to aspects of contemporary culture. To help define the attitude of global technology giant Nokia, DesignStudio created a series of short films that explore the idea of everyday adventure. Sending a series of documentary filmmakers to explore the alternative culture in cities like Shanghai or Istanbul, it sought to connect the brand to innovative culturally diverse youth cultures. The agency has also been involved in the design and production of Nokia's brand magazine, *Uusi*, which explores similar ideas through photography, illustration, and creative journalism.

Red Bull

Probably the most notable example of a brand that has successfully built a cultural ecosystem around itself is Red Bull. It produces little traditional advertising, choosing instead to develop initiatives that "give wings to people and ideas," such as Red Bull Music Academy, Danny MacAskill's Imaginate, Red Bull Flugtag, and Felix Baumgartner's Red Bull Stratos mission. In alternative sports such as skateboarding, BMX, and mountain biking, as well as cultural events, Red Bull supports the most exciting and interesting practitioners. Not only does it have the world's most popular energy drink, but it's established an independent media company—Red Bull Media House—that produces, publishes, distributes, and licenses sport, culture, entertainment, and educational programming across the full spectrum of platforms to global media such as NBC, Discovery Channel, N24, Globosat, and BT Sports.

Red Bull lives the "brand as action" maxim, and many within the industry, such as Adrian Ho, strategist and founding partner of Zeus Jones, see it as a "mentor brand." He describes three reasons for this:

1. Its content business is on track to become larger than its drinks business. As a result, the things that it has traditionally done to raise awareness of its product are on track to generate more income than the drinks themselves.
2. It has carved the position for itself in the global sports market. Up until that point you would have assumed that this was impossible because Nike owned sports.
3. It doesn't leech off of culture. Rather it finds early nascent examples such as extreme sports culture and seeks to develop this culture collaboratively. It does this in a sympathetic and nurturing way so that the members of that culture align themselves with the brand.

7

8

Logos are what designers want to create, not what the public wants to see.

In Conversation

with Simon Manchipp,
founding partner,
SomeOne

Simon Manchipp is one of the founding partners of London-based creative agency, SomeOne, whose clients include O2, Eurostar, the 2012 Olympics, Sky Sports, and Accenture. Manchipp is famous for suggesting that the logo is dead and he is a regular speaker at design conferences around Europe. He enthusiastically advocates that designers embrace more flexible and responsive approaches to brand identity.

someoneinlondon.com

Manchipp started off by talking about how our relationship with brands has changed.

"We have moved from reverence to reference. We trusted what brands told us, but now we reference this against what people are saying on Trip Advisor or Facebook. We have shifted from trusting brands to trusting people." Brands need to communicate with people on their level; they needed to invite them in and create a world that they want to be part of. This means creating culture.

"Clients are often programmed into buying a logo and a set of guidelines. They are not programmed to buy culture . . . but the thing is, there is little to interest the public in a consistently applied logo, a set of colors, and a typeface—it does not make financial sense to invest in the surface. Sooner or later, clients realize that they need more."

To overcome this problem, designers need to be able to explain their ideas on their clients' terms. They need to be able to reassure clients who are inherently terrified of creativity. Creativity is all risk—and business is all risk averse.

Manchipp reminds us, "It's not what you say it is—it's what Google says it is. When we first meet a client, we often get them to type the name of their brand into Google or Twitter to see what comes up. If they don't like what they see, then we talk about how we can help them change it, [which] generally involves a lot more than tweaking a logo. . . . Via a rebrand, they will sometimes get a new typeface, a new logo, and a refreshed color system—but these days that's not enough because we are in such a multichannel culture. . . . So we advise them that we will also need to create a broader set of assets to connect the many channels together. It may cost a little more, but it will last considerably longer and will connect with audiences more deeply. What's not to love! . . . Many start skeptical, but gradually, as we work with them, they start to realize the advantages.

"There is a reason why the creative industries are outperforming the finance sector, for example. There is a reason why we are

generating more value and hiring more people. And this is due to the fact we make brands and the owners of those brands very rich—we provide a competitive advantage."

Manchipp was part of the team that created the Meerkats for comparison website Compare the Market, and the benefits that this campaign has had for the business is there for all to see.

Unlike some designers, Manchipp feels that the ability that the Internet provides to get public feedback on one's work is a positive thing.

"The old way of doing things would be to pay a lot of money for a logo, spend a year crafting it, and be wedded to revering it. You no longer need to do this, you can publish the things you do, you can get feedback, and you can gauge the reaction to understand how people feel. If you provide your client with adaptive systems, this means you can take the feedback on board to give your client more of what they want and less of what they don't."

He points out that the reaction to visual work is not always logical, and sometimes the only way to understand the way people feel about something is to ask them. "Ideas and artistic justification are one thing, but the emotional response to something doesn't always work to the same logic."

Manchipp also feels that there has never been a better time to be a graphic designer.

"Graphic design does what other things cannot do and more importantly has become a bolt on to other sexier, more easily quantifiable stuff, for example digital—this is the one thing that everyone wants—but for digital to really work it needs charming, entertaining, involving, and inventive graphic design—the two things together make the experience and the brand identity more powerful."

He believes that the success of digital creativity lies in a much more collaborative approach to design as a whole. "Digital has to collaborate. And as you remove the walls and start to collaborate people realize that the product improves exponentially, that you have more fun, that you relax, and above that no one has to be an auteur—you don't have to do it all yourself. . . . Great work comes from teamwork—Richard Rogers says that no architecture can be achieved by a single person: it's too complex. The same can be said of creating a brand. We see every client we work with as a collaborator. At Eurostar, I almost had a desk in their head office I was there so often. I wanted to understand their culture, to go socializing with them, to attend their meetings, and to find out how they approached things that were not related to design. The insights that I drew from these observations were what we built our design work around. The best part of design is that you get to find out about lots of different businesses and lots of different areas of practice."

"A designer can very rapidly become the most interesting person at any dinner party because they've worked with so many different companies." Good designers should be interesting people, they should read weird books, and they should do things that are outside the mainstream to avoid creating a cultural echo chamber.

Unlike some bigger consultancies, SomeOne believes that designers should be client facing. They do not see the value in a third party who manages the client relationship. They also believe that designers should be involved in creating the conceptual direction for a project.

"At SomeOne we have [a] 90/10 split between designers and non-designers. Of the 30 to 35 people [who] work here, we have five or maybe six project managers—the rest are designers. We do not have traditional strategists. The most senior designers are strategists, and all of the designers are strategically led. This is because we believe that if you have worked in design for long enough and you're actively involved in business change, you can add considerable value strategically. . . . Designers are known to be very good with pictures. But the best ones are also really good with ideas." Manchipp believes that designers should be able to think beyond the surface.

"I am interested in designers who have an intellectual position," in designers who make a contribution to the debate around the subject.

"The best brands put design in the boardroom and they respect it. As soon as design becomes seen as an asset and not a cost, it becomes boardroom worthy. When a designer gets involved in a project intelligently and can be articulate enough to talk to the CEO in a reassuring and encouraging manner, he has the ability to move mountains."

Simon Manchipp's ten principles to creating engaging brand communication:

1. Be coherent, not just consistent.
2. Create more than a logo.
3. Brand without badging.
4. Bring charm to charmless categories.
5. Create ownable moments.
6. Remove clients' fear.
7. Weird stuff works for brands.
8. Curate choice.
9. Create assets, not costs.
10. Finally, always remember we are not in the design business— we are in the people business.

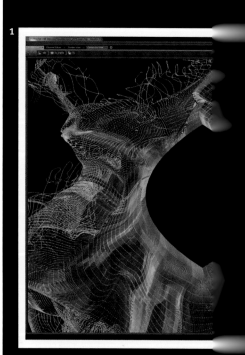

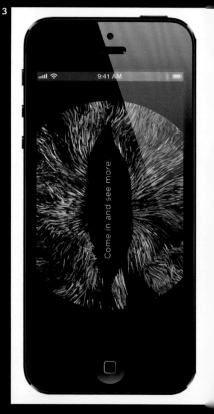

1. Generative wireframes created by Field.

2. Examples of some of the iterations of the iris created for the project.

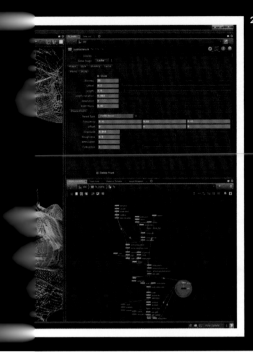

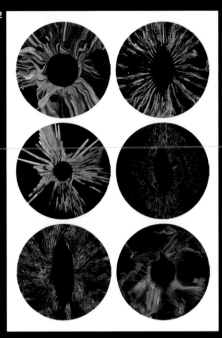

2

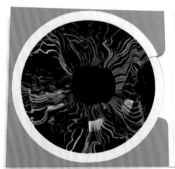

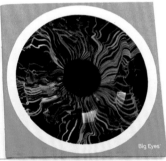

Case Study: Big Eyes

SomeOne was asked to brand a start-up advertising agency, originally called "Monster." After some initial research, which included drawings of monster eyes by Simon Manchipp's five-year-old son, they started to explore the patterns held within the iris. Using the child's drawings for inspiration, they approached generative designers, Field, to create "something innovative and daring using eyes as a metaphor." In response, they developed a "metaphorical representation of the iris in a 3D environment." The digital iris design emulates the muscular construction of biological eyes, creating unique designs for each context and application. They can mirror visiting clients and be activated by data. This generative system provides a flexible source of imagery that remains visually coherent across its media iteration. Using this, SomeOne has created a brand world that manages to balance a consistent tone of voice with a visual dynamism that gives the brand a life beyond well its launch.

someoneinlondon.com/category/projects/data-powered-branding-big-eyes

3–5. The Big Eyes visual identity applied to a website, specially created vinyl album, and promotional bags.

Authenticity

Brands seek to create a sense of honesty, transparency, and a connection to how something is made.

Over the last decade there has been a backlash against the digitization of the design process. Working on a computer provides the opportunity to endlessly correct a piece of communication, and this process inevitably leads to a visual perfecting than can leave work feeling sanitized and impersonal. In the eyes of the public, perfectly contrived digital slickness can be the signifier of the faceless corporation. As a result, brands are seeking to distance themselves from it. There is desire among designers to achieve a sense of "authenticity"—of honesty, transparency, and a connection to how something is made.

Brands are careful not to talk to us in a voice that feels too authoritative and aloof. Instead they strive to appear friendly and humane. To compliment this tone, rounded sans serif typography and hand-rendered letterforms are the order of the day. When asked to redefine the visual voice of the Macmillan Cancer charity, Wolff Olins created an awkward hand-rendered font to deliver messages in the first person, stressing that "WE are Macmillan."

Good writing is essential to the success of these strategies, and few brands have been able to create copy that is as down to earth as Innocent Smoothies. Their drinks are brought to you by "the makers of trees and stuff!" or "from a product range that includes the Brecon Beacons," and their seasonal range includes "the perfect smoothie for a summer season of flip flops, freckles, and rained off barbeques."

1. Examples of Wolff Olins' award-winning identity for Macmillan Cancer support applied to information leaflets.

2. Letterheads carrying the hand-drawn logotype of the Lyric Theatre in Hammersmith, created by Multistorey.

3. The Lyric identity applied to communication aimed at children.

SEARCH: Blu animation; David Crow; *Eye 70* "Digital Craft"; *Eye 70* "Make it Real"; Michel Gondry; Chrissie Macdonald; Multistorey/ Lyric Theatre; Ann Odling Smee "New Handmade Graphics"; Wolff Olins/ Macmillan; Innocent smoothies; Job Wouters ABCDEFGH…

Multistorey's rebrand of the Lyric Theatre in West London is a good example of something that communicates an informal honesty. Harry Woodrow and his team have created a unique visual personality for the theatre by utilizing "a handwritten system to become both the signature logo and the general voice of its presentations.' As their website points out, "The idiosyncrasies inherent in the mark-making of spontaneous handwriting are key to reflecting the personality of the Lyric." Evidencing the hand of the maker in a piece of communication provides a connection for the audience. It also helps us more easily understand the work that went into its making.

In a world where the computer takes much of the effort out of the creative process, something that has been made with obvious care and effort engenders a certain respect. Much has been written in the design press about the resurgence of traditional craft skills, and brands have been quick to utilize its power. This is evident in the popularity of the calligraphy of Job Wouters or the handmade constructions of Chrissie Macdonald. In the world of animation, it can be seen in the popularity of stop-motion animators such as Blu. This phenomenon is more than a style driven trend and is not limited to the analogue world: In *Eye 70*, David Crow draws attention to the craft involved in digital design. He points out that, "Craft is so often described as a practice surrounding a specific set of materials. But in truth it is less the material that defines the practice as the process of play, experiment, adjustment, individual judgment, and love of the material." These qualities can be part of the digital creative process. Matt Rice, founding partner of digital agency Sennep, echoes this sentiment: "The best apps are the ones that feel like all the team that produced them care and have put some love into them. You can feel it in the extra non-essential details they have added. Little personal touches that evidence that the developers have really thought about the experience of the user."

4 & 5. Multistorey's hand-rendered typography applied to a series of promotional posters.

5

Orange, I Am by Chrissie Macdonald with photography by John Short

Very soon after graduating in illustration from Brighton University, Chrissie Macdonald went to see an art buyer at the advertising agency Fallon with her portfolio. A decade later, Fallon was asked to pitch for a new campaign for the telecommunications giant Orange and built its proposal around her hand-crafted models.

Fallon won the job, and in a conversation with the author from 2013, Macdonald describes how the project developed.

"The original concept was based on collections; a group of individual elements illustrating one theme composed on a tabletop. This developed over time and was used across a series of billboards as well as online, point of sale, direct marketing and so on. The process began with the copy line and initial ideas from the creative team (a copywriter and art director), often using metaphors to represent different aspects of the mobile network. I'd respond with a list of ideas that we'd develop together to illustrate the concept most effectively, to be agreed and signed off by the client who was refreshingly open-minded . . . soon a visual language started to develop.

"Although some pieces were based on sketches, others were designed as they were created; I enjoy how materials and their constraints can steer

6

7

8

the direction of the design, particularly with the family of characters. These developed by combining different shapes and materials as a kit of parts, the whole process was very organic. . . .

"After lighting and shooting all the elements, the photographs went into postproduction retouch. Here John would work with the retoucher to strike a balance between being able to see the hand in the objects' creation and a clean, neat aesthetic."

"The success of what they created meant that what started as a three-month commission eventually developed into a three-year collaboration that forced Macdonald and Short to take on a larger studio just to accommodate the amount of work that was involved."

6. Drawings of initial ideas from Chrissie Macdonald's sketchbook.

7. One of John Short's photo shoots from the project.

8. Color swatches from the model-making process.

9. One of the illustrations for the Edinburgh Festival that inspired the project.

10 & 11. Some of the models that were used in the I Am ads.

12 & 13. Some ads from the Orange campaign.

9

10

11
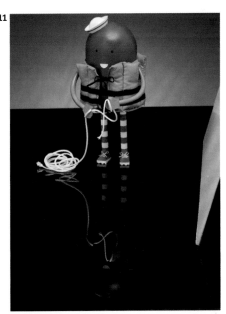

12
13

Heritage

At its best, a visual heritage grows organically from how a brand behaves.

1

2

SEARCH: Michael Bierut "Helvetica period!"; "Austerity Graphic Design" Patrick Burgoyne/ the *Creative Review Annual*; Labour and Wait; Peyton and Byrne; Grainedit; Draplin Design; Sign Painters; Coca-Cola Santa Claus; St. Peters Brewery; Ortiz tuna; Moving Brands E. Tautz/ Norton and Sons

We talked earlier in the chapter of how in the 1950s the International Style cleansed American corporate communications of nostalgic idiosyncrasy in a single-minded pursuit of modernist clarity. To a certain extent, the design community has never lost this evangelical zeal, but there has been a cyclical questioning of the universal benefits of this approach. In the early 1970s, Push Pin Studios' decorative quirks became the order of the day, and soon after, Wolfgang Wiengart pioneered more obscure and discursive forms of visual communication. More recently, there has been a revival of some of the design values of preceding ages. *Creative Review* called this "Austerity" graphic design, and after judging entries to the 2013 annual, Patrick Burgoyne remarked in the editorial that he "felt like he'd stepped into a design time machine and emerged in the mid fifties," because so much of the work was "nostalgic for an austere post war era in British life."

The success of brands like Labour and Wait and Peyton and Byrne in the UK or blogs like *grainedit*, studios like Draplin Design, and the documentary film *Sign Painters* in the United States testify that this is not an isolated local trend. There seems to be a longing among consumers for visual messages that have the authority and integrity of a simpler bygone age. Whether this will last is another matter, but there is definitely a sense that a perception of heritage has currency with the contemporary audience.

Too often, however, heritage is applied as a veneer of faux letterpress typography and decorative borders plundered from Google's never-ending supply of reference material. A more intelligent approach develops a visual narrative that explains the inherent values that have built a brand. Coca-Cola utilizes its history to confirm a place at the heart of recent American culture by reminding us of its role in creating the modern Santa Claus, and craft brewery St Peters uses its historic pub, the Jerusalem Tavern in Clerkenwell, London, and traditional bottle designs to connect with the heritage of British cask-conditioned ales. The key is applying this approach with integrity so the message is not perceived as contrived or falsely constructed. At its best, a visual heritage grows organically from how a brand behaves. Spanish fish manufacturer Ortiz packages its products using visual iconography that has evolved gradually since the 1930s. The design of Ortiz's cans draws a direct visual parallel to the meticulous care and respect for tradition that goes into processing their sustainably caught anchovies and tuna. In a market where ethical concerns have more and more significance, audiences are increasingly receptive to this narrative.

E. Tautz/ Norton and Sons

The heritage of a brand offers an intrinsic link to something that has authority and lasting meaning. An intelligent designer sees this as a valuable communication tool and something that need not inhibit the creation of fresh, contemporary design. A good example of this is Moving Brands' re-brand of Savile Row tailors, Norton and Sons.

Established in 1821, Nortons has a long history of providing tailoring to clients bound for Africa, India, and the near East and developed an expertise in lightweight clothing. Lord Carnarvon was dressed by Nortons when he discovered Tutankhamen's tomb, as was Henry Stanley when he met Dr. Livingstone. Unfortunately, Nortons fell on hard times—its suits were made so well that they were handed down through generations, and new customers were proving hard to find. Its brief to Moving Brands was simple: Find us a way to get some new customers because our existing ones are dying!

Moving Brands sought to build out from a tradition rather than set up a new one. From the beginning of the project, they sought to understand the heritage of the company and build an identity that allowed customers to understand its richness and quality. The agency was given access to Norton's archives and found a wealth of historic material to draw inspiration from. It created an identity that reflects the idiosyncrasies of this material—even including an upside down S that had been incorrectly replaced when the shop's signage was repaired after the war.

The re-branded Norton and Sons has become one of the best-known and most successful of a new wave of Savile Row tailors, and it has returned to Moving Brands to help it create new a ready-to-wear brand called E. Tautz.

1. The classic Ortiz can, utilizing original artwork from the brand's history.

2. Labour and Wait have built a very successful business by tapping into perceptions of heritage and authenticity.

3. An original ad for E. Tautz from 1912.

4. These Norton and Sons suit labels incorporate handwritten details of the tailor, cutter, and cloth supplier.

5. The identity for E. Tautz, which is Norton and Sons ready-to-wear brand, was also designed by Moving Brands.

6. A wall of reference material from the E. Tautz project in the Moving Brands studio.

3

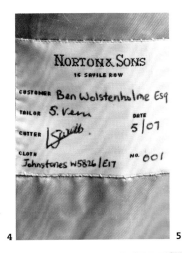

4

5

6

In developed economies, marketing and client service budgets are moving from brand and traditional advertising into the social web and rich Internet applications. It's difficult innovative work that involves making tools and platforms for people to use, not making finished messages shouted from megaphones or oratorical asides expecting no reply. William Owen in "Messy Medium," *Eye 64*

During the 20th century, the way messages were consumed became more and more complex. In his groundbreaking book *The Medium Is the Massage*, Marshall McLuhan charts the move from communication via images, words, and an alphabet to what he calls "electric circuitry." He charts how radio, film, and television communicate through combinations of senses and involve us much more immersively—stimulating new forms of behavior. At the beginning of the 21st century, the Internet and digital technology took this a stage further, enabling interaction through responsive media and giving us the opportunity to reshape the messages we were consuming.

Initially there was a clear divide between those who worked in experiential media, such as radio, television, and film, and those involved in graphic design, creating layout and typography for print-based media. For graphic designers, there was always an expensive technical hurdle to jump if they wanted to employ motion or sound.

The development of desktop computers in the 1980s and '90s meant that screen-based media was now accessible for those who were once confined to two dimensions and print.

Gradually, technology has blurred the boundaries between graphic design and media design. Those who were traditionally defined as graphic designers have become more and more involved in the creation of experiences that appeal to a much wider range of senses. Sound, moving image, animation, and more recently, interaction, responsive media, and social networking have all conspired to create communication that evolves through complex connections between different channels. As a result, designers have adapted the way they work from broadcast to conversation and from transmitting messages to orchestrating experiences.

Motion Graphics

In the last 20 years, motion design has become a core activity for a majority of creative agencies.

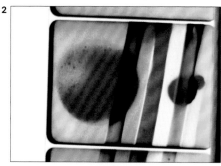

1–3. Stills from Len Lye's revolutionary film for the Post Office Savings Bank, *Rainbow Dance*. Examples of his early experiments with painting on celluloid.

4. Stills from some of Bernard Lodge's groundbreaking title sequences.

In the article "Images Over Time" in *Eye 60*, Matt Soar and Peter Hall attempt to define a series of milestones in the development of what has became known as "motion graphics." For starting points they go back as far as Marcel Duchamp's *Anémic Cinéma* and Man Ray's *Emak-Bakia* pointing out that this heritage is "nearly as old as graphic design itself." Oskar Fischinger's motion-based abstraction in the 1930s and 1940s, Len Lye's experiments with painting on celluloid, Saul Bass's groundbreaking title sequences for the films of Oscar Preminger and Alfred Hitchcock in the 1950s, and Bernard Lodge's work for *Doctor Who* in the 1960s all demonstrate the potential communicative power of motion-based graphic elements when combined with sound. Until the 1990s, however, this area between moving image and graphic design remained fairly niche due to the highly specialized skills and extremely expensive equipment it required. More watershed moments came with Terry Gilliam's stop-motion animations for Monty Python and the surreal explorations of Czech and Polish animators such as Jan Svankmajer and Walerian Borowczyk. This work provided inspiration for identical twins, Steven and Timothy Quay in the UK to produce a series of influential films including *Street of Crocodiles*, which was selected by Terry Gilliam as one of the best animated films of all time.

The development of desktop filmmaking tools during the early 1990s provided an outlet for a new generation of filmmakers, who were able to bypass what up until this point had been a long apprenticeship into filmmaking. The work of Bass, Svankmajer, Gilliam, et al. now provided exciting reference points for time-based visual experiences made by artists who had not been to film school. The new technology enabled them to create work without the expensive inconvenience of a studio and provided the tools that would nurture an underground digital filmmaking culture.

The influential film festival ResFEST in the United States played a major part in showcasing digitally made films. Equally groundbreaking was the UK digital arts festival onedotzero, which supported and showcased more experimental explorations into digital motion. Between them, these festivals provided platforms to support a group of artists who would create work that defined an era.

At this time, new freedoms and economic prosperity had led to the establishment of a global youth culture, and the launch of TV stations like MTV provided an insatiable demand for short-form, visually led films that could accompany the pop music that formed this audience's staple diet. As a result, the pop promo became an important new format and ResFest, onedotzero, and Mirrorball at the Edinburgh International Film festival helped establish some of its most significant protagonists. The likes of Michel Gondry, Spike Jonze, Chris Cunningham, and Jonathan Glazer were all able to gain wider exposure through the support they received from these festivals.

In the years that followed, software platforms such as Director, Premier, and After Effects led to the establishment of motion graphics as a recognized discipline within the graphic design industry. New studios

SEARCH: Marcel Duchamp's "Anémic Cinéma"; Man Ray's *Emak-Bakia*; Jan Svankmajer; Walerian Borowczyk; onedotzero; Resfest; Terry Gilliam; Antirom; Audiorom; Tomato design; The Light Surgeons; D-Fuse; Spin design; Why Not Associates; Oskar Fischinger; Bernard Lodge; Saul Bass

4

such as Spin and Why Not Associates in the UK began to offer motion design as a viable addition to conventional communication design formats, creating title sequences, moving logos, and even commercials. Graphic designers were able to bring the sensibilities of their discipline to what had been a highly specialized medium until this moment. Today, motion design is a core activity for a majority of studios. It not only provides a communication option that compliments print and online applications, but is also used as a research tool providing mood films that are used to illustrate a creative direction.

Parallel to the conventional commercial development of motion-based graphic media, onedotzero championed more experimental explorations. Creative collective Tomato had been exploring exciting cross-disciplinary collaborations since the early 1990s fusing sound, image, film projection, and animated typography into pop promos and live performance. Tomato's work went on to inspire other cross-disciplinary collectives, some that

were short lived but highly influential such as Antirom and Audiorom and others that survive to this day such as The Light Surgeons and D-Fuse. These early innovators have spawned a use for motion-based graphic media that places it at the center of more immersive digital experiences. onedotzero created onedotzero industries to take advantage of the commercial opportunities that were being created for the artists that they had nurtured through their festivals. Huge stage shows by the likes of George Michael, U2, and the Rolling Stones provided an exciting testing ground for these new audio-visual combinations. The area continues to expand, and the further development of technology has enabled physical interaction and motion tracking to be incorporated alongside animation and moving image. Directors like Kate Dawkins are now able to create work that coordinates motion design across a variety of screens and into mechanisms that allow users to shape its nature.

5

6

5–7. Experiments in digital motion, projection, and interactive filmmaking showcased by onedotzero.

5. United Visual Artists live stage show in Taipei.

6. "House Of Cards" for Radiohead, by James Frost + Aaron Koblin.

7. "Body Paint" by Mehmet Akten.

7

Case Study: Adidas Innovation Kin with Kate Dawkins

Kin was approached by M&C Saatchi to create a series of interactive experiences for Adidas. "Adidas lab" was the first in a series of innovation events showcasing the brand's future products and celebrating its continued commitment to pushing the boundaries in performance technologies. This first event focused on innovation in football and took place over the UEFA Champions League Final weekend. Kate Dawkins joined the team at Kin as design director, overseeing the look and feel of all the content for two of the largest interactive activations at the event.

In the days that led up to the 2013 Champions League Final in London, invited participants took part in a series of football-related interactive activities. The main experience The Track, used RFID technology to personalize the experience, with X-Box Kinect cameras tracking their movements as live data was streamed to screens that Dawkins designed to be a backdrop to their activities.

She worked alongside a team of developers who used processing to translate the data into visual imagery that was incorporated into the framework that she had created. The balancing of these volatile user-generated elements into coherent motion graphics proved highly challenging, but as Dawkins points out, "When you're working with live data, you can't just hope it works on the day. These projects take an immense amount of planning, checking, and testing."

Having completed The Track experience, a football shoe was identified that would best suit the participants' performance. Their scores were then placed into the daily and overall leaderboards and a film of their performance was uploaded to YouTube.

katedawkins.co.uk/project/
adidas-lab-london/

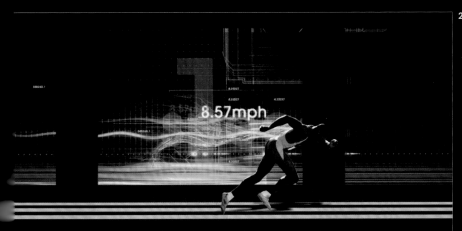

8.57mph

2

6.28mph

4

the track leaderboard - day 1

1 12. greg marshall	2 25. tony radcliffe	3 14. karl johnston	4 02. robbie reily	5 22. james byrne	6 18. neill colman	7 03. evan stephens	8 12. david peterson
› predator - the technical wizard › 31.04	› f50 - the speed demon › 31.38	› predator - the technical wizard › 32.18	› nitrocharge - the engine › 32.47	› nitrocharge - the engine › 33.56	› f50 - the speed demon › 34.02	› f50 - the speed demon › 34.38	› predator - the technical wizard › 34.25
9 21. conor carlton	10 17. ross maples	11 04. dave donhou	12 13. keith warren	13 21. conor carlton	14 17. ross maples	15 04. dave donhou	16 13. keith warren
› f50 - the speed demon › 34.46	› nitrocharge - the engine › 35.10	› predator - the technical wizard › 35.16	› predator - the technical wizard › 36.02	› f50 - the speed demon › 36.50	› nitrocharge - the engine › 37.22	› predator - the technical wizard › 37.36	› predator - the technical wizard › 37.58
17 21. matthew aylsbury	18 17. tommy fallon	19 04. ray white	20 13. oliver callan	21 21. lee reynolds	22 17. cain lewis	23 04. john dillon	24 13. karl case
› predator - the technical wizard › 37.45	› nitrocharge - the engine › 38.01	› f50 - the speed demon › 38.06	› nitrocharge - the engine › 38.23	› predator - the technical wizard › 38.45	› f50 - the speed demon › 39.11	› predator - the technical wizard › 39.15	› nitrocharge - the engine › 39.49

1 & 2. User-generated data was integrated with predesigned motion graphics to form a live moving visual backdrop for participants.

2. Daily leaderboards recording the scores of individual participants. Films of performances were also uploaded to YouTube.

3. Careful planning enabled X Box Kinect cameras to motion track the performance of participants and feed data into live visuals.

We were like an early warning system for the way the industry was changing.

In Conversation

with Shane Walter,
co-founder, onedotzero

Shane Walter is co-founder and creative director of onedotzero—internationally recognized as one of the most important influences on the development of digital culture. Its annual festival, Adventures in Motion, champions innovation in moving image and interactive arts. Over the past 16 years, it has reached more than 150 cities, building unparalleled relationships with creators and audiences worldwide.

onedotzero.com

onedotzero's first festival took place in 1997 over a long weekend at the ICA and tapped into an underground culture that was utilizing newly available digital filmmaking tools. In many ways it foresaw the desktop digital revolution—and the potential for what Matt Hanson, director of the first festival, called "the film studio in your flat" and "The End Of Celluloid" It also created a platform to explore moving image across single screen, interactive, and live audio-visual formats. Walter describes how onedotzero "set out to showcase non-traditional filmmakers. People who were not just using digital tools, but who were using these tools to make things that have never been made before." Very soon after the first festival, its mission became an international one, when in 1997 they were invited to take part in the Festival of Cinema & New Media in Montréal.

In the years that followed, onedotzero was able to provide a showcase for a burgeoning group of talented pop promo directors such as Spike Jonze, Chris Cunningham, and Michel Gondry and in many ways presided over the "golden age" of this form. As the tools for the creation of digital film and motion-based graphic design became more available, designers and illustrators became more interested in using them. Walter explains how this talent needed some encouragement.

"We worked with lots of people who came from a design background. Tomato were involved along with people from illustration backgrounds such as Andy Martin, and this meant that in the end, lots of the films we showcased were visually led."

Indeed, targeting and encouraging new talent was a central aim of the festival. "We were always a producing festival. Most film festivals collect work together and showcase it, but we were always interested in doing a bit more than this. We wanted to encourage and help talented people make work and then provide a platform and showcase for it."

As a result, onedotzero provided the first opportunities for some of the most influential practitioners within the digital creative scene to get their work acknowledged internationally—these include UVA, Johnny Hardstaff, Digit, Tomato, Karsten Schmidt, Shynola, Quayola, and Jason Bruges Studio.

Walter talks about the festival being a platform for change, and those who took part in it were encouraged to use it as such. "We were like an early warning system for the way the industry was changing."

They acted as a testing ground for many of the ideas and principles that are now central to contemporary creative practice. As Walter points out, "We were called a digital film festival, but we could also be called a festival of creative convergence or a festival of non-linear filmmaking. We also could have been called a festival of digital creativity. All of these things were accurate, but it was just an easier sell to call it a 'digital film festival at that time.'"

Walter makes a distinction between between using digital technology and creating digital culture. "One of the problems with digital is that people cannot separate the tools from the culture." The significance is that using digital tools engenders new ways of working and thinking, and onedotzero picked up on this really early. "There is a cultural and artistic way of expressing yourself that is shaped by digital technology, that uses code, that uses generative systems, that's collaborative, that works across disciplines, that involves the user, etc. This is what is significant."

Collaboration and creative convergence were inherent to the culture that onedotzero set up, and Walter describes how "one of the wonderful things about onedotzero was that you met people you hadn't known before and that you wouldn't have met in any other context. So maybe you walked in as an illustrator but at the festival you met an architect and then a filmmaker and as a result you wouldn't walk out in the same direction."

Walter also talks about observing the emergence of a different mindset around ownership and how the principle of sharing what you make and not keeping it to yourself is at the heart of digital

culture. He describes how the newness of digital technology and the fact that everybody was learning how to use the tools together meant that there was much more of an incentive to share skills and expertise.

"You'd ring your friends and ask how you use a tool or whether you have a trick for hacking a piece of software. In this scenario, suddenly it's not just about what you know, it's about what your network knows and how you share that knowledge. . . . This was the approach we took to our festival—if we found this really amazing creative person, we wanted to share that information. We wanted to tell the world about them."

Each festival provided panel discussions and forums that Walter says were designed to "demystify this black art of digital." These discussions were an opportunity to develop an interface with educational establishments. At the same time, economic necessity and the demand for the talent that onedotzero was showcasing created opportunities to broker commercial projects.

Walter is very open about the importance of this to nurturing the artists they worked with. "I have never seen commerce as working in opposition to working creatively or personally; I've always seen it as just another platform and got excited about it because it might mean working with bigger budgets and gaining more exposure or more interesting connections."

These factors led to onedotzero developing three strands to their activity: showcasing talent through its festivals; onedotzero industries— working with the likes of George Michael, U2, the Pet Shop Boys, and the Rolling Stones; and what eventually became onedotzero cascade—developing educational platforms to explore the ideas that were being revealed at the festivals.

In 2007, onedotzero moved its London festival to the BFI in London's South Bank Centre. Having largely championed digital cinema and motion graphics and live audio-visual work, these new venues provided the opportunity to present a much broader cross-section of digital culture's output. This included

live interactive installations and discussion events that examined the significance of the work on show.

In 2003, onedotzero had also begun working with the V&A, and in 2006 it was offered the opportunity to curate Friday Late. This event became "onedotzero_transvision" night, featuring the first public installation by United Visual Artists. This is still the most attended Friday Late in the V&A history, with almost 6,000 people attending.

At the V&A it featured and became recognized for championing installation and intervention. In 2009, Walter cocurated "Decode: Digital Design Sensations," a collaboration between onedotzero and the V&A—the first major retrospective of work in this area. Decode looked at three themes within digital design—exploring the utilization of code, interaction, and networks. The success of this exhibition at one of the world's most significant art and design institutions confirmed Walter's position as a leading figure within digital culture and cemented onedotzero's significance in its development.

Case Study: onedotzero responsive identities

From the very beginning, onedotzero commissioned identities that worked across platforms and disciplines. Initially this meant the creation of something that could be animated and would work in print, but in later years the studio developed identities that were responsive to user input. Walter, onedotzero co-founder, has commissioned a series of studios to work on this project, and new interpretations of its identity became a feature of its festival at the BFI.

In 2008, it worked with award-winning experimental technology studio Troika on an identity that included the creation of a fully functioning zoetrope! In addition to motion graphics and print,

Troika describes this on its website as a "spinning poetry device that displays, one after another, text-based narratives of five individuals living in the city." It was inspired by Shane's exploration of urban living—"citystates." The onedotzero logotype was concealed within the piece, appearing at various points. The zoetrope formed an installation at both the BFI and as part of the Decode exhibition at the V&A and inspired a custom logotype, animation, and printed iconography.

The following year it embarked on an ambitious collaboration with international advertising agency Wieden & Kennedy (W+K). Computational designer and "borderline genius" Karsten Schmidt (see pp. 117–119) was brought in to work on the project, and W+K provided Nokia as a client. Together they created an "open source, remix-able identity" that responded to user input via the onedotzero communites, online activity. The constantly evolving identity could be freeze framed to produce assets for printed media, recorded for motion: during the festival at the BFI it formed a live projection displayed on a 50-m screen, creating a huge interaction in the middle of London utilizing the Nokia N92 handset. All of the source code that Schmidt created to power the identity was open source and made available for public download.

vimeo.com/8693818

1 & 2. The 2008 onedotzero Adventures in Motion identity.

1. This "spinning poetry device" built by Troika displayed urban narratives to accompany the 2008 Adventures in Motion festival.

2. The visual identity of the festival was then inspired by how these spinning elements separated and combined.

3–5. The 2009 onedotzero Adventures in Motion identity. Live data from social media was incorporated into a living logotype, which was projected onto the exterior of the BFI on the South Bank in London. This projection could be manipulated using a Nokia smart phone.

6. An earlier onedotzero identity applied to the felt cover of the "Motion Blur 2" publication.

Environment

Spaces can respond to the user to create experiences that are both seductive and informative.

Over the last 20 years environments have made an increasingly valuable contribution to the way messages are communicated to an audience. International multidisciplinary design company Imagination is highly influential to the development of this area, creating groundbreaking retail and exhibition spaces. Founded by Gary Withers in 1978, Imagination soon developed a reputation for design that incorporated exhibition, interior, architecture, graphics, and product design with a touch of theater. Ron Herron, originally part of legendary experimental architecture group, Archigram, designed their headquarters in London's Store Street.

Key to Imagination's success is its use of architectural space to imbue an experience with ideas and values, for which the hypothetical structures created by Archigram could be seen as inspiration. Former employee and founder of Kin Kevin Palmer explains how there was also a sense of theater in the work that Imagination produced, and many of the senior designers had experience designing within this context.

"Imagination were doing experiential design before the term was coined. They were able to bring theatre to the corporate world. They had a stage production ethic using lighting, projection, and sound from very early on. As digital technology developed they were able to take advantage of this expertise using huge video

1. The "Window of Intensity" by AllofUs for Carte Noir augments the movements of passersby using motion tracking, sound, and visual effects.

1

2 & 3. Some of the responsive exhibits created by AllofUs for the "Who am I?" gallery at the Science Museum in London.

2

3

walls alongside physical interaction. They could then add in live performers or even a full dance troupe."

The Science Museum in London has also made a valuable contribution to the evolution of communication environments. Over the last 70 years they have worked with some of the world's leading designers to create a series of exhibits that use innovative design to open up science to a wider audience. More recently, the museum's galleries have provided a testing ground for the potential of creating spaces that respond to the user in ways that are both seductive and informative. In 2000, UK studio Graphic Thought Facility (GTF) worked with exhibition designers Casson Mann to create "Digitopolis," a gallery designed to explore the future of digital technology. The designers used electro-luminescent lamps for the signage and information boards, adapting this technology to produce a typographic system that uses a single modular circuit to create the characters D, I, G, T, O, P, L and S. Individual letterforms were created by breaking the circuit with a hole punch, at different points to selectively illuminate. Later GTF and Casson Mann worked on the "Who am I?" and "Energy" galleries, which also feature responsive experiences that were created by interaction studio AllofUs.

AllofUs was formed in 2000 by five former employees of award-winning digital agency Digit, and it has since developed a reputation for innovative combinations of physical and screen-based interaction. The Science Museum was one of its earliest clients, and an ongoing relationship has allowed for the exploration of how new technologies might be applied to enhance the "visitor-interpretation" process.

AllofUs have also been able to apply the lessons learned from this work to a commercial context through installations such as the "Window of Intensity" for coffee brand Carte Noir in London's Westfield shopping center. This piece features a five-meter-wide window display that reflects the street. Movements of passersby are augmented and transformed using motion tracking, real-time effects, generative visuals, and sound effects. The installation engages on a scale and with a playfulness that the public finds irresistible, and the promotional video on the AllofUs website records the pleasure people derive from interacting with it. The audience's everyday experience is intensified in the same way the coffee brand would like to have us believe its product does.

SEARCH: Archigram; Imagination Design; Ron Herron; The Science Museum: Who am I?/ Digitopolis/ Energy/ Atmosphere; AllofUs Science Museum; GTF Science Museum

Case Study: Vital Arts
The Royal London Children's Hospital, Barts Health

Vital Arts is the arts organization that serves the Barts Health NHS Trust in London and is charitably funded to deliver arts projects that enhance the well-being of patients, staff, and the wider hospital community.

In the Royal London Children's Hospital in Whitechapel, Vital Arts has created a series of projects designed to stimulate moments of intrigue and wonder

for patients at the hospital. The artworks commissioned are part of a wider creative strategy to put art and design at the heart of improving the patient environment for the NHS Trust. A range of artists and designers from the local East London creative scene have taken part in the projects and included the likes of Ella Doran, Blaise Drummond, Katharine Morling, Morag Myerscough, Chrissie Macdonald, and Andrew Rae for Peepshow Illustration Collective, along with Lemn Sissay, Bob and Roberta Smith, Chisato Tambayashi,

Jessica Voorsanger, Chris Watson, and Joby Williamson. Together these practitioners have created what are hoped to be transformative experiences for the patients.

Three projects in particular illustrate this strategy:

Morag Myerscough, Cottrell & Vermeulen: playroom

The playroom at the Royal London Hospital is probably the most striking of Vital Arts' commissions at the hospital. It was designed by

1–3. Eddie the Tiger and Twoo the Owl provide inspiration for storytelling in the extraordinary oversized children's activity space of the Royal London Hospital.

award-winning architects Cottrell & Vermeulen in collaboration with the designer Morag Myerscough and forms an extraordinary activity space. Resembling an oversize living room, it features an enormous storytelling chair and television. The huge scale of these objects creates a surreal Alice-in-Wonderland atmosphere for the room and provides an environment full of stimulating distractions for children and adults. The room also features huge rag dolls—Eddie the Tiger and Twoo the Owl—designed to stimulate storytelling. Patients and caregivers can also step inside the TV to enter a digital play space, where games created by Nexus productions are projected onto the screen.

Ella Doran: curtains and bed furniture
Interior and product designer Ella Doran created a series of designs based on views of London that were then printed onto custom curtains for ward beds and bedside furniture. As part of the commission, Ella engaged in discussion with patients and staff in order to tailor her designs to their needs. Using her findings, she created extraordinary panoramic views of the River Thames full of details that could be used to distract patients from the treatment they were receiving. The designs are printed on the inside of the curtain (rather than the outside as is traditional) in order to be seen and used by the patient.

vitalarts.org.uk/hospitals/
childrens-hospital-royal-london/

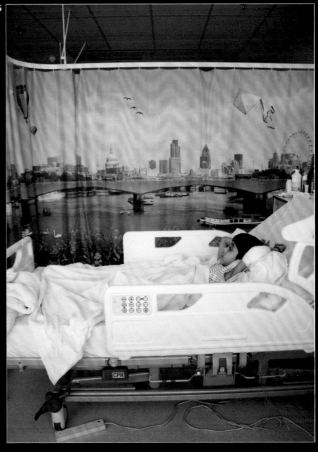

5

4 & 5. Panoramic views of London applied to curtains and bedside furniture by designer Ella Doran to provide visual stimulation in the children's ward at the Royal London Hospital.

The activity space is a unique play concept providing important respite treatment and medical intervention for children and their families.
Barts Health Children's Group Director Jane Hawdon

Motion graphics used to stand alone, but now it exists in a context provided by new technologies.

In Conversation

with Kate Dawkins,
designer and director

**On her website, Kate Dawkins
notes that she "delivers design led
content for activations such as brand
campaigns and digital films to large
events and interactive experiences."
She has been involved in innovative
and often groundbreaking projects
with a series of high profile clients.
She provided the lead art direction
for the giant 360° audience pixels for
the London 2012 Olympic Opening and
Closing Ceremonies and has worked
for the likes of Adidas, Ford, BBC, GSK,
Elton John, and the MTV European
Music Awards.**

katedawkins.co.uk

Dawkins began her career in
the early 1990s at Intro and was
interviewed and eventually employed
by one of the founding partners,
Adrian Shaughnessy (interviewed
on pp. 182–185) Intro had gained a
reputation for creating cutting-edge
packaging for leading international
bands, and at that time it was
starting to move into creating the
accompanying music videos.

As Dawkins points out,
"Once such an impact is made with
a record cover or a visual language,
it is obvious that somebody at the
record company is going to ask 'Can
you apply the same language to a
video?' At that time there was an
understanding that, as a band, you
needed to have a holistic approach to
the way you promoted yourself. . . .
If you look at the work that Julian
House did for Primal Scream for
example, you can see that he created
a visual language that worked across
a number of albums. This gave them
the rare gift of immediate recognition
in a world of short attention spans."

After working with director
Julian Gibbs on a number of projects,
Dawkins was given the opportunity
to direct the promo for the rerelease
of Elton John's "Are You Ready for
Love?" and the success of this project
led to a commission to design and
direct the live performance visuals
for his Red Piano show at Caesars
Palace in Las Vegas. This show
proved a breakthrough moment for
her. It was directed by world-famous
photographer David LaChapelle and
gave Dawkins the opportunity to see
her visuals played out on the largest
HD LED screen in the world at that
time. Her work was part of a complete
stage concept, which required her to
consider how her work sat within this.

"I realized that the animation
needed to be a holistic part of the
show and not simply a backdrop: it
wasn't just about bits of animation
and flat screens." She soon began
to develop an innate understanding
for the particular challenges of this
type of work. "Although essentially
we were working with static
screens, the scale of the event might
have caused some complications,
but somehow I understood it
and was able to visualize it."

Soon after, she was asked to
produce the performance visuals
for the MTV European Music
Awards in Munich. This involved
the coordination of a series of bold
and immersive graphic animations
displayed across a variety of
screens. Once more, Dawkins found
herself having to rise to a complex
challenge. As audio-visual technology
has developed, she has gained a
reputation for being able to work on
projects that were at the leading edge
of what this technology could provide.
In 2012, this reputation led to her
being chosen to provide the design
and art direction for the opening and
closing ceremony audience pixels at
the London 2012 Olympics Games. She
points out that, "large-scale projects
require an understanding of how
particular screens might coordinate
together within an environment.
I enjoy the challenges that projects
such as these bring, having to
consider the screen as part of a
bigger production, not in isolation."

The scale and complexity
of these projects means that
Dawkins has learned to collaborate
with multidisciplinary teams, and
part of her role is dependent on
the ongoing relationships she has
developed with a range of diverse
and talented practitioners. "Trust
is really important in this industry.
When you are building a team that
can work on a very complex and
demanding project, you need to
know that its totally fit for purpose."

Her move into the creation of
immersive experiences has involved
the development of new working
relationships. "I work alongside
people that really understand
experiential technologies, and
working in a small team with these
people means that I have developed
a much deeper understanding of
this area. Motion graphics used to
stand alone, but now it exists in
a context provided by these new
technologies. I work at an intersection
where design and technology meet.
This is really exciting because it
means that I am creating motion
graphics and films for a world
that's very new and challenging."

Dawkins stresses that it is really
important to strike a balance between

what the technology enables and the creativity that shapes how it is used.

"As a creative, I would always want to be brought into a project early so that I can have some input into defining the project from the ground up. Sometimes projects are driven by what the technology can do and sometimes they are driven by a creative idea, but to be honest I think it should be defined by what's best for the project and outcome.

"People have asked me what I'm going to do after the Olympics, but to me its not about the size of the screen or the profile of the environment. The same creative process applies to a handheld device or the largest screen in the world. What I like is the challenge. It's all about an audience or a user, how you can engage with that audience, interact with them or inform them. There are lots of questions that you need to ask beyond what shape or size the screen is."

Her interest in new and challenging contexts means that the nature of Dawkins's work is constantly changing. As technology develops, she is often asked to work with new processes and tools, and it would be easy for her to be deterred by the challenges that this brings. "The scale of these projects means that they are delivered by a skilled team, and it is the combined experience that rises to the challenge. You could never take on a project of these sizes and do it alone: its about teamwork." She also has the confidence and determination to find out how to do new things. "If you think you've learned everything you need to know, you are on a hiding to nowhere. Every day should be a learning process, and I am excited by each day that I am faced by the unknown and learning something new."

Case Study: 2012 Olympic Games Audience Pixels
The audience pixels consisted of 70,500 small "paddles" each containing nine powerful lights, attached to each audience seat. These resulted in the audience seemingly disappearing and being replaced by a giant screen covering the entire audience area. Crystal CG was the Official Digital Imaging Service Supplier to the London 2012 Games, and Dawkins was employed by them as lead art director, working on both the Olympics Opening and Closing Ceremonies, designing, directing, and with the team helping, delivering more than 100 individua pieces of content.

1

2

The pixels idea was director Danny Boyle's brainchild. His vision was one of inclusiveness, integrating the audience in a way not seen before, blurring the boundaries between spectator and spectacle. As lead director, Dawkins was quickly confronted with an array of problems related to the scale and ambition of the project. Not least of these problems was how to visualize what was being created, which was vital to aid the creative process and also to facilitate viewing the work and sign-off stages. It was only after they had begun working that a full visualization of the stadium was created, enabling the team to test animations. This model was updated and perfected as more information became available about how the stadium and the pixels would work.

As the date of the opening ceremony rapidly approached, Dawkins and a team of experienced animators and producers worked through a continuous stream of project requirements. "It was a very experimental process, very different to other projects I'd worked on and hugely exciting. We used so many different processes—creating elements in open-source processing, motion capturing, 3D modeling, and a live-action green screen shoot—what we produced is certainly not just typical animation or motion graphics."

Facilitating this work became a task of mammoth technical proportions. Just supervising the rendering of the animations was a 24-hour job, and an extremely large render farm had to be brought in just to get the animations rendered in time to meet the ceremonies' deadlines.

In the end, all of the stress and hard work were worth it and the stadium pixels were received with widespread public acclaim. For Dawkins, "It was a fairly stressful but highly rewarding experience. I suppose the only downside really was that we missed out on seeing the Olympic Games because we were too busy working."

katedawkins.co.uk/project/london-2012-opening-and-closing-ceremonies/

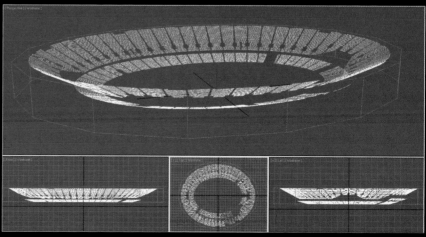

1 & 2. The Olympic Stadium at the 2012 Olympic Games was turned into a giant animated screen to provide a powerful visual message of inclusiveness.

3 & 4. Some of the animation team's original artwork.

5. A powerful "render farm" had to be brought just to process the animations.

6. The computer visualization of the stadium needed to be created to preview the animations.

Play

Suddenly you could publish games yourself and sell them through the App Store.

Developing Own IP games and apps was a way of us showing our clients, ourselves, and the industry that we care about what we do. That we care about it so much—we are prepared to invest in things that do not necessarily make immediate financial sense. We are seeing the benefit of this risk to all areas of our business. From recruitment—where we can employ great people because they want to be part of a business that is creating interesting things—to the skills that are nurtured in the games area and then applied in the other things that we do.
Mills, co-founder of ustwo

1

SEARCH: Pong; Pac-Man; Space Invaders; Asteroids; Atari video games; Matthew Smith Manic Miner; *From Bedrooms to Billions*; the Sega Mega Drive; Nintendo Game Boy; Sony PlayStation; Xbox; Sennep; Macromedia Flash; the Designers Republic/ Wipeout video game; Attik; Me Company; ustwo Granimator/ Mouth Off!; Sennep Seeds

We have been playing screen-based games since the 1970s. Whether in an arcade or through consoles, games such as Pong, Pac-Man, Space Invaders, and Asteroids are part of the fabric of our youth. From the Atari video system to the Sega Mega Drive, Nintendo Game Boy, Sony PlayStation, and the Xbox the memories of each recent generation are colored by playing computer games. In addition to this, in the UK, Clive Sinclair created a culture of do-it-yourself game programming through the release of the ZX Spectrum computer. The accessibility of this machine allowed teenagers in their bedrooms, such as Matthew Smith, to create globally significant games like Manic Miner and Jet Set Willy.

As the console gaming industry developed, however, it did so at a one step remove from the mainstream design and communication industry. Even for established interaction designers, such as Matt Rice, co-founder of Sennep, game design was never something that seemed an option when he was studying design. He talks of being inspired by the early CD-ROM created by people like the designers at Digit—even though they explored levels of interaction that were at best rudimentary compared to what he experienced everyday on his Nintendo.

"We grew up with gaming—gaming was something you did. We had always played on a computer or with our Game Boys, but somehow what Digit were doing was far more interesting—this was interaction that did not have a defined purpose. It was more abstract and therefore more interesting. It also seemed a little more achievable than the things we were importing from Japan at the time."

The creative output of this first generation to have grown up with computer games was obviously informed by the experience. Initially this manifested itself in an aesthetic—Designers Republic, Attik, and Me Company all produced graphic design that looked like it could have been screen-grabbed from a game. They even made decorative use of Japanese letterforms. The game industry picked up on this, and soon Designers Republic was providing the visual styling for the Sony PlayStation game Wipeout. Then, the development of ActionScript within Macromedia Flash enabled mainstream designers to experiment with simple gameplay and learn skills that could be incorporated into their commercial work. By the time Apple released its first touch-screen devices, there was a community ready to create content for this environment. Suddenly you could publish games yourself and sell them through the App Store. Companies like ustwo, who had been designing themes for mobile phones up until that point, suddenly saw the opportunity to apply their expertise to a new area—the creation of what became known as "Own IP products" (IP standing for intellectual property).

Neil MacFarland, creative director at ustwo games, explains, "We had been creating themes and other forms of content for Sony Erikkson when the App Store opened and Apple released the 3G iPhone. Suddenly there was a new outlet for the content we were creating and a platform that we could publish it through. Very soon we had established a ring-fenced area of the business in which people could focus on

1. The Sony PlayStation game Wipeout, with visual styling provided by the Designers Republic.

2. The sleeve design for Bjork's "Army of Me" by Me Company carries obvious references to computer game iconography.

3, 4, & 5. ustwo's Monument Valley is an evolutionary milestone in the visual design of mobile games, called "possibly the most beautiful game of 2014" by Wired magazine.

this new area. Early apps like Granimator and MouthOff proved that there was a market for this work, if not at that point a great deal of financial income."

This opportunity allowed a much wider range of people to break into gaming design. People like MacFarland, with a degree in film and scriptwriting, a love for comics, and professional experience producing illustration and animation, found themselves working alongside more traditional game designers. Within this melting pot, studios like ustwo were able to build teams that used expertise gleaned from console game design and applied it to experiences that engaged much more intuitively, such as MouthOff, Nursery Rhymes, and Whale Trail.

ustwo also creates user experiences for clients in the business world, and learning to understand gameplay and the mechanics of the intuitive interaction required by an app provides them with valuable lessons into how to effectively engage a user. In the world of gaming, there is always a tension between intrigue and disengagement. The user is enticed in and develops a familiarity with the language of that particular interactive environment. This enables them to solve problems that gradually become more complex. All of this requires highly sophisticated user-experience design skills that can then be applied to other aspects of their business.

The design of Own IP digital products also fulfills a marketing function. Each game or app that they release is a demonstration of what they can do—something that allows future clients to experience their work in a way that provides instinctive understanding. Founding partner of ustwo Mills points out how the games they design also offer a seductive draw for clients who have grown up with gaming and that they are often reference points for conversations that start to shape the products and services that these clients end up commissioning.

Case Study: OLO

OLO started as one of Sennep's "Seeds" (see p. 84)—an R&D (research and development) project designed to explore the potential of the newly released HTML 5. It was a simple game that proved instantly addictive for those in the studio. Sennep decided to prototype it as a web app and then put it out for user testing. At this point, the project was picked up by the gaming blogs, and soon around 50,000 people were playing it. Matt Rice explains, "One of the things that was great about OLO is that it doesn't conform to the other gaming formats that are so prevalent in the iPad environment." Its popularity led to Sennep investing the time to

1

develop it in iOS so that it could work natively on the iPad. Their developers had to learn new skills to make this happen. The whole process took six to eight months, but at the end they had a fully functioning, fluidly interactive game.

At the same time, Sennep's visual designers had worked up a marketing strategy—creating a brand identity, website, and a short-release video. The name and logo are a condensed representation of the game. Two OLOs divided by the center line, one player on each side. It's more obvious if it's spelled OlO (with lowercase l). They even created ideas for bolt-ons and merchandising, developing amusingly crafted gameplay themes related to robots, safari, fairy tales, or horror films and commissioning a group of musician friends to create the soundtrack.

The game was launched with a party that featured OLO-themed food, OLO tournaments, and a live jazz band riffing to the theme music. Just before the game's release date, Sennep received an email from Apple expressing an interest in the development of the product and asking what their plans were after release. They were then asked to provide artwork, and on the day of its launch, the game was featured on the home page of every App Store around the world. Before the day was out, they had sold 25,000 games and had generated enough income to cover the costs of OLO's development.

sennep.com/work/ologame

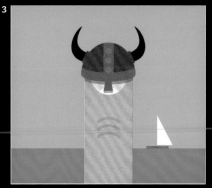

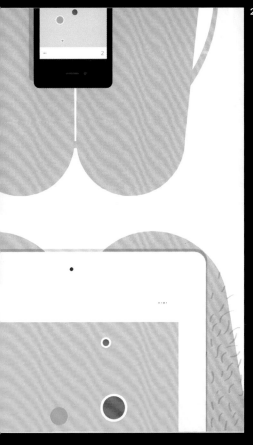

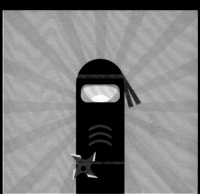

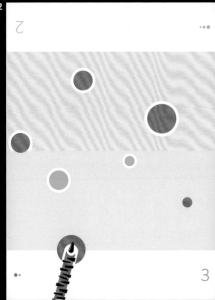

1. A still from the animation that Sennep created to promote OLO.

2. Downloadable gameplay themes for OLO include robots, fairy tale, horror, or this one, safari. All have hilarious matching sound effects.

3 & 4. Some of the achievement icons for OLO.

5. OLO was the App Store's favorite game during the week of its release.

6. Some of the OLO-themed food from its launch party.

It's about a network of people that can enable things to get done—a network that, based on past experience, tells us that we can deliver anything.

In Conversation

with Kevin Palmer and
Matt Wade, co-founders,
Kin

Kin has defined its own place within London's creative industry by combining digital and physical outcomes to create work that simultaneously explores interaction, motion, and environment. Its work has been widely recognized as groundbreaking within the design community, and it has won a coveted D&AD Yellow Pencil as well as being featured in the Design Museum and in *Time* magazine's Top 10 Everything 2010.

kin-design.com

Matt Wade and Kevin Palmer are both graduates with honors in design at Goldsmiths, University of London, and this has obviously been instrumental in shaping the development of their careers.

Palmer describes how "the great thing about that course is that it made you realize that design needs to have a purpose and not just be about style. It made you understand that it can change the world, make lives better, and be socially conscious. I must confess I wasn't really looking for this at the time but it opened a whole new world to me."

Wade explains how, "It was about design futures—about the things you make in the world. There was no specialism. You got a brief and could answer it any way you wanted—you could make a piece of furniture, you could create a magazine, you can make some posters or make an object."

Texts such Victor Papanak's *Design for the Real World* informed the curriculum at Goldsmiths and Kin continues to rationalize what it makes through theoretical reference points. *The Practice of Everyday Life* by Michel de Certeau and *A Pattern Language* by Christopher Alexander have helped to define a desire to understand human behavior, which is still at the core of their work. "There are patterns that exist in the way people behave, and by observing them and by understanding them we can exploit them and use them."

Palmer graduated four years before Wade and describes how he had become "interested in the link between digital interaction and physical interaction, how you can think about behavior and what influences how somebody interacts with an object. . . . At that time, the digital world and the physical world were very separate, but obviously today that's all changed. Now Wade and I don't really like talking about the real and the virtual. They don't have a divide anymore."

After graduation Palmer worked at Fitch before going on to Imagination, working in its newly formed multimedia studio designing large-scale motion graphics and later touch screens and interactive

video walls. Palmer returned to Goldsmiths each year to set a project to the students, and it was during one of these projects that he met Wade, at that time still a student. Wade secured a placement at Imagination and later a full-time job. Working at Imagination taught Wade and Palmer about how to engage an audience with physical and environmental storytelling. Palmer talks of learning how to temper his use of technology with experiences that were more human. "The tendency is for digital to be about cold, hard experiences, whereas if you add moments that have clearly been touched by the human hand, then you can achieve surprise and engagement."

Wade began to realize the significance that coding could have in the creation of digital experiences. "At Imagination, I actually found the developers more interesting than the designers. I realized that there was another way of making things, that you could make stuff with numbers, maths, and behavior, and by using this I could create both visual outputs and tangible objects."

To explore these ideas further, Wade left Imagination and enrolled in an MSc in Adaptive Architecture and Computation at the Bartlett School of Architecture. There, he began to program interaction that explored the relationships between space, form, and behavior and unearthed a series of ideas that are still at the heart of Kin's work.

Soon after leaving the Bartlett, Wade landed a job at Moving Brands. At that time they were just beginning to engage with responsive branding, and Wade was offered the opportunity to lead this area, working alongside a young designer named Mat Heinl (see pp. 23–25). This was a time of exciting opportunities and steep learning curves that in many ways has provided him with the confidence to take on the unknown.

At this time, a chance meeting reignited Wade and Palmer's friendship, and while talking in the pub they began to hatch a plan to start their own studio. They decided to call their business "Kin." As a noun, this word means "one's family and relations," and as an adjective, it means "kindred/ related/ allied/ cognate." Wade explains why this was relevant to what they were trying to do.

"Kin is about the relationship between me and Kev—our shared philosophy about design: the friendships that we share, the extended connections between the people we know. It describes the relationship between things in space and the way they connect with each other. The relationship between the surface of an object and the things it does. How an object relates to its surroundings and how people relate to it. It's also about a network of people that can enable things to get done, a network that based on past tells us from past experience that we can deliver anything."

Case Study: Kin Says "Hello"

The designers at Kin often find themselves working in virgin territory, working across a range of disciplines and media. It is therefore really important that they explain what they do clearly and seductively. "Hello" is a presentation that allows them to do this. In many ways it feels like a blueprint for a future-facing communication design practice.

The presentation describes Kin's ability to create "smart spaces, interactive objects, and installations" and how the studio is at the "heart of their practice." Distributed across three floors this "multi-functional space . . . serves as a platform for prototyping, project development, and material-led creative thinking." A team made up of designers, developers, and makers uses this environment to create work that the document organizes under five themes:

Attractors

Kin produces work that takes advantage of "the point at which you grab the attention of a viewer and draw them in." For example, giant responsive cassettes for Tommy Hilfiger and a clock for Ted Baker on Fifth Avenue, New York, with a variety of faces and interchangeable numerals.

Collaborative Games

In the studio's work, Kin uses play to "engage a young audience with a story or message" and "often use[s] the mechanics of play to construct experience[s] for different audiences."

Interactive Surfaces

Kin has created a number of "interactive tables" in places that encourage the audience to "pause and engage with content."

Embedded Technology

Kin often "likes the technology in our projects to take a back seat so that the user can concentrate on the interaction."

Customization and Personalization

New manufacturing and distribution systems have enabled the possibility for experiences to be tailor made, and as Kin points out, this is a powerful tool for drawing people into a brand or experience.

kin-design.com

3. The working mechanism of Kin's clock for the Ted Baker flagship store on Fifth Avenue, NYC.

4. The environment design for the Compass Lounge of the National Maritime Museum in London.

5. The interactive learning tablet that Kin designed for the National Maritime Museum.

1. Some of the oversized cassette cases that Kin created for Tommy Hilfiger.

2. Projections for the Sony IFA Exhibition in Berlin.

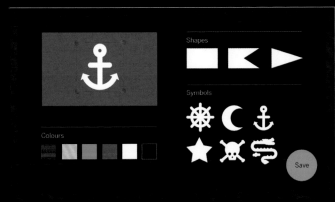

Touch

Print is now an option rather than the only solution, but as a result designers have started to better understand its inherent strengths.

Print is a true craft. Our technologies are advanced but that's not the point. Achieving the subtleties of finish and finesse still calls for extreme skill of hand and eye, and genuine care in the process. The creative agencies, fashion labels, and luxury brands that repeatedly trust us with their most important work all crave craftsmanship.
From the website of Identity printing

1

For over a decade now, design commentators have talked about the end of print, but each year more books are bought than at any other point in history. Print is now an option rather than the only solution, and as a result designers have started to better understand its inherent strengths as a medium. We now need a rationale to use it and have begun to appreciate why people might be attracted to what is essentially a tactile experience. Print creates objects that engender an intimate relationship, and its tactility offers an extremely valuable way to create a physical connection with an audience.

Tim Milne is one of the early innovators in this field and founded the Artomatic library in 1998 in order to store his extensive print sample collection in a place where the designers he was doing business with could access it. Talking with his friend Malcolm Garrett, Milne identified that the most significant shift in the function of printed media since Gutenberg's invention of the printing press was taking place.

If you look at what Gutenberg did, its real significance was that he provided a way to distribute information cheaply, efficiently and accurately. His invention was the best way of doing this until we invented the Internet. . . . Print innovation up until the invention of the Internet had been related to improving speed and efficiency, but once we came to realise that the value of print was no longer in the transmission of information people started to focus on its ability to define physicality. . . . Objects are fundamental part of the human experience. Human beings are conditioned to read objects. But in modern communication objects are given secondary importance. We tell people things using words and pictures.

Milne believes that by being freed from the shackles of reproduction, print can start to fulfill a much more interesting and powerful function. "If you create an object that has value in and of itself—rather acting as a reproduction of something else—that object is going to feel more special to the recipient."

The size, shape, materials, and construction of an object tell stories that are understood instinctively. Milne refers to Daniel Kahneman's Nobel Prize–winning book, *Thinking, Fast and Slow*, to demonstrate the significance of this. Kahneman proposes that perception is derived from two modes of thinking: "System 1," which processes information quickly and works subconsciously with little or no effort, and "System 2," which requires our attention to analyze information logically. System 1 thinking provides an instinctive and emotional background that informs the effort of our System 2 analysis. Milne points out that, by giving us words and pictures to decode, a majority of communication design is perceived through System 2 thinking, which requires effort and our full attention. Tactile objects, on the other hand, are perceived mainly through System 1 thinking and engender an instinctive, less effortful response to form, texture, weight, and materials, thus providing a powerfully influential context for our System 2 analysis.

Printers and paper suppliers have responded to these realizations with innovations in production techniques. In the global creative centers, new businesses have sprung

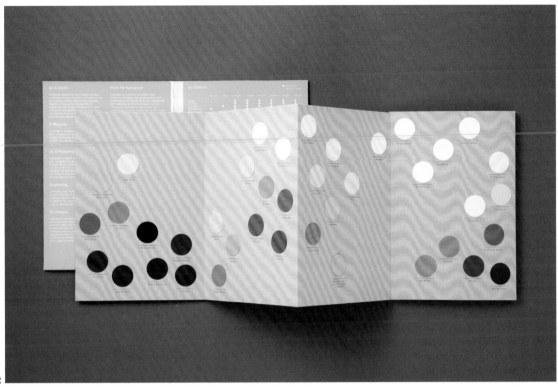

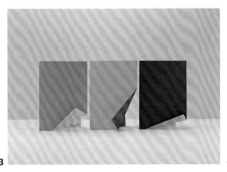

2

1 & 2 Paper samplers designed by Madethought for GF Smith.

3

4

3 & 4. Invitations for GF Smith's "Beauty in the Making" use minimal typography and simple folds to show off the Colorplan paper range.

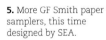

5. More GF Smith paper samplers, this time designed by SEA.

6. 10,000 digital textures were generated as part of this collaboration between Field and SEA.

5

6

up offering high levels of technical finish and the ability to create objects that communicate through seductive relationships between ink, paper, varnish, and custom binding techniques. In the UK, boutique production houses and specialized printers such as Thinktank Media, Progress Packaging, Generation Press, K2, Push, Identity, and Benwell's work with creative studios to lead the world in innovative print and packaging design.

Independent British paper supplier GF Smith has created a sophisticated support structure to enable designers to demonstrate the potential of print and paper to their clients. They also work with leading studios such as SEA and Madethought to create beautifully designed sample books and guides. They have become the byword for innovation in this area, and in 2012 sample packages designed by SEA were selected as one of the Design Museum's Designs of the Year. This project provides an excellent example of how digital technology can be integrated into the print process. SEA worked with Field to create a generative system that enabled the creation of 10,000 digital textures that were then applied to custom packaging. Madethought worked with GF Smith to create the invitations, an identity, and a series of samplers that were used to market their "Beauty in the Making" exhibition in Central London. They used minimal typography, die cutting, and folding to allow the quality of the paper ranges to take center stage. The influential graphic design blog *September Industry* said of this project, "When a product is intrinsically beautiful,

its important to allow the product to speak and not apply excessive layers of graphics or design trickery."

Creative studios sometimes create in-house projects that provide physical examples of what can be achieved through the print process. Over the last eight years, designers at London-based creative studio Accept & Proceed have engaged in a studio project that involves the creation of a set of artworks that describe amounts of daylight for the forthcoming year. These "light calendars" are expertly printed by local screen printers K2 and Bob Eight Pop before being sold in selected galleries around London.

It is clear that in the more progressive parts of the industry the opposition of print and digital media is an anachronistic irrelevance. Designers understand that each medium has attributes that are appropriate to different types of communication. A physical object like a book has a permanence that digital communication could never achieve. Digital is by its nature transient and updatable— it therefore does not have authority of the printed page. The process of editing and perfecting prepares print for a much longer life. The expense of print and its ability to create seductively tactile objects has found a perfect home at the luxury end of the market. In recent years, up-market estate agents, luxury fashion brands, and boutique hotels have all utilized print finishing techniques such as screen-printing, foil blocking, and lazer etching to create tactile promotion that feels reassuringly expensive.

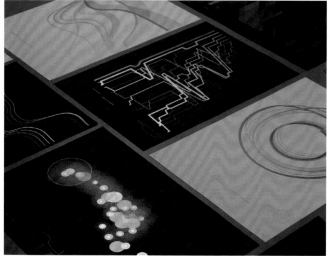

7

8

9

10

11

Container

Tim Milne continues to explore the future potential of print and his latest project, CONTAINER is "a magazine made of objects." As his website says, "Inside the first edition of CONTAINER is a collection of 10 bespoke, exclusive conceptual physical objects, each created by an individual contributor around a specific theme— 'Hot&Cold'. The objects are packaged in a suitably temperature-related container—an expanded polystyrene box. The objects in CONTAINER are designed and executed exquisitely in a wide range of materials and processes (67 in total)."

Container #1 featured work by the likes of Daniel Eatock, one of the founding partners of Poke, Nick Roope, Mother, Malcolm Garrett, and the artists Rebecca & Mike. It also features a stainless-steel mapping of the North and South poles created by Accept & Proceed. This piece demonstrates the layers of instinctual communication that physical objects are able to inspire. The cold hard steel is used to hint at the physical environment being depicted, and this is contrasted with precision-crafted intricate lines detailing territorial borders and the tracks of explorer's expedition routes that are created at high temperature using lazer etching.

CONTAINER is published in a limited edition of 200 and retails for £200. It is designed to illustrate how "objects tell stories" and in delivering this intention it explores the latest innovation in high-end production techniques.

7 & 8. Some of the screen-printed posters created by Accept & Proceed that cleverly combine ink and paper to create seductively tactile data visualizations.

9. GPS by James Bridle. A 3D printed model of the earth's GPS satellite network.

10. *So Hot Right Now* by John Willshire. An exploration of perceived and actual value, and a joke that gets funnier as it gets older.

11. *The Temperature of Things* by Leila Johnson. Temperature readings taken of the artist, printed onto thermal paper.

12. All the storytelling objects in the CONTAINER package.

12

Experiential Marketing

Seductively crafted experiences engage without demanding to be understood and as result are able to elicit an instinctive emotional response.

In the last section, Touch, Tim Milne refers to Daniel Kahneman's *Thinking, Fast and Slow*. The book explores the relationship between the two different cognitive systems of the human brain. Kahneman's proposition is key to understanding many of the ideas that are currently informing communication design. Broadcast messages involve an audience engaging in System 2 thinking, which requires effort and our full attention—a luxury in the crowded communication landscape. Today, more effective communication utilizes System 1 thinking, enabling an effortless impression that will instinctively inform our understanding, thus, providing a highly influential context for our rational decisions. Seductively crafted experiences engage without demanding to be understood and are able to elicit an instinctive emotional response. A website that functions perfectly, a payment system that is painlessly efficient, or an intelligently thought out activity are able to instinctively engage an audience and win their trust.

Mills, co-founder of user experience and user interface designers, ustwo (see pp. 89–91) explains, "Doing throwaway campaign-based work is not something we are interested in—other companies can deal with that. I am interested in marketing, but it has to be relevant. We are trying to create experiences that people genuinely want such as 'Ping it!'—which allows people to transfer money really easily. We want to educate our clients that

1–3. R/GA's groundbreaking Nike+ system: a range of products that enable Nike customers to record their physical activity competitively.

4 & 5. Barclay's Pingit! enables quick, easy money transfers and in doing so provides an experience that helps market the products and services of the bank.

1

2
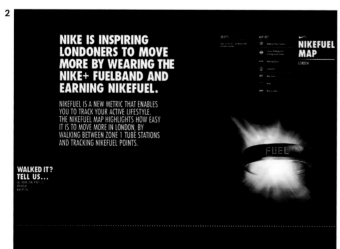

3

if they spent some of the marketing budget they have put aside to promote the service we have created for them on making that service better—then this would represent a more intelligent use of their finances. The product or the service that we have created is the advertising and marketing. The best marketing you can have is to create a great user experience."

Explaining what you do is not the best way to get somebody to understand it. Far more effective is to let them experience what you do and form their own opinion. Experience engenders a deeper and longer lasting understanding.

Designers are ideally placed to create these experiences and have become very successful at siphoning off the marketing budget for themselves. Agencies such as Ideo and Frog utilize "design thinking" to create products and services that define experiences are designed to connect with consumers' needs and desires. Tim Brown, president and CEO of IDEO, explains on the IDEO website that, "Design thinking is a human-centered approach to innovation that draws from the designer's toolkit to integrate the needs of people, the possibilities of technology, and the requirements for business success."

Digital agencies like R/GA, ustwo, and AKQA create products that define experiences around a brand. Working with the sports mega brand, R/GA created Nike+,

a range of products that track activity with NikeFuel a universal way of measuring and recording movement. These devices enable Nike customers to record their physical activity competitively and be healthier. Nike+ demonstrates a brand presented through a product that brings its values to life and, as such, has taken the industry by storm, redefining the way we think about branding and marketing. Brands are now queuing up to create a digital product that will become the next Nike+.

Hashem Bajwa, former digital strategist at Droga5 (interviewed on pp. 109–111) in NYC, launched DE-DE, a studio that Droga5 has created to explore the potential of digital products. He is wary of seeing them purely as an add-on marketing tool, pointing out that product development is challenging within an advertising, marketing, or branding-agency model. He finds the concept of using one product to market another potentially problematic. He stresses that marketing as well as design expertise needs to be brought to bear on the development of a company's digital products in order for these products to deliver an experience that has marketing benefits. "The product strategy and the marketing strategy are inherently linked. The engineer who is building a new future into their product and the marketing person who is developing communications about the product need to be working out of the same core ideas."

To illustrate this he uses the example of a carbon calculator that another digital studio, AKQA, developed in association with Fiat. He points out that Fiat came to them to look at ways that the USB port in their new car could be used. AKQA proposed a tool that would help drivers understand the way their car works and in particular its efficiency in terms of carbon emissions. Not only was this product innovative and useful, but the experience it engendered tied in with perception of sustainable innovation that Fiat wanted to create around its car.

4

5

SEARCH: DE-DE; Hashem Bajwa; Nike+/ NikeFuel; AKQA; R/GA; Droga5; IDEO; Frog Design; Daniel Kahneman *Thinking, Fast and Slow*; ustwo; user centred design; William Owen "Messy Medium" *Eye 64*

Conversation

The alphabet and print technology fostered and encouraged a fragmenting process, a process of specialism and detachment. Electric technology fosters and encourages unification and involvement.
Marshall McLuhan,
The Medium Is the Massage

Developments in communication media have created a landscape of connected channels. This process has had irreversible effects on how media is experienced and also the way it is created. The hierarchy of the relationship between producer and consumer has shifted, transforming dictation into dialogue. In a networked world, the audience is much more active—able to provide instant response and opinion. This means that data revealing the effectiveness of a piece of communication is more available than ever before.

Social networking provides endless opportunities for audiences to register their opinions, and the backlash to an ill-thought-out creative decision can be instant and overwhelming. Brands need to be more accountable and carefully nurture public opinion. Our relationship with them has moved from reverence to reference, and anything they tell us is cross-referenced before being deemed credible.

While some designers are inhibited by this feedback, others have built it into their working process and engage with audiences proactively to continually adapt and perfect what they are producing. In the digital arena, new design methodologies have been developed that respond to the specific qualities of the medium. Iterative processes allow outcomes to evolve by using prototypes that are tested by users and improved at each stage from their input. The principles that drive these new approaches are also increasingly applied to the design of physical outcomes. As a result, production processes have become more agile, and open-ended collaborative making is now embraced as the creative industry standard.

Collaboration

Successful contemporary
design practice is moving away
from a production-line approach
to take advantage of the
potential of collaborative making.

1

1. This painting by
illustrator Nic Tual
was created as part
of a collaboration
with interactive
designers Sennep.

**Designers and technologists must share know-
how and experience to come to grips with the
opportunities created by networked social media
and that the best way to do this is through the
collaborative making, not specifying.**
William Owen, *Eye 64*

SEARCH: Mills ustwo YouTube; Moving Brands;
Web 2.0; Sennep; studio culture; field generative
design; BERG/ BERG Cloud; hack days; hack
manifesto; Raspberry Pi; Open IDEO/ IDEO

The communication landscape we inhabit is made up of complex open networks. The model of the lone egocentric specialist is not suited to this environment. Mills, co-founder of ustwo (see pp. 89–91), illustrates this point: "There is no space for ego at ustwo. Here it's about teamwork, and people can only work in teams. Digital design is about generosity and empathy." Contemporary communication works across media in ever-changing contexts and employs a range of skills and disciplines. The success of companies like ustwo and Moving Brands (see pp. 23–25) is based on the recognition of the potential of the different qualities within a team coming together to solve problems, not in the form of a production line but through genuinely collaborative creative activity.

The creation of a vibrant studio culture is fundamental to this approach, and as Matt Rice, founding partner of Sennep points out, "The culture you establish in the studio is really important, and as our studio grows we think about it more and more. I think it starts by getting the right people. The people establish the culture. I'm not sure we can really say that the culture is engineered— it's more that we just get on and enjoy talking to each other about the things we're working on. . . . We all work facing one another around a big table—so we talk to each other. Everybody's ideas are welcome, all of the time."

Contemporary practice is often structured around a small core of permanent employees complemented by regular contributions from known freelancers. These freelancers work within a community of like-minded studios, and the connections will sometimes extend to collaborating on jobs where specialized skills are required. London-based digital studio Field has gained a reputation working alongside more traditional studios using coding to program generative design outcomes. They worked with Bibliothèque to create the Ollo logo (see pp. 16–17) and SomeOne to create the imagery for their Big Eyes identity (p. 33).

Another London studio, BERG, takes this idea of collaborative making a stage further by developing BERG Cloud. This is a development platform that makes the same technology, tools, and user interface that was used to deliver its own digital products available for other developers to use. According to CEO Matt Webb writing on the studio's website, by putting this "operating system for connected products in a social space" they hope to create a space where "new product categories are born and new business models are enabled." (A more detailed conversation with Webb about BERG Cloud is featured later in this chapter.)

Hacking
BERG opens up the studio to the general public for "hack days" and "After School Clubs" and many technology companies also use this approach. Moving Brands, ustwo, and bigger names such as Dropbox and Google have identified the value of hacking in helping them explore new potentials for their technology. Moving Brands uses hacking as a way of trying out new ideas. In a recent project, they hacked the Kinect camera (the camera that provides motion tracking

2 & 3. Collaborative client workshops from Moving Brands.

4. Collaborative screen-based interaction by So Touch + Mindstorm.

Our business is inherently multidisciplinary, inherently complex and inherently involves lots of people who are not from the design industry— so it is really important that to be part of this you need to understand and feel capable of operating in a team.
Mat Heinl, CEO of Moving Brands

for the Xbox 360) to create a typeface that was based on gesture. There is even a "hackday manifesto" that can be found at http://hackdaymanifesto.com/.

Hacking has become a lo-fi science movement promoting the do-it-yourself adaptation of technology in an attempt to make it work better. More and more people are interested in trying to get technology to do new things, and hack events provide a way of sharing and developing skills and ideas. Academics in the University of Cambridge's Computer Laboratory have even invented a computer that is designed to promote hacking in schools—the Raspberry Pi. This single-board credit-card sized computer was created to adapt and subvert its technology to a wide variety of unseen uses. Costing between £20 and £30, it is priced to encourage use by young children and those wanting to experiment with computer technology on a budget.

5

Open IDEO

Award-winning global design firm IDEO has developed a reputation for what it calls a "human-centered, design-based" approach to innovation, and collaborative making has always been at the core of this approach. To add an ethical dimensional to its design business, it has developed Open IDEO—according to the website, it is an "open innovation" platform that uses a global community of collaborators to "solve big challenges for social good."

Members of the public are invited to take part in a variety of challenges; which are regularly posted at OpenIDEO.com. These challenges are then taken through three development phases—inspiration, concepting, and evaluation. Members of the OpenIDEO community sign up to take part in this process and can contribute in a variety of different ways—from posting inspirational observations and photos and sketches of ideas to business models and snippets of code. Sometimes contributors provide a comment that enables an idea to move forward, while at other times they might submit their own project proposal. Between each development phase, IDEO helps shape the journey by framing the challenge, prototyping, and facilitating the discussion. Eventually a number of concepts are chosen by the community to take forward and are presented on the website as raw material to be put into practice by funded interest groups or corporate partners.

6
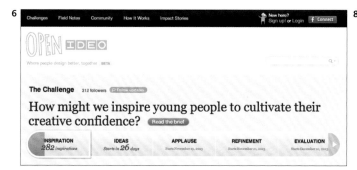

7

8

5. Collaborative prototype development at interaction design studio Sennep.

6–8. Pages from the OpenIDEO website:

6. An OpenIDEO challenge.

7. Collaborator profiles.

8. Stages in the OpenIDEO design process.

Part of what we do is make tools that will allow us and other people to experiment individually.

In Conversation

with Matt Webb, CEO
and founding partner,
BERG London

**Influential London-based product and
design consultancy BERG has worked
with major global names such as
Apple, Google, Intel, Twitter, and the
BBC. It is probably best known for the
creation of its web responsive printing
device Little Printer. One of BERG's
aims is to move beyond isolating
screen-based interfaces and create
web-based products that enable more
social interaction. Its consultants
believe we are now in a position to
develop an "Internet of things" that
would enable physical products to
be more social and more alive.**

bergcloud.com

In our interview, CEO Matt Webb
talks about how when they began
in 2006, he and BERG co-founder
Jack Schulze were interested in
technology that existed in a social
space, in how technology can
humanize, but when they began to
try to create the physical technology
to enable these ideas, their
development process was too slow
and laborious. As Webb points out,
"If it's slow and difficult, it means
that you can't experiment, you
can't get your hands dirty,
you can't feel the grain of the
material in your fingers."

To overcome this, they
developed BERG Cloud to help speed
up the process and provide some
"scaffolding" that they could build
from. What they created acts as both
a development platform and the
operating system for their products.
It has the potential to act as a
"nervous system for connected
products," and they envision its
potential beyond their own use. Webb
observes, "If it was scratching an itch
for us and it was scratching an itch for
our clients, then it could also scratch
an itch for other people." As a result
BERG Cloud was created as an open
platform, "so open that creators of
new products will just naturally use it
as a prototyping tool."

It was crucial to the success of
BERG Cloud that new users could feel
comfortable on the platform, so the
consultants at BERG asked, "How do
you end up in a place where people
are familiar, happy, inventive, and
sharing? . . . How do you get to the
place where you have the chance
transmit the culture of BERG Cloud?"
The consultants see the mechanisms
to enable the transmission of this
culture are as important as the
technical support they offer. Webb
talks about "project Dutch," the idea
that as a group of people get involved
in a project they start to develop a
language that only they understand.
He observed that learning to use
this specialized language becomes
fundamental to being part of the
project. To be involved in BERG Cloud
you need to learn a little "project
Dutch," and BERG has created
mechanisms that will allow you to
do this.

The ability that language has
to unlock or obscure understanding
is something Webb refers to often.
At certain points in a project he
feels that it is important not to try
to describe something through
language but to value an unspoken
understanding. "I have this idea that
it's good to be able to experiment
and get your hands dirty and learn
material without having to say it
out loud. Your language always
comes from your past, and if you're
inventing, that's something that
is going to exist in the future—so
almost by definition we won't have
language to describe it yet." The act
of describing something using words
can hinder a deeper understanding.

Webb still feels that there
is a need for solitary, head-down
investigation—especially when
learning to work with a new
medium like the iPad or connected
devices. "These things are cracked
at two in the morning with coffee
and cigarettes. In most cases real
discovery, real insight happens at
an individual level." Once the insights
have been gained, then the individual
might develop the vocabulary to
articulate them. This is where project
Dutch kicks in, followed by a point
where outsiders can be brought on
board to push discoveries forward
or apply them to a context.

It is only through discovering
it for yourself that you can really
understand "the grain of a medium."
This is why BERG often creates tools
that enable clients or collaborators
to make discoveries for themselves.
BERG breaks client projects down into
three stages:

1. **Materials exploration.**
   This is a place for individual
   discovery and getting to know
   the grain of the medium.
2. **Production, design development.**
   This is broken down into
   two-week sprints, with core
   corrections made along the way.
3. **Tuning in communication.**
   This is a period at the end of the
   project that enables the team to
   work out how to introduce it to
   other people.

Interestingly, on client projects Webb points out that they are not always able to plan for further iteration. Increasingly however, they are developing BERG Cloud along with their own products, and in this area of their business they plan a continuous evolution—both for digital and physical products.

"One of the things we are doing with BERG Cloud, Little Printer, and connected products is discovering that physical things are no longer finished." Just like digital products, they develop through use. For example, "When we brought out Little Printer, we saw it has a mini newspaper; then somebody created a publication called *monster of the week* and we received a picture of one of the monsters colored in by a child and pinned on a fridge. We realized in that moment that kids loved Little Printer, and this discovery has informed its future development in a massive way. Since then, we have gone about redoing it for families. Its behavior has changed. If you look at Little Printer now, it's not in the newspaper delivery business—it's lots of things and one of those things is a fax for kids."

Case Study: Little Printer

Little Printer is a product of now. It is a "product," a tangible thing, but is also a "product" in the sense of a consequence of contemporary culture. It humbly and accessibly exemplifies how physical and digital have merged to become one, to become hybrid objects, to demonstrate how objects might become networked, and how domestic objects might behave.
"Little Printer, A Portrait in the Nude," *Domus 965*, Dan Hill interview with Jack Shulze

Put very simply, Little Printer is a web-connected, responsive printing device. It was developed using BERG Cloud, and anyone can create publications for it using its API (application programming interface). BERG calls the pieces of software that produce content that can be printed on Little Printer "publications." A good way to understand how publications work with Little Printer is to think about how apps work with an iPhone or iPad.

BERG is keen to create a community of people publishing to Little Printer. As it says on the website, "We wanted to open up

1

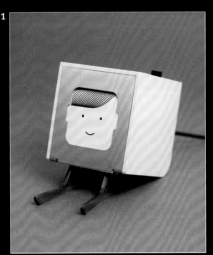

1. The Little Printer is, in effect, a till receipt printer that has been ingeniously repurposed.

2. Little Printer enables you to add "Publications" using your smartphone.

3 & 4. Publications provide everything from a daily puzzle to an update on your running progress.

5. A drawing challenge from the Little Draw publication.

2

publication to the kind of person who can cope with installing WordPress on their shared server, but who doesn't have the time or inclination to learn to code."

They also run hack days and after-school clubs where they can help potential collaborators work with their API at first hand. According to BERG, these events "help us with the development of our own API, and it's exciting for us to see people getting involved and getting their hands dirty with code and design."

littleprinter.com

Little Draw

Ruckus is two recent graduates of Central Saint Martens, London: Anisha Peplinski and Cally Gatehouse. Soon after graduation, they attended a Hackney House Creative Day and heard BERG's talk about Little Printer. Soon after, the two women started a conversation with BERG via Twitter and started to work on ideas for a Little Printer publication. "I wanted to do something that made proper use of the medium, not something that just enabled you to print your last five Instagram photographs." They created a pitch and sent it to BERG, who replied saying that they loved the idea and wanted Peplinski and Gatehouse to move forward with it. After a bit of initial coding, Peplinski

and Gatehouse then went along to one of BERG's After School Clubs, where they received firsthand advice that helped them produce some test prints and perfect their publication so that it connected to the BERG Cloud. After approval from BERG, Ruckus's publication was made available for download to the mobile devices that connect to Little Printer. Little Draw is a weekly drawing game delivered by Little Printer for children aged four and up. Little Draw has been a runaway success, and Ruckus now commissions illustrators to create imagery for it.

littledraw.co.uk

5

Iteration

New ways of communicating have brought with them new ways of working—ways of working that might not have defined beginning and end points.

If you're making a physical product the development cycle is much longer—you spend more time perfecting and developing the product before you release it. But in the digital sphere, the development cycle is very different. You have to see people interacting with your product and then you incrementally improve it as you go along.
Hashema Bajwa, CEO, NYC digital production studio DE-DE

In the days when designers were mainly focused on the creation of physical artifacts, it was necessary to work through a linear process that was gradually perfected toward a final, permanent outcome. The growth of digital design has brought with it a new creative process. The nature of digital technology means that design outcomes are continually perfected and adapted to account for new uses, new users, and new purposes.

A linear process is well suited for the creation of broadcast-based communication. However, today digital communication channels enable conversation. As a result, a more complex process of development is required. Digital communication does not have the permanence of analog forms. Outcomes change and are adapted by both the creator and the user. The working process for creating this sort of communication often does not have defined beginning and end points. Outcomes are in a constant state of flux. Here, iterative processes with a series of outcomes that are adapted and evolved take advantage of opportunities to make and remake.

Digital design outcomes continue to evolve even after publication. A recent development in digital production proposes the creation of what is called "a minimum viable product" or MVP, created as quickly as possible and released into the market to be perfected through user feedback. Further versions can then be shaped in response to audience recommendations.

Recently, this digitally native attitude of iteration and outcome evolution has begun to influence design in the

1 & 2. Visual icon development sheets from Moving Brands.

3. Prototyping drawings from the Compass Lounge project by Kin.

4. Some of the 365 logo iterations created by Kin for the Third City PR company.

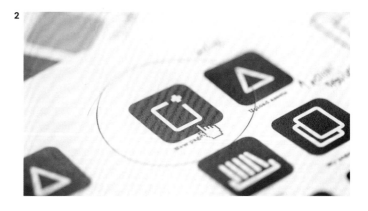

SEARCH: Hashem Bajwa; digital products DE-DE; ustwo Mills; Matt Rice Sennep; iterative development/ design process; minimum viable product; digital production

I've always welcomed the ever-evolving nature of digital design. The idea that you would print something that is finished and you're be stuck with makes me very nervous. The thing with digital is that even at the last minute you can make it better. . . . Actually even after its launch you can make it better. You can improve it as you use it and as you see other people using it. I feel much more comfortable with this way of working.
Matt Rice, founding partner, Sennep

physical world. More agile and sophisticated production processes enable analog products to adapt and evolve through use. The new design attitude is user centered, and contemporary designers are motivated by the desire to create things that people genuinely want to engage with. As Matt Rice points out, "Iteration is really just building small things, looking at them, trying them out, and seeing what happens. It's about getting a response from people and, in light of that response, adapting what you do. On the one hand, there is a strategic way of thinking about developing something but also on the other hand, there is an emotional, intuitive feeling of creating stuff that people respond to."

These principles are benefitting all areas of creative practice. It makes sense across all disciplines to be open to new ways of doing things, prepared to constantly evaluate what you do, to respond to evidence, and to make the changes that are necessary. Within new digital companies such as ustwo, these principles are also applied to the organization and management of the business. Often having grown very quickly, these companies are agile and responsive, employing new and exciting systems to manage people and motivate their employees. They are made to feel included in the business because it responds to their needs in positive and dynamic ways. In the brave new world of tech, recruiting the right talent is a major challenge; as a result, user-centered design is often created by employee-centered businesses.

3
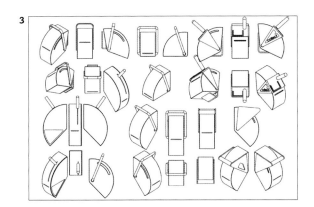

4
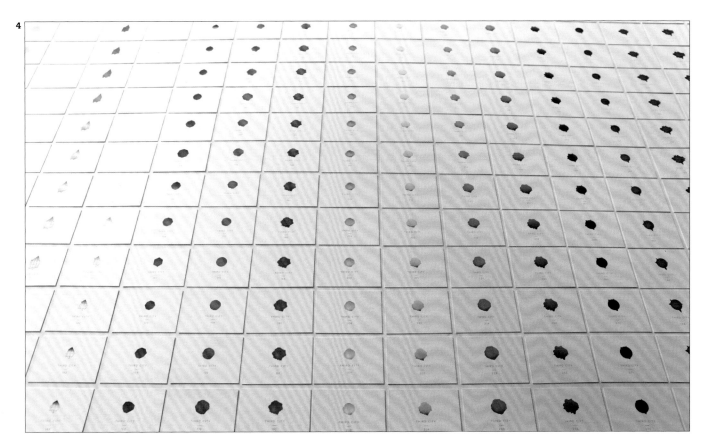

Prototyping

This is a key principle of the iterative design process.

Go as far as you can with paper—the crudeness of the medium makes you focus on what is really important, and that is the movement and interaction.
Neil MacFarland, creative director, ustwo

Iterative design processes require the creation of prototypes that can be tested, adapted and developed. Each prototype is a step to perfecting an outcome. Digital design studios in particular engage in a process of making and testing in order to assess suitability and functionality. The prototypes they use to do this are often quick and dirty, created to test and move on. This "build mentality" provides a competitive advantage by enabling a client to experience how something works rather than simply being told.

Prototypes can also be used as a tool of strategic planning because they allow for the testing of ideas and principles in real time. The speed and economics of digital production mean that instead of hypothesizing about something, you can just build it.

Outside of client-led projects, prototyping has a research-and-development function (R&D). It is a way of exploring what is possible as well as building skills and technical know-how. Sennep regularly creates in-house projects designed to test out and demonstrate technical expertise. They call these Sennep "Seeds" and document them on a website of the same name (http://seeds.sennep.com). Founding partner Matt Rice explains that these projects also have benefits for recruitment. "We want to give out the message that we are consistently doing interesting things with new technology. This is good for PR, but it also really helps us to engage with the development community and get the attention of the exciting developers. Getting good developers is really, really important to us."

Moving Brands has a similar approach to R&D and runs a series of studio projects aimed at developing skills related to pieces of new technology. These projects have enabled Moving Brands to explore the use of technologies such as the Kinect camera, 3D printing, generative manufacture, and augmented reality using outcomes such as a 3D gestural typeface, a scarf created from user-generated pictograms, laser-cut electronic lanterns, and a book with living content. As Mat Heinl says, "We approach innovation from a prototyping perspective— if we want to try something out, we make it." (see pp. 105–107 for more about Moving Brands R&D projects).

1. Motion mapping from an interactive 3D music video for the band Duologue created by Moving Brands.

2. Kinect cameras like this one (which comes free with every Nintendo Xbox 360) have recently become a key component in the prototyping process for the design of interactive experiences.

Prototyping a Simple App

Design specialist and ustwo legend Gyppsy
talks through how to prototype an app.

1. **Paper prototyping**

   First you need to create paper-based mock-ups of
   what you want the app to look like and do. This means
   sketching, folding and sticking elements together. Neil
   MacFarland, the creative director of the ustwo games
   team, always encourages his team to take their idea as
   far as possible on paper.
   Test and discuss.

2. **Visualize screens**

   When you are happy, you can design your screens—
   this means creating visuals in Photoshop. These visuals
   will define an overall look and feel in terms of color,
   typography, and graphic devices.

3. **Prototype links**

   Then think about how these screens might interact
   with each other. For very basic interaction, you could
   create a Keynote, PowerPoint, or PDF presentation to
   do this. There are also a number of prototyping apps
   available online such as Pop App or Field Test App
   (https://itunes.apple.com/gb/app/pop-prototyping-
   on-paper/id555647796?mt=8). New tools are being
   developed all of the time.
   Again, test and discuss.

4. **Cut up for coding**

   You will then need to separate your designs into
   different layers to enable each element of interaction
   to work separately.

5. **Link and animate**

   The separate elements involved in the design can then
   be linked and animated in something like Xcode—the
   iOS development environment. This is free to download
   from the Apple website (https://developer.apple.com/
   xcode/) and there is a similar platform available for
   Android. Depending on how involved the interaction
   is, you may or may not need to write code at this stage.
   A working prototype may be achieved by simply
   changing settings in Xcode or Quartz Composer.

6. **User test**

   At this point you should have something that you can
   user test or possibly even present to a client.

7. **Code**

   To take your prototype beyond this stage and make
   the software run correctly and smoothly will involve
   writing code. But there are lots of online forums and
   tutorials to help you do this. https://developer.apple.
   com/resources/ is a good starting point here.
   Alternatively, you could do what Gyppsy does and give
   it to a developer.

3

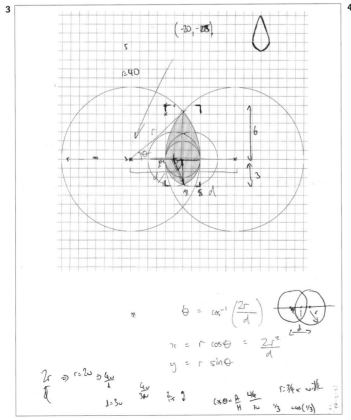

4

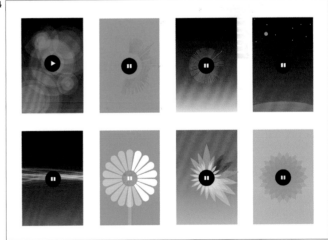

3 & 4. Examples
of prototyping and
development drawings
from BERG.

Case Study: Rando by ustwo

From an interview with Jack Maxwell, visual designer, ustwo

Rando is an app "where serendipity rules the day and users send and receive random photos to and from random people all over the world." Its development process also explores the potential of live iterative prototyping. The project was developed by Malmö-based developer Kenny Lovrin and visual designer Jack Maxwell in downtime between client briefs. It demonstrates the importance to technology-led agencies of creating research and development opportunities that will enable the discovery of new processes and working methods.

Stage 1: Interaction design

At a company like ustwo, interaction designers normally provide wireframes that describe the required interaction diagrammatically for visual designers to work on.

1. For Rando the interaction was fairly simple, so visual designer Jack Maxwell handled this part of the process himself.

Working quickly in his notebook and on-screen, Maxwell generated ideas for the app's desired functionality.

2. Simple wireframes were then worked up in Illustrator and InDesign. They included text, images, icons, buttons, positioning, and how a user flows from one screen to another.

1

When we pitch for a job, we do not visualize as some agencies do. We build something that works for a client to play with. This is a very important factor in their decision-making. From this point it is a much shorter step for us to create a finished outcome.
Gyppsy, design specialist, ustwo

2

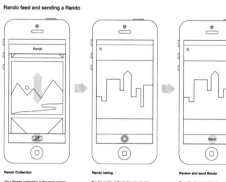

Rando feed and sending a Rando

Rando Collection

'Your Rando collection' is the main screen. From here the main action will be to tap the action bar along the bottom to initiate sending/recieving a Rando, which will take the user to the photo capture screen.

Rando taking

Tap the centre of the bottom bar to take photo. Hit the 'X' to return to the rando collection screen.

Review and send Rando

Once the photo is taken the user can review the image and tap the center of the bottom bar again to send.

Pressing 'X' would take the user back to their collection.

Stage 2: Visual design

Visual designers put together the visual assets for a piece of interaction design and will often come from graphic design or illustration backgrounds.

Working from the wireframes, Maxwell developed four routes, exploring visual metaphors for what the app does.

3. He looked at a paper airplane metaphor to represent the act of sending the photograph.

4. Another route developed the voyeuristic idea of looking through a peephole into the lives of others. When initial trials were placed on the wall of the studio feedback from both the senior team and other ustwo employees was that this was the route to follow.

Stage 3: Working with a developer

5. After the approval of the visual designs, Maxwell created all of the project assets in Photoshop. These included interface, different screens, buttons, and press states. These designs were then cut up in Photoshop, exported as PNG files, and sent over to the developer in Malmö. Since the development of the retina display size, all artwork must be set-up at both normal screen resolution (72PPi) and retina screen resolution (144PPi).

Maxwell accompanied his artwork with an InDesign document describing the flow of interaction and specific actions. This document included a specification with the measurements and pixel dimensions.

Stage 4: Release and iterative development

6. An interactive prototype was then developed for discussion between Maxwell, the developer, and the senior team. Once everything was agreed, the app was released through the App Store and the process of iterative development began. Feedback was gathered through Twitter, the ustwo blog, the Apple Store reviews, and friends and associates, enabling Maxwell and the developer to further improve the project.

Since its release in March 2013, Rando has been a worldwide hit and according to its website is "probably [ustwo's] 'most successful app release ever.'"

Our style is that we do not have a style. We are about the user. We find out what the user needs because we want to create something that they will love.

In Conversation

with Mills, founding partner, ustwo

Two best friends, Mills and Sinx, founded ustwo in 1998 with £5,000 (about $8,500) borrowed from their parents. At the time of writing, ustwo employs more than 150 people in London, Malmö and New York. Over the years, contrasting personalities of these two friends have come to define the secret of their company's success.

ustwo.com

Mills explains that right from the start, the partners had differing interests—Mills was the visual designer and Sinx the interaction designer/developer—but it was this mixture of creativity and technical innovation that enabled them to define a distinctive place in the market. Mills is an exuberant larger-than-life extrovert; he is the "head wonka" and ustwo's cultural ambassador—whereas Sinx shies away from the limelight and likes to lead at a client/project level. Working together, they have developed a seemingly schizophrenic business that creates off-the-wall digital games, apps, and their own IP products, but also offers high-end interface and user-experience design for a range of high-profile corporate clients.

Mills comments, "You shouldn't be able to build a gaming team and create products like Whale Trail and at the same time work for a big bank like Barclays, create Ping It and work on multi-million pound trading platforms. People say that you should specialize and be either one or the other."

He also talks about how ustwo has focused on developing a build mentality and that this has enabled the company to ensure a high level of technical functionality. Its team has developed in-house tools that provide platforms for internal communication and financial record-keeping and have developed a set of highly sophisticated in-house skills from doing this.

As Apple opened the App Store and released the iPhone, Mills initiated Content With Attitude—an area of the business set up to realize the potential creative opportunities that these new platforms might provide. The two sides of the business now feed each other's existence— they are symbiotic. The income from interface and user-experience design provides ustwo with a level of financial security that in turn enables them to also work on more speculative projects. The release of apps such as Granimator, Nursery Rhymes, Mouth Off, Whale Trail, and Rando fulfills the dual function of providing exposure and explaining through experience what they can do.

The two contrasting sides of ustwo's business create a unique opportunity to keep teams motivated through a system of "project holidays."

"We need to be doing big projects, but the problem with these is that they take years to complete. People can't possibly stay focused and motivated on a project that goes on forever. It doesn't matter whether it's for a client or a game—even something like Whale Trail gets boring after a while. We move people off projects and give them a two- or three-week break doing something completely different. They might go on to another project or they might just do some research. We created the sound for [the app] Blip Blup by using somebody who had been working on Ping It, for example. He was interested in sound design so we gave him this task to work on this as two-week project holiday."

While the specifics of what they create might be different, the two sides of ustwo are linked by a concern for the user and a rejection of style-based approaches to design. "I grew up loving the Attik, Designers Republic, and all of these style-based graphic design companies, but now I think you have to be absolutely moronic to try to adopt a style. Our style at ustwo is that we do not have a style. I love the fact that we can do Whale Trail and we also do Ping It. We are about the user—this is a user-centred design company. We find out what the user needs because we want to create something that the user will love."

Mills is currently working on a redesign of ustwo's identity. Originally, he commissioned one of his design heroes to work on the project, but this strategy failed. The designer created a series of visual solutions that were inspired by his (rather than ustwo's) vision of what the company was about. They believe in a rigorous examination of user need, so Mills felt that any identity strategy should start with the people who work for him, who he calls "the ustwobees."

As a result, he terminated the project and began working with a researcher to instigate a series of discussions with his employees that were aimed to identify the core values of the business. This process enabled ustwo to establish a way of describing themselves. They became the "dreamers and doers"—a group of people able to apply a build mentality but also able to understand the power of play and innovation, a studio able to create irreverent but highly engaging digital products while at the same time producing sophisticated functional services for serious financial institutions, a company able to post YouTube videos of Mills riding a mobility scooter in a pink wig without jeopardizing the patronage of their fee-paying corporate clients.

Case Study: Whale Trail
As with most digital games, Whale Trail started with "a mechanic," or set of actions that a gaming experience could be built around. Pac-Man eating power pellets, Super Mario jumping from platform to platform, or an explorer running/ jumping/ sliding through an ancient temple in Temple Run are all examples of successful game mechanics. The mechanic for Whale Trail started with the gentle undulation of a bird in flight. While the game designers were brainstorming this movement, someone jokingly suggested creating a flying whale. Thus the surreal humor of Whale Trail was born, and from this point the game almost designed itself.

The next step was to visualize the world that Willow, the flying whale, would inhabit along with characters and environments that he would interact with. Working prototypes of this world produced by the development team enabled them to test animation and interaction. A team of user testers were then recruited using Twitter with the

additional benefit that they could promote the game on social media. Further publicity was gained by recruiting Gruf Rhys, formerly of the band Super Furry Animals, to create a soundtrack for the game. This track, "Space Dust #2," was released as a single to coincide with its launch.

The success of Whale Trail led to ustwo being approached by Penguin to buy its publishing rights; and an e-book of the game simplified for children was released as a joint venture. ustwo is now working with children's TV production company Absolutely Cuckoo to turn Whale Trail into a TV series. A pilot was created in 2013 featuring full-sized live-action puppets who inhabit a digitally animated 3D world. At the time of writing, MacFarland and the team have just returned from Cannes where they have been pitching their pilot to leading TV executives.

www.youtube.com/
watch?v=r8bJs8opqRw

1

1. The promo screen of the Whale Trail game.

2. Initial sketches of Whale Trail created by Neil MacFarland from ustwo.

3 & 4. Tests from the development of the Whale Trail game.

5 & 6. Stills from the "Whale Trail" TV pilot.

7. Green screen puppetry from the filming of the TV pilot.

User Testing

The strategic starting point for a piece of design is often user behavior.

Can you empathize with the users' experience, and therefore come up with new features, new ideas, new things, and then understand it sufficiently to execute and engineer them?
Hashem Bajwa, CEO, digital product development studio, DE-DE

1
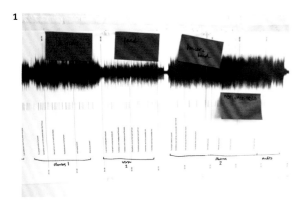

2

Design used to be about individual creative genius. In the 1990s, David Carson famously designed a page of *Raygun* magazine in unreadable dingbats just to make a creative point. Today, designers can no longer afford to ignore the user's needs. The development of social media has empowered consumers and enabled them to enter into a conversation about the products and services they consume. In the world of digital media, the user has a direct input into shaping the design outcome. Immediately accessible feedback data means that audience response need never be second-guessed.

Companies like ustwo position the user at the center of their design strategy, but founding partner Mills (interview pp. 89–91) is keen to stress that this does not mean simply reacting to demands. "We are not in the business of just providing people with what they want. . . . User testing gives you a grounding, but ultimately we make the decision whether to act on it."

Engaging the public in the development of a design outcome can also help recruit advocates that will generate positive feedback on social media. Mills points out, "When we created Whale Trail, our user testers helped market the product. Very early on in the development of the game, we put messages out on Twitter asking people if they wanted to test it. . . . We set only one rule and this was that they had to be honest and they had to be very vocal about it on social networking sites. This worked really well in creating a buzz around the product." Before the product was released, ustwo had recruited an army of people who already identified with it, felt like they were part of it, and were prepared tell the world about it.

Methods for User Testing

Gov.uk defines user testing as "a 'qualitative' research method, used to gauge how easy and intuitive a product, service, website is to use and whether it supports the needs of its intended audience," and says that "user testing measures how well participants respond in the key areas of: efficiency, accuracy, recall and emotional response."

Studios employ a wide range of methods for user testing—here is a description of how two of the studios we spoke to go about it:

Gyppsy and Mills from ustwo (see interview, pp. 89–91) describe four main sources for generating user feedback:

1. Feedback from the Apple Store and websites such as Tech Crunch (techcrunch.com).
2. Twitter hashtags and a network of Twitter followers who provide feedback on the work they produce.
3. Specialist user testing labs provide more formalized research into how a user reacts to a product. These labs create reports from test scenarios during which members of the public are observed working from instruction scripts.
4. They have also set up their own informal user testing groups, using friends and people who work for them. As digital companies grow they tend develop their own user testing infrastructure.

SEARCH: User testing ustwo; David Carson Raygun/ dingbats; ethnography; Hashem Bajwa; user journeys; user centred design; user experience; user research; ustwo nursery rhymes; WW. Denzlow; ustwo nursery rhymes

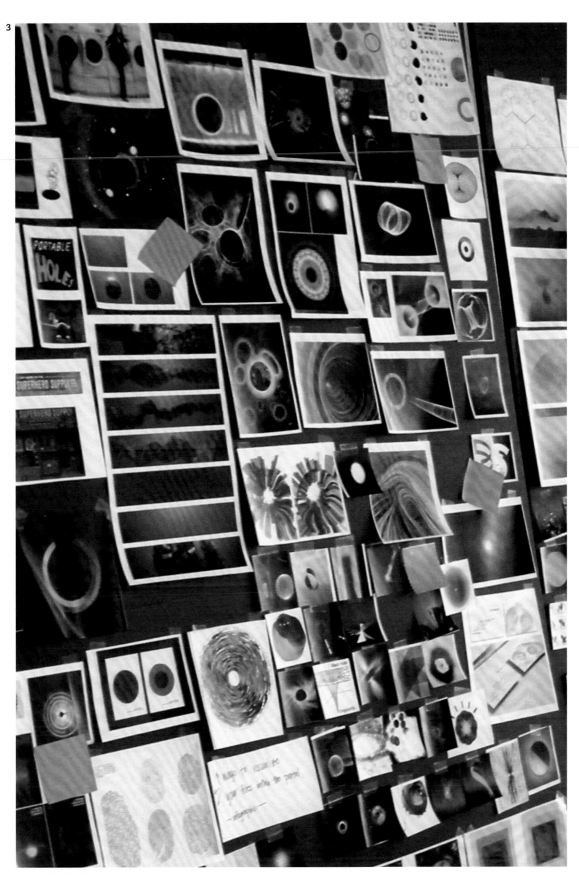

3

1. Sound tests from Moving Brands

2. The antithesis to user-centered design: 1990s design superstar David Carson once created this spread for *Raygun*, replacing type with Dingbats to make the feature impossible to read.

3. Mood boards like this one from Moving Brands are used to define a visual direction for the client.

Mat Heinl CEO of Moving Brands (see pp. 23–25) describes three user testing models employed by his studio:

1. **Persona:** Essentially this is audience profiling; it is driven by personality rather than data and seeks to predict how different types of people react in set situations. This is a subjective form of testing and relates to the team's knowledge of human behavior. Members of the team or an external sample are asked to role-play the use of a prototype or act out a reaction to a piece of communication.
2. **User journey:** This looks at the moments involved in an interaction and considers the structural logic of how a prototype might be used. It is far less emotive than persona testing and employs logical patterns to run through user scenarios.
3. **Ethnography:** This is the study of human behavior. In a user-testing scenario, ethnographic research techniques are used to look at how a sample of group will react in certain situations. This often involves workshops or play-oriented sessions with focus groups.

There are many more approaches in use across the industry, but what seems clear is that anybody wishing to work in the digital design industry needs to be regularly user testing what he or she creates. It is not enough to produce something that your friends feel works, because your friends are likely to be much more tech savvy than the average member of the public. Experienced digital designers such as Gyppsy from ustwo recommend using your parents to user test because they are least likely to have any specialist insight.

Case Study: Nursery Rhymes

Nursery Rhymes was developed by ustwo in partnership with Chris Stephens from Atomic Antelope, originator of the best-selling app of Alice in Wonderland. It uses the copyright-free content of traditional nursery rhymes such as Humpty Dumpty, Jack and Jill and Three Blind Mice and remakes them "for the iPad generation."

The look of the app was inspired by the drawings of William Wallace Denzlow, the American illustrator, most famous for creating the illustrations for *The Wonderful Wizard of Oz* by L. Frank Baum. Images created by ustwo creative director Neil McFarland conjure ideas of antiquarian bookshops and Victoriana and were hand drawn and distressed before being colored in Photoshop. They were then "sprung animated" by ustwo's developers using the open source cross-platform game engine cocos2d. Each page of interaction is loaded with a series of hidden opportunities to engage with the artwork. These interactions gradually evolved through user testing with young children. Suggestions from the testers such as being able to cut the tails from the three blind mice and pin them back on were incorporated into the app to create a wonderfully rich experience that could only exist on an iPad.

On its release, Nursery Rhymes was a runaway success and disrupted the traditional publishing industry to such an extent that it was featured in the *Guardian*, the *Evening Standard* and Reuters. It became the highest grossing app in its category in both the United States and the United Kingdom.

itunes.apple.com/gb/app/nursery-rhymes-storytime/id423322533?mt=8

1–3. The visual elements for Nursery Rhymes were drawn out with a brush and ink before being assembled and animated digitally.

4 & 5. Animated screens from the final app.

6. Nursery Rhymes featured Story Time, which enabled the user to read to their children remotely.

7. The Nursery Rhymes screen icon.

Participation

What we are calling
participatory culture is
a culture where everyone
has the potential to produce
and contribute creatively—
where everyone contributes
to the production of
knowledge and exchange
of information—is
precisely about being able
to rewrite and rescript
the environment around
you, to remix the media
that comes into our lives.
That is in some sense
a modern definition
of what the consumer
does in a digital age.
Dr. Henry Jenkins

The media we use influences our cultural behavior. Marshall McLuhan realized this as far back as the 1960s. His predictions were played out across the latter part of the 20th century and continue to be relevant today. Printed words and images defined a culture of individualized passive consumption. Objects and artifacts had a central role and the makers were revered without question.

As new technologies developed, they created an environment that provided opportunities for audiences to contribute. First, projection and amplification enabled greater communal involvement. Then, with economic prosperity came a wider participation in culture creation and increased outlets for its consumption. More recently, networked computing has created opportunities for an audience to influence and distribute creative content, and this audience has gradually become influential contributors to its form.

Participation culture did not start with networked computing. As far back as the 1950s, cultural commentators described a momentum that was leading to the development of cultural forms that embraced an openness and multiplicity of meaning. Robert Venturi's *Learning from Las Vegas* sought inspiration from architecture that had developed organically through use. Umberto Eco's *The Open Work* examined the benefits of creating work that is unfinished and open to interpretation. Fluxus and the Situationists specified artwork for construction by an audience. More recently, Nicholas Bourriaud's theory of relational aesthetics described an opportunity for artists to create a social circumstance, orchestrate what surrounds them, and become a conduit for the experience.

Networked computing has accelerated the evolution of these ideas through heightened opportunities to adapt, contribute, and redistribute. Today postmodern ideas such as intertextuality, deconstruction, hybridization, appropriation, and recontextualisation all seem like they were coined to describe post- rather than pre-Internet cultural activity.

"Participation culture" is a term first proposed by American media scholar Henry Jenkins. In his 2006 book *Convergence Culture*, he describes how consumers have become "active participants in shaping the creation, circulation, and interpretation of media content." In this brave new participatory world, the nature of creative outcomes is not solely controlled by the expert. Instead it is as likely to be governed by the contribution of an audience. As a result, creative authorship now needs to develop out of empathy, interpretation, and orchestration. In his 2008 essay for *Interactions* magazine, "Design in the Age of Biology: Shifting from a Mechanical-Object Ethos to an Organic-Systems Ethos," Hugh Dubberly, former creative services coordinator at Apple and founder of Dubberly Design Office, describes a shift from a "mechanical object ethos to an organic systems ethos" as we evolve new models for production, distribution, and consumption. He proposes that it is the coordination of these organic ecosystems that will evolve cultural outcomes rather than rigidly controlling specified outcomes and artifacts. These ideas seem set to become increasingly influential in shaping practice within the creative industries as the 21st century evolves.

Behavior Change

A sophisticated manipulation
of our instinctive behavior
is increasingly being used to
influence our decision making.

1. *Nudge* by Cass
Sunstein and Richard
H. Thaler heralded
a new approach to
influencing public
behavior.

2 & 3. By printing
a fly in the men's
urinals, the authorities
at Schiphol Airport
cut their cleaning bills
by 80 percent.

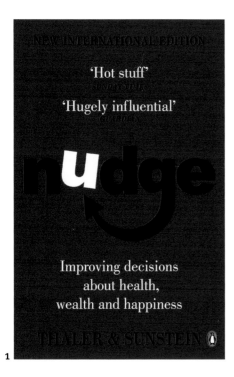

1

SEARCH: Don Norman "Why Design Education Must
Change"; Daniel Kahneman *Thinking Fast and Slow*; Graham
Lawton Behavioral Economics; Cass Sunstein *Nudge*;
Aad Kieboom fly; OgilvyChange; Rory Sutherland

In a world where an audience participates in shaping and redistributing of culture, design is much more dependent on the subtle orchestration of their involvement. This audience wants to feel that they have retained ownership of their input and that this input has been shaped by their own free will. Engineering audience involvement is a complex task that requires skills that go beyond those we traditionally associate with a designer. As a result, design commentators such as Don Norman have called for design education to embrace the development of an understanding of areas such as psychology and applied social and behavioral science.

For much of the 20th century, economic thinking described a consumer who made decisions based on a logical analysis of cost against materials, labor, and availability. This gives a priority to what Daniel Kahneman in his book *Thinking Fast and Slow* calls System 2 thinking: the focused, rational way our brain forms perception. As we have seen earlier in this book (see pp. 66–68), the problem with System 2 thinking is that it is slow, inefficient, and requires 100 percent of our attention. Kahneman points out that, in a world where our busy lives are bombarded with multiple messages, we are not always able to assign the effort and attention required by System 2. As a result, our instinctive perception (what he calls System 1 thinking) is an equally important shaper of our decisions. The science of behavioral economics seeks to understand the complex interrelation between the instinctive perception, emotional preference, and rational analysis that shape our decision making. As Graham Lawton explains in a recent article in *New Scientist* magazine, "Human behavior is irrational but predictably so. It is this predictability that convinced behavioral economists that it should be possible to change behavior." Strategies for influencing this behavior have become known as "nudges."

The "nudge" is an idea coined by U.S. legal scholar Cass Sunstein to describe the sophisticated manipulation of our instinctive behavior in order to influence our decision making. A great example of the nudge, and probably one of the first cases to be widely recognized, happened at Schiphol Airport in the Netherlands in 1999. The airport authorities were looking for ways to save money on their cleaning bills, and economist Aad Kieboom targeted the men's urinals as being a particular problem. He proposed that by getting men to pee more accurately they could save on the floor-cleaning bill. The rational solution to this would have been to put up some signs asking men to aim more accurately, but as Kieboom pointed men were not making a rational decision to pee on the floor. Instead, he suggested that they etch a picture of a fly into the toilet bowl and instinctively men would aim at the fly. Amazingly it worked, and the cleaning bill was cut by 80 percent.

The global advertising and PR agency Ogilvy and Mather have set up a specialized area of its business called OgilvyChange that engages with a "community of behavioral economics experts consisting of leading professors from around the world to create strategies that positively influence behavior," according to its website.

Most importantly, nudges must be freedom preserving, which means people remain at liberty to make the wrong choice.
Graham Lawton, the *New Scientist* magazine

2

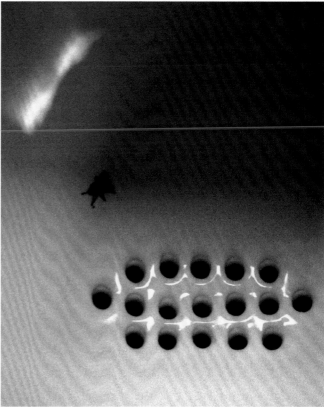

3

One of its founders, Rory Sutherland, has also delivered a series of very popular TED talks on the subject, the first being "Life Lessons of an Ad Man" in 2009. His TED profile describes him as "standing at the center of an advertising revolution," and Ogilvy's groundbreaking status has been reflected in a wealth of awards. In 2013, it was globally the most awarded agency at the Cannes International Festival of Creativity and one of its Golden Lion winning projects, Immortal Fans, (featured on pp. 164–165) used Brazilian football fans' instinctive loyalty to their team to encourage them to sign up with an organ donor registry.

Tara Austin, senior planner at Ogilvy & Mather UK, describes ten factors that influence how we make decisions that inform the work of OgilvyChange:

1. The endorsement of someone we trust can positively influence a decision.
2. Fear of losing something is more influential to a decision that the desire to gain something.
3. We are more likely to make a decision if we see those around us making it too.
4. We are reluctant to pull out of a process. Organizations will often automatically opt us into something with the knowledge that we are unlikely to opt out.
5. Information is better understood if it is delivered at the point where it is needed.
6. Subconscious cues can influence our decisions.
7. We respond to emotional connections.
8. A public pledge is much more likely to be acted upon.
9. We like decisions that make us feel morally good about ourselves.
10. We prefer to commit incrementally rather than through one conclusive decision.

All of this might sound a little like George Orwell's Big Brother, but it is important to remember that these strategies will not work if people feel like they are being covertly forced into something. As Graham Lawton points out in the *New Scientist* article mentioned earlier, "perhaps most importantly, nudges must be freedom preserving, which means people remain at liberty to make the wrong choice."

In almost every area, there are people out there creating amazing content, and they would jump at the chance of creating content for your brand—if your brand is meaningful.

In Conversation

with Adrian Ho, strategist and founding partner, Zeus Jones

Before founding Zeus Jones in 2007, with Christian Erickson, Eric Frost and Rob White, Ho worked at Fallon, Goodby, Silverstein & Partners and Anderson & Lembke. Based in Minneapolis, the company has grown quickly to become one of the most influential agencies in the Midwest, working for clients such as Nestlé Purina, 3M, Nordstrom and Betty Crocker; and in 2014 it opened a second office in the San Francisco Bay Area. Zeus Jones questions traditional views on how a brand might be structured drawing a distinction between "classic brands" that establish trust through authority, deliver a promise, communicate through consistent messages, strive for perfection through control, and establish relationships that are based on transaction and the "modern brand," which is guided by a purpose, establishes a culture built around multiple coherent ideas, creates a community, delivers an experience, moves forward through iterative development, and gains trust through transparent communication.

zeusjones.com

Adrian Ho began our interview by expanding on some of these ideas:

"We believe brands come to life through what they do. They should be built around ideals and purpose so that people can participate with them, be they consumers or strategic partners. This purpose should inform everything that a brand does, from the way the boardroom is laid out to how the representatives of the company behave.

"Some brands have a communications mindset. They believe that a brand is supposed to say things. But if you define a brand in this way, then you automatically end up saying that the brand needs to stand for one thing. You end up wanting to be consistent, saying the same thing over and over again in order to be understood. But if you buy into the idea that a brand is understood by its actions, then this deters you from making one simple promise. A simple promise such as 'we make whiter whites' doesn't have any scope for an audience to participate."

Ho believes that how a brand defines itself needs to be richer and more complex in order to enable the alignment of "different people, partners, disciplines, and functions.

"You can't do anything on your own. You've got to build coalitions of people in order to turn something into a movement. There has to be benefit for all of the participants, and when this happens you have something really powerful.

"A traditional business is one dimensional—it defines itself through that product and creates a transactional relationship with its customers. A modern business is one where you create an ecosystem of different partners and all of those partners win. A good example of this is the iTunes Store, which creates a platform where bands can market themselves and sell their product. iTunes is not about a one-to-one transaction.

The same could be said of the App Store, which supports and nurtures the creation of the content that enables products like the iPad to come to life. Both iTunes and the App Store have created communities of vested interests that contribute to the success of Apple and the products its teams create.

"This concept [the idea of brand as a collaborative platform] is true at all levels of a business. We apply these principles to our work with a brand. Advertising or approaching an advertising agency has always been a very one-dimensional experience: you give the agency a problem and they produce a piece of communication that solves that problem. Instead of simply getting our team to produce content, [Zeus Jones] thinks about other content creators. In almost every area, there are people out there creating amazing content, and they would jump at the chance of creating content for your brand—if your brand is meaningful.

And when you consider the reach that your brand has through its website, media, packaging, retail store, etc., your brand can offer many of those content creators distribution for their content that up until this point has not been possible for them to achieve. One of the major advantages of this model is that you are able build content that is more authentic and more believable, and typically far less expensive, than any content that has been created by an advertising agency. What's more, this content is in turn attractive to other advertisers.

"Zeus Jones can broker a partnerships [that] will allow you to develop a range of really interesting content on the behalf of your brand. Once you have all of this interesting content being created, you can then package it up and approach a media company. These organizations are always looking for interesting content to fill their media space. The key is to define an idea that relates to your brand, informs your brand, and informs ideas around your brand.

"The foundation of all of this is the brand purpose. It outlines the big mission that the company has in society, it tells everyone what the company hopes to do, and, importantly, it also tells people how they can participate. A strong purpose allows us to reach out to other people who share our beliefs and who may want to help. To do this, we create what we call a manifesto, which is really a statement of intent. It is also extremely important that these manifestoes feel visually right. Often what something looks like can help define an idea better than words. A manifesto could be film or a series of pieces of design, but its purpose is that it will help partners contribute cohesively to a vision. Unlike traditional graphic standards, our manifestoes are designed to tell you what you can do rather than tell you what you can't do.

"It's very easy for you to build graphic standards that only you can execute but much harder to build graphic standards that allow different contributors to bring their personality in. It's one thing creating a series of adverts that will work together, but [it's] incredibly difficult to have a whole battery of partners all working toward the same thing and to have that feel coherent. So we work hard to create an infrastructure [that] is defined in writing, in design, in establishing a tone of voice, in setting direction, and so on.

"Ultimately it's about defining a vision that can be individually interpreted."

Case Study: Betty Crocker

When Zeus Jones started to work with Betty Cocker, its brand was built around a very traditional idea of the American family home. Betty Crocker approached Zeus Jones asking its creative team to help create a more progressive perception.

Betty Crocker has always been a brand that helps homemakers. The team discovered that the need to enable homemakers to do more hasn't gone away, but the individual definitions of a homemaker have changed. Research into the life of American families today revealed that they've changed so much that there is a need to redefine what it means to "make home." As an icon of homemakers, Betty Crocker could help gather this information and share it with the world—to demystify what it means

to be a successful family today and help everyone talk about their challenges and their strengths.

Zeus Jones co-founder Adrian Ho explains, "We decided to make Betty Crocker into a brand that is associated with a progressive idea of the American family—the family of the future. And instead of simply talking about the family of the future (which actually means next to nothing) we chose to demonstrate it, and design is a really excellent way to do this."

To execute their idea, the Zeus Jones team created a report, in conjunction with family studies expert Dr. Stephanie Coontz, on the modern family with the purpose of celebrating the differences that make families great. They talked to four unique families about what makes them strong and worked with filmmakers Group Theory to put together documentaries about their experiences. They then made a video that captured Betty Crocker's

new philosophy and shared it on YouTube. Finally, they put all of this together into a website and approached bloggers and content creators who were commenting on issues such as same-sex marriage or single-parent families to create content for it that would stimulate debate.

zeusjones.com/work/betty-crocker-families-project/

4

Watch the films at:
bettycrocker.com/familiesproject
#familiesproject

Where there's a family, there's a home. And where there's a home, there's a homemaker.

Everyone is part of a home, one way or another.

1 & 2. To understand the potential of the Betty Crocker brand, Zeus Jones conducted some research into the state of the American family and published a report.

3–5. They then used the findings of the report to celebrate the differences that make families great and position the brand at the center of this celebration.

Generative Systems

Designers can create systems that synthesize the individual contributions of an audience into something far greater than the sum of its parts.

Although connected media channels allow the contemporary audience to actively reshape and redistribute media content, this does not mean they always want to create it from scratch themselves. The tools to generate content are readily available to all. A new generation of digital devices enables high-quality image capture, sound recording, and video editing on the move in a form that can be instantly uploaded. However, the untrained hand does not always have the expertise or confidence to fully utilize what they have created. Designers have a new role in orchestrating this contribution: creating systems that synthesize the individual contributions of an audience into something that is a far greater than the some of its parts. Design during the 20th century was framed through the control of media and process, but now we are seeing this control reframed to encompass the orchestration and manipulation of audience input. At its best, this alchemy can transform the throwaway act of the untrained amateur into outcomes that seductively compete with those created by experienced professionals. In addition, the involvement of an audience creates a vested interest in the contributors and a ready-made team of advocates that provide free PR and viral marketing.

To productively orchestrate user-generated content requires the coordination of interconnected organic systems that allow a theater of intrigue to build incrementally and provide the motivation for an audience

1

2

3

SEARCH: *Wallpaper** custom covers; Kam Tang; James Joyce; Anthony Burrill; Hort; Nigel Robinson; Dubberly "Design in the Age of Biology"; Moving Brands Snowflakes; MB Weare™; MB Joule; Matt Wade Karsten Schmidt Processing; Kongsberg cutting; Kin design *Wallpaper**

to devote precious moments of their busy lives to small manageable inputs. Around these inputs, designers build networks and communities bonded by the incentive of what their efforts might build. The 20th-century mentality of the lone ego with highly developed specialist expertise is not best suited to the challenges of this task. Today designers need to have empathy with participants in the systems they orchestrate and an interest in areas of expertise that will help them understand and predict behavior. Contemporary design practice increasingly revolves around the development of software and services that are given form through use, and a basic knowledge of areas such as psychology, ethnology and applied social science are increasingly seen as a valuable compliment to the designer's traditional skillset.

MB Weare

There are few precedents to draw from as these new areas of practice define themselves. Studios like Moving Brands are continually learning what works within these new paradigms and as a result have developed R&D strategies that help them make and record discoveries. Over the last 15 years Moving Brands has created a series of themed R&D projects that are built into their seasonal calendar. Many of these projects have specifically focused on creating systems that elicit, collect, and synthesize user-generated inputs.

From fairly early in its life, Moving Brands used the window of its London studio, which looks out onto a busy street in East London, as a vehicle to interact with the public at Christmas. At that time, Matt Wade (see pp. 63–65) and Karsten Schmidt (see pp. 116–119) were design directors at the company and were using the open-source programming language and development environment called Processing as a prototyping tool. Wade and Schmidt had already used it to create a mechanism that transformed text messages into digital snowflakes that were then projected from a screen in the window. Following this project, at the end of 2007 they decided to do something that explored more fully how the public might become involved in the design process. The aim would be to create something that was "socially sourced and user created."

Over the Christmas period, they set up a grid of fairy lights and launched a simple website where anyone could create messages and graphic icons and add them to an online gallery, which then populated an (unedited) electronic display in the studio window. All the contributions (without editing) were used to create a scarf. Moving Brands then sent the scarf out as a Christmas gift to clients, friends, and collaborators and sold it through its website and independent design stores. The icons have since been used in the Moving Brands Artist's Pack for the Granimator iPad app produced by ustwo.

1. Moving Brands used the window of its London office to display pixel drawings from the general public on LED screens.

2. Images submitted were incorporated into a pattern that helped conceal the less politically correct iconography.

3. The patterns became the basis for a scarf that was sent as a gift to friends and associates.

4. The pixel drawings were created using an interface that could be accessed through the Moving Brands website.

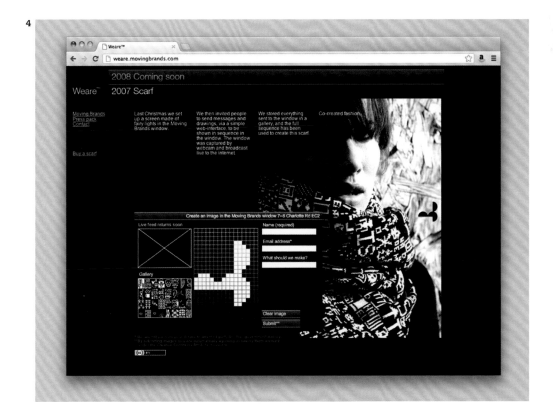

5. Moving Brands created the MB Joule to explore opportunities created by emerging technologies related to custom manufacture and small-scale production.

6. Once the joules were folded and assembled, a circuit created by screen-printed conductive ink was joined and they lit up.

7. Laser and "Kongsberg" cutting were used to create intricate custom patterns for the individual joules.

5

6

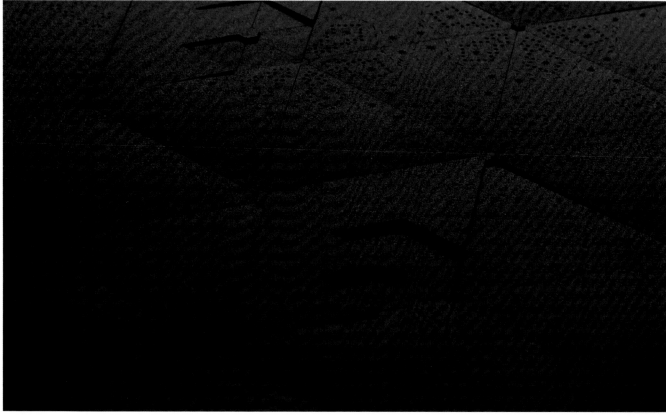

7

8. *Wallpaper** subscribers were invited to use this custom interface to create their own cover of the magazine. They were able to choose elements designed by the likes of Kam Tang, Anthony Burrill and James Joyce to arrange, recolor or resize.

9. Individual covers of the "Handmade Issue" were then applied to the magazine and sent out to their creators.

10. Some of the subscriber-designed covers.

MB Joule

Moving Brands has also been quick to recognize how the growth of digital printing and other bespoke small-scale manufacturing processes are leading to a disruption of the financial advantage of large-scale manufacture and production. In 2012, it created the MB Joule, a paper-crafted electronic ornament that combines design, digital manufacturing, code, and hand assembly. The joules were crafted as a special holiday gift to the friends and partners of Moving Brands with more than 500 meticulously created, individually designed cards to send out. This was a lesson in the patience required by small-scale production and manufacture for the Moving Brands team. Designs for the card were inspired by the snowflake project described previously. Their production involved laser cutting, "Kongsberg" cutting, screen-printing, conductive ink, and finally hand assembly. To bring in a wider participatory element to the project, visitors to the Moving Brands site and staff in their offices around the world were then asked to create their own joules through a custom-built website.

Kin *Wallpaper** Custom Covers

A year after working on the MB Weare project, Matt Wade left Moving Brands and founded Kin with his partner Kevin Palmer (see pp. 63–56). One of Kin's early projects clearly demonstrates the lessons of Weare and Wade's ability to create tools that actively engage the user to participate in the generation of an outcome. At the end of 2009, Kin was commissioned by *Wallpaper** to design and program an application that would allow all 20,000 subscribers to create their own unique cover design for the magazine.

Subscribers were invited to a website where they were able to use a simple intuitive interface to manipulate and arrange a series of assets commissioned by contemporary designers and illustrators such as Kam Tang, James Joyce, Anthony Burrill, Hort, and Nigel Robinson. Each one had a specific use, from icons to resize and manipulate, to patterns that users could recolor. Kin created specific interaction methods for each element, along with ways to combine them. So, for example, users could fill a James Joyce shape with a pattern by Kam Tang or one of Nigel Robinson's textures.

As a result, more than 20,000 unique designs were then digitally printed by F.E. Burman and bound along with the interior of the magazine, which was printed using traditional lithographic techniques.

8

9

10

Digital is not just another communication channel—it is the communication channel because it is the channel that drives all other communication channels.

In Conversation

with Hashem Bajwa, former CEO of DE-DE and director of digital strategy, Droga5

Hashem Bajwa started his career in the communications department at the United Nations and progressed via McCann Erickson to become digital strategy director at Goodby Silverstein & Partners. In 2009, he moved to Droga5, where he helped design and lead the award-winning "Decode Jay-Z with Bing" campaign. He is a highly respected figure in the industry, and Timothy Shey, director of YouTube Next Lab at Google says of him, "Hashem is one of those rare movers in the creative industry who makes the right things happen—he has an innate insight as to what's next and what's most valuable amid the overflow of new ideas in new media."

hashembajwa.com

Hashem Bajwa is convinced that "digital is not just another communication channel—it is the communication channel because it is the channel that drives all other communication channels." Expanding on this, he describes three major ways that digital media contributes to marketing:

1. **Digital can act as the vehicle for a message.**
   For example, YouTube ads, web banners, emailers, etc.

2. **Digital can be the center of a marketing experience.**
   This means more than taking a message and packaging it in a digital context. It involves creating an entirely new way of interacting with the product and creating an experience related to the product that is enabled through digital media.

3. **Digital can act like a product in its own right.**
   This means creating new products for clients that work through digital media and that are designed to deliver an experience that has a marketing objective. Examples of this is are the digital products that have been produced to support Nike+.

Earlier in the book, we talked about how products (and particularly digital products) can define experiences that are highly influential in creating a perception around a brand. The success of Nike+ has led the advertising and marketing industries to focus on the development of digital products in an effort to provide new opportunities for its business model. However, as Bajwa points out, there are many difficulties in trying to replicate the Nike+ phenomenon. In principle, it can work, and there are various successful historical precedents of products and services that have been used to market other products and services.

He refers to the example of the restaurant and travel guides that Michelin developed to promote its tires. These guides eventually became multimillion-dollar businesses in their own right by drawing attention to and enhancing the freedom and discovery that motoring makes possible. The Michelin Guides demonstrate a very smart alignment of a secondary product to a set of marketing objectives—framing the benefits of the experiences that Michelin products enable.

It is clear that when employed intelligently, digital products are a way of defining the values of a brand. Unfortunately, as Bajwa points out, "The marketing model (and the way clients think about marketing) means that there is always a pressure to include a message about buying a product, and at that point the power of an experience related to a product is compromised because the audience feels like they're being sold something. Marketing and digital media can be really powerful in defining the purpose for a brand, creating a clear message for it, and delivering that message in more innovative, interactive, valuable, exciting ways. They can create content and experiences that the consumer will seek out, but the interrelationships between the marketing objective and the user experience need to be carefully managed."

"The interactive element really needs to be driving the program, and often this will happen through a system of things. Not through the old school idea of 360-degree marketing where you define a message and put it in as many different boxes as possible. That model is dying out. A new idea that can be seen in campaigns like Decode Jay-Z with Bing is much more complex and multifaceted."

Along with many in the industry at the moment, he questions the traditional advertising agency model, pointing out that "the hierarchy of an advertising agency is orientated around the creation of the message and the delivery of that message, which is quite a linear process. It is also full of vested interests that do not orientate themselves around fluid R&D-based development."

Digital products and the objectives that govern their creation need to evolve together. Bajwa says, "I would like to see agencies develop and evolve so that they can shape the development of existing products—not create new products and try to bolt them onto existing products.

"My view is that the product strategy and the marketing strategy need to be inherently linked to the point where they are inherently the same thing. The engineer building a new future in their product, whatever the product is, and the marketing person who is developing communications about the product need to be working out of the same core ideas."

Case Study: DE-DE
At the time of interview, Hashem Bajwa was the CEO of a new studio associated with Droga5, specializing in the development of innovative digital products. DE-DE (standing for DEsign & DEvelop) is a technology-based innovation studio that creates "great products with an understanding of how to form a market around the benefits of these products." They were set up from a desire to give Droga5 an influence beyond the marketing room.

"Our model is one where we are trying to identify people who are extremely creative, who can come up with a solution to a problem in the world and design, develop, and employ that solution into the market." Bajwa describes

how they are not looking for people who can be given a problem to solve, they are looking for people who can identify the problem themselves and solve it."

DE-DE works from the premise of trying to set up an innovation-orientated studio with a start-up mentality alongside a more established agency. The people who work for them are offered a stake in the business. Their attitude aspires to the mentality of the likes of Twitter or Skype when they were initially building their businesses.

Bajwa talks about a friction between the inspiration and uncertainty that is at the heart of the start-up mentality and the efficiency of an established methodology, which minimizes risk through repetition. At DE-DE they

are trying to balance these qualities and, as far as possible, to "capture lightning in a bottle" and be able to do this again and again and again.

"DE-DE's mission is to create a portfolio of Internet-fueled, technology-driven products that do solve problems in the world and have some value exchange for us." They currently have three core products that have gone through their development cycle and are being taken forward to a point where they have been released into the world:

Birdseye
Birdseye is the first email client built from the ground up for tablets. It takes advantage of this new environment to utilize gesture-based interaction. It provides a finger friendly visual overview of your inbox with intuitive actions for each message to cut through the overload. It is built out of the insight that email is a stressful, time-consuming thing to manage for anybody who leads a busy life.

Pling
Pling is a push-to-talk voice messenger that helps teams and individuals communicate quickly and naturally. It allows the user to send messages to individuals or groups with the speed and brevity of a text message and the personality and ease of a human voice.

Thunderclap
Thunderclap synchronizes messages across different social networking platforms to enable a piece of communication to have more impact. It has been extremely successful, with more than 1 billion users, including some of the highest-profile people and organizations in the world, such as Barack Obama, Major League Baseball, the UK government, the White House, Levi Strauss & Co., and the United Nations.

Bajwa defines the success of these products not only through the financial income they generate. "An Internet product needs to create financial value, it needs to create utility for yourself and for other people, and it needs to create widespread adoption in the market; and finally, it needs to have great technology underpinning in order to make it unique and distinct."

de-de.com

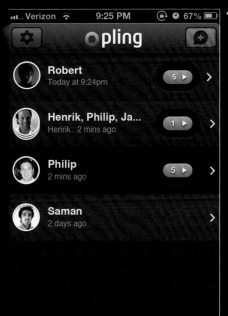

1 & 2. Birdseye is an email client specifically built for use on tablets. It takes advantage of gesture-based interaction to cut through the message overload.

3 & 4. Pling is a voice messenger that is designed to update the text message format and allow messages to be sent to individuals or groups.

5 & 6. Thunderclap synchronizes messages across different social networking platforms and has been used by the likes of Barack Obama and the UK government.

Participation and Advertising

Today's audience wants to create, engage, and share. Successful campaigns focus on facilitating this creativity by building transactional experiences that have value to both the consumer and the client.

Up until the launch of YouTube in 2005, advertising was largely based around the "interruption model"—messages delivered between media content via an attention-grabbing "big idea." Video sharing changed all of this. All of a sudden home movies such as *Charlie Bit Me!* were achieving more viewers than expensively produced TV ads without having to be sandwiched between other content. The industry regrouped and set about populating this new media channel with brand-sponsored material. The smarter producers realized that this new environment worked on a different paradigm. This was a much more democratic environment, where audiences directed each other toward content and their reasons for doing so were not always governed by slick production values or catchy straplines. Interviewed in "Make it Real" by Steve Hare in *Eye 70*, Ed Robinson from the Viral Factory explains that the Internet is "a direct window on the world. There's no real filter between the audience and what's on screen. So they trust it more; its how the world really is." Through this realization, companies like the Viral Factory began to develop content that was designed to resemble something that the audience could make themselves.

After the launch of YouTube, advertising and marketing campaigns drew inspiration from viral home movies, influential bloggers, or what is trending on Twitter. The hierarchy of cultural evolution is no longer from high to low culture or from professional to amateur. *Charlie Bit Me!* has had more viewers than the first moon landing, and unemployed body builders, the Hodge Twins, have gone from posting home videos to setting up their own YouTube channel. They now have more than 600,000 subscribers and are managed by the multichannel network Big Frame who "connect advertisers with targeted audiences through influencers they trust."

Crude video mash-ups, screen-grabs, and photographs accompanied by comments or crude straplines have developed into the phenomenon of the meme and have spread across the Internet to command massive audiences. So much so that websites such as Know Your Meme (knowyourmeme.com) have been developed just to track their progress. Viral Internet phenomena such as LOLcats (comments applied to pictures of cats), Rickrolling (ironic humor connected to Rick Astley's pop hit "Never Gonna Give You Up"), and chocolate rain (parodies of the "I move away from the mic to breathe" caption during Tay Vonday's viral film) are now viewed by audiences that are larger than many expensively produced advertising campaigns. Interestingly, many memes are designed to echo traditional advertising in their image/ text/ punchline composition, but unlike many ads their lack of craft or artifice communicates a spontaneity and irreverence that encourages reaction, response, and contribution.

Droga5: The "No Bollocks" Subtexter

Contemporary agencies such as Droga5 are alive to this viral power and have used it to inspire campaigns that have the same infectious irreverence. As part of the "No Bollocks!" campaign for Newcastle Brown Ale, they launched the Subtexter in 2012, which allows

1 & 2. These posters created in 2008 by Multistorey for the 2008 AV International Broadcast Festival of Electronic Arts, Music and Moving Image describe the new dynamic between broadcaster and audience.

3–5. Elements from the Droga 5 Newcastle No Bollocks! Subtexter campaign.

Companies that desire to understand the "flow" within the ever-quickening media environment need to understand how these changes are generating a rapid movement from impressions to "expressions," and intellectual property to "emotional capital." Such approaches maybe key to breaking through a cluttered and fragmented media environment, relying on consumers themselves to help knit together information and impressions gathered from multiple media experiences.
MIT Convergence Culture Consortium

friends to expose the social media pretention of the photos they post on Facebook. With an obvious visual reference to memes, the campaign invites users to expose an unsaid social-media photo "subtext" by adding a statement to the photograph and then sharing it via the Facebook timeline. The campaign was then taken into the real world where street-art-style artwork was created with ready-made subtext for people to pose in front of, photograph, and share via social media.

In his 2006 book *Convergence Culture*, Henry Jenkins describes how, as consumers explore the new range of resources available to them, they "become active participants in shaping the creation, interpretation of media content" and how "such experiences deepen the consumers' investment in the media property and expands their awareness of both content and brand." In a later essay, "Confronting the Challenges of Participatory Culture: Media Education for the 21st Century," he describes how "a participatory culture is also one in which members believe their contributions matter, and feel some degree of social connection with one another." These findings obviously have powerful implications for the advertising and marketing industries.

Small digital agencies initially led the line in taking advantage of this new relationship with the consumer. Agencies such as AKQA, Glue, Dare, R/GA, and Poke have built a reputation for creating strategies that although digital at their core, encourage users to contribute to the development of experiences that evolve outside of this environment. These studios develop interconnected systems that utilize user generation, viral filmmaking, and games and grow organically to create opportunities that tap into an audience's desire to grab their five minutes of fame. Tom Roope, one of the founders of Poke, has launched a new studio, the Rumpus Room, and the statement of intent published on the company's website describes the potential of this new approach perfectly. "We were founded to harness the power of participation and help align this activity with brand communication. We think today's audience wants to create, engage, and share. We also think successful campaigns focus on facilitating this creativity by building transactional experiences that have value to both the consumer and the client."

The big names at the heart of the traditional advertising industry like Wieden + Kennedy, Fallon, BBH, Ogilvy, and newer key players such as Mother and Droga5 are learning from the example of what smaller digital agencies have achieved. They are now creating participatory campaigns interconnected by digital media but underpinned by the production standards that we associate with traditional advertising.

Droga5: Decode Jay-Z with Bing
In 2010, Microsoft's search engine, Bing, approached Droga5 to trial and market its Search and Maps function with the aim to increase its relevance and use by a younger audience. At the same time, Jay-Z had begun talking to them about helping him launch his autobiography *Decoded*. Droga5 saw an opportunity to harness a unique moment in the history of pop culture

1–4. Some examples of the site-specific artwork created for the Decode Jay-Z Bing campaign including:

2. A customized Cadillac at the birthplace of hip-hop;

3. A typographic piece on the bottom of the pool of the Delano Hotel in Miami; and

4. A custom Gucci jacket with text from Jay-Z's autobiography embroidered into its lining.

5. Reactions to the Decoded campaign on social media.

6. Bing Search and Maps in action during the campaign.

to give millions of people a reason to use Bing, and in doing so it created a new demographic for the search engine. In the month before the release of the book, the agency displayed each of the pages of *Decoded* on specially created, site-specific artworks in relevant sites across the United States and around the world. In addition to conventional billboards, Droga5 also created unique collectable objects and large-scale pieces that transformed their environment. These included exclusive Gucci jackets lined with words from the book, a bronze plaque in the Marcy Projects where Jay-Z grew up, a typographic piece on the bottom of the pool of the Delano Hotel on Miami Beach, and a Cadillac wrapped in a page of the book parked at the birthplace of New York hip-hop.

At the same time, Bing created an online gaming experience that allowed fans to search locations from clues that were posted daily on Facebook, Twitter, and announced on the radio. The system that housed this experience was based on Bing Search and Maps. Every person who found an artwork had the opportunity to win the page that it referred to, signed by Jay-Z. The most loyal players were then entered for the ultimate prize—a lifetime pass to all Jay-Z's live performances.

Fans were able to document their finds through photographs, and in the days before the launch, they assembled the book digitally at bing.com/jay-z. The whole campaign was an unprecedented success, and the statistics that describe its success on the Droga5 website make pretty astounding reading.

1. The average player engagement time on the website was 11 minutes.
2. The campaign achieved 1.1 billion global media impressions.
3. Jay-Z's Facebook followers grew by 1 million.
4. *Decoded* was in the global best sellers charts for nine straight weeks.
5. Bing broke into the top ten most visited websites for the first time.

Bing had become part of the pop culture conversation and had transformed its perception with the youth audience. All of this was made possible by an exciting, engaging participatory experience engineered by Droga5. Needless to say, the project won a Gold Lion at Cannes.

Technology sets us apart as a species. It should be in everybody's hands.

In Conversation

with Karsten Schmidt (aka Toxi)

Karsten Schmidt was born in Chemnitz in the former East Germany and began programming at the age of 13. A few years later, he was in London interning at web developers Omniscience and was soon subsumed into the chaotic but highly creative melting pot of Shoreditch in the late 1990s. Adopting the alias "Toxi," he split his time between playing techno records at parties and using his coding skills to define early digital creativity at agencies such as Zinc and Lateral before joining Moving Brands in 2005. He contributed to the development of the open source programming environment Processing, and alongside fellow creative director Matt Wade at Moving Brands, he pioneered its use as a prototyping platform. In its Winter 2009 Reputations profile, *Eye* magazine referred to him as a "virtuoso among new-media designers." Over the last ten years Toxi has been at the heart of code-based innovation in the UK and has worked on iconic projects such as the generative identities for the 2009 Adventures in Motion festival with onedotzero and Wieden + Kennedy and the Decode exhibition at the Victoria & Albert Museum.

postspectacular.com

Karsten Schmidt sees creativity as being led by the understanding that evolves from the expertise of making.

"You gain understanding by being involved in building something and by figuring out what works physically and what works virtually. Without knowing how to assemble things in detail, you will never learn how to be a designer. Reading about something or attending lectures that explain how people have done it in the past is not the same as sitting down and actually doing something.

"There are a lot of people who think that there is so much value in just having ideas. It is often said that we live in an ideas economy, [in other words], the better your ideas are the better off you are financially. But this is totally divorced from any form of hands-on skill: it reduces hands-on skills to implementation. Anybody can have an idea, but an idea will only stand up through the discoveries of the people [who] make that idea work."

He seeks to understand the interconnection between these different aspects of creative making and also how digital technology connects to the world it is shaping.

"There is no such thing as digital culture, all our lives are digitized in some way."

Schmidt believes the true potential of digital technology is not being realized at the moment. "We are sold the myth that digital technology is something that you consume, something that other people have put into the world for us to use. The mobile revolution, the iPad, the iPhone, and a majority of the digital devices we use are about media consumption. Their main effect on people's lives is to just to get them to consume more. These devices are not used to discover something totally new or to create new skills that might enable the transformation of somebody's life."

The key to unlocking the true potential of digital technology lies in the mass acquisition of programming skills—"a key skill to decipher the world we live in." It is as fundamental to our society as the alphabet was to preceding societies.

"Technology sets us apart as a species. It should be in everybody's hands. To see technology as something that geeks involve themselves with is a form of brainwashing. Education is something that all of society goes through; it is meant to teach us life skills. If this process engenders people to fear technology then there must be something wrong with it."

He points out that programming creates tools and systems that guide outcomes and maybe, more significantly, behavior, and if all we do is use software created by corporations then we are being controlled by these corporations. It is important to understand that when Toxi talks about programming, he is describing a way of thinking, not just the use of a prescribed mechanical language.

"Programming is not just about machines. It's about shaping behavior, PR is programming, rhetoric is programming. . . . It's about thinking about the world around you as a system or a number of processes that are all interconnected and A, understanding that those connections exist and B, understanding what happens when you manipulate these connections. It has nothing to do with machines—machines are just a means to an end."

The mind of a programmer breaks down the creative act into a series of choices and actions that branch out from each other. Schmidt notes, "On a fundamental level, everything boils down to very primitive tasks. This is the nice thing about code, because within any idea, no matter how complex, at some point in the hierarchy of the generation of that idea, it's just zeros and ones. . . . Every process fulfills one little role. When you program, it literally is arranging processes in a structure."

Breaking down the creative act in this way has led Schmidt to question conventional ideas around creative ownership. "Every idea we have is actually a product of our own idea and ideas that are in the environment. Each product is the result of the accumulated thought of thousands of minds. As a very rough model of creativity this works really well." Open source thinking embraces this principle rather than slavishly laboring toward the myth of originality. From this starting point, it then proposes each stage of the process is opened up for others to use "to implement an idea in such a way that you can build other things in the future using the same principle.

"You have a path that you have followed to get to a particular mental state: there is nothing wrong in the fact that this path has been explored before. How can anybody say that they have explored that path and discovered everything that can be discovered there? This is not possible. Open source is a leveller for this sort of opinion about originality. It makes it obvious from square one that you are benefitting from previous knowledge, and by using those open source tools you already acknowledge that you will not be the full author.

"Digital making . . . offers an opportunity that has never happened before—to stand on the shoulders of giants. If you think about the millions of man-hours taken up by something like [the open source library of programming functions] Open CV [http://opencv.org] and the sheer amount of intellect that has contributed to this one project. You could never achieve that sort of insight and perfection in a whole lifetime. So to have that sort of potential at your fingertips should give everybody goose bumps!"

Case Study: Toxiclibs

Toxiclibs is a personal project that Karsten Schmidt has been working on for the last seven years.

"Often I find it very hard to say that my process is finished. The only reason why work is finished is because there is a deadline to meet. If I had the opportunity, most of my projects would go on much, much longer. The great thing about Toxiclibs is that it is open ended, and I really enjoy that open ended nature. I know that it will never really be finished."

Put as simply as possible, Toxiclibs is "an independent, open source library collection for computational design tasks with Java & Processing" that can be used for a range of different things, including education workshops. To explain this, Schmidt gives a basic lesson in programming, "Every process fulfills one little role. When you program, it literally is arranging processes in a structure." This is where Toxiclibs comes in: it provides hundreds of primitive elements of code that can then be

1

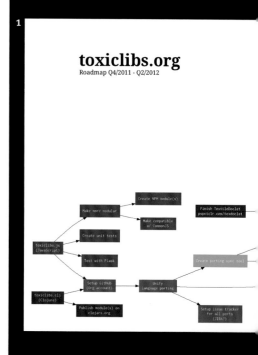

assembled in infinite different ways. Central to the idea behind Toxiclibs is that the members of the community will not only submit elements to the library, but will also combine these elements to create new processes.

Schmidt uses the analogy of the computer game Minecraft to introduce the building potential of Toxiclibs but goes on to explain that the forms that it is able to create are far more complex and dynamic. Rather than "building blocks" he prefers to use the analogy of sand to explain this potential. He also points out that, as people develop expertise in using the materials he provides, then the potential of this material will become more apparent and outcomes will move beyond a defined aesthetic. He also demonstrates how Toxiclibs can be used to create 3D structures that can then be manufactured in the real world, both on a 3D printer and in traditional materials like paper.

toxiclibs.org

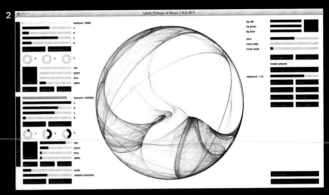

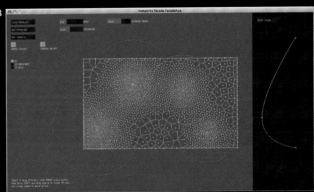

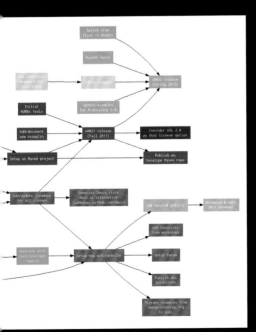

1. A self-portrait of Toxiclibs: this complex map of interconnecting lines and shapes and words describes all of the different categories of elements available within Toxiclibs. Lines, polygons, rays, color palettes, 3D free-form surfaces, nodes, meshes are all arranged to demonstrate how their interconnections call them to take on different forms and behaviors.

2–5. Some of the forms and behaviors from the Toxiclibs open source library collection.

Open Source

Releasing the potential of
the accumulated thought
of a thousand minds.

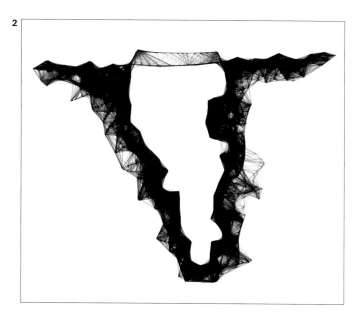

The open source movement is founded in the belief that the source code of computer programs should be freely accessible to all. This principle has significance far beyond the world of software development. It is built on the proposition that each stage of discovery involved in any creative act be opened up in order that it might provide starting points for new creative acts. Open source programmers like Karsten Schmidt talk about the potential of being able to "stand on the shoulders of giants" and how the progress of humanity might benefit from "the accumulated thought of thousands of minds." The potential of this philosophy could be not only to multiply understanding and accelerate progress but also to trigger an attitude of open, shared collaboration, which could define new, more sustainable forms of human behavior.

The roots of the movement can be traced back to 1983, when activist Richard Stallman launched the GNU project as the first completely free and open operating system. This operating system was improved and perfected by a growing community of developers and acted as a beacon to like-minded programmers. Very quickly the movement was rubbing itself up against economic interests terrified of such an open approach to ownership. As a result Stallman wrote the GNU General Public License, turning copyright law on its head and creating a new set of agreements that became known as "copyleft." Copyleft licenses mark a creative work as freely available to be modified and in addition require all modified and extended versions of the work to be made free for utilization by other users. As an extension of this work, Harvard Law School professor Lawrence Lessig founded Creative Commons (CC) as a nonprofit organization devoted to expanding the range of creative works available for others to build upon legally and to share. They provide copyleft licenses free of charge to the public. These licenses "allow creators to communicate which rights they reserve and which rights they waive for the benefit of recipients or other creators."

In 2001 two MIT Media Lab graduates, Casey Reas and Ben Fry, initiated a project that brought open source development to the attention of the communication design community. Processing is an open source programming language and "integrated development environment" designed to support the exploration of the fundamentals of computer programming within a visual context. UK-based computational designer Karsten Schmidt was involved in writing parts of the graphic engines of earlier versions of Processing. At that time Schmidt was the design director at Moving Brands, and they began to use the platform as a prototyping and production tool. Processing is now used by "tens of thousands of students, artists, designers, researchers, and hobbyists . . . for learning, prototyping, and production," according to its website.

Open source platforms such as Processing avoid the controlling aesthetic of major software platforms by giving designers more creative control in adaptation and development of platforms to suit individual needs. Scriptographer, a project initiated by Jurg Lehni and Jonathon Puckey, creates a scripting environment for Adobe Illustrator. Their website http://scriptographer.

SEARCH: Karsten Schmidt; Richard Stallman; GNU/ copyleft/ Creative Commons; Lawrence Lessig; Creative Commons; MIT Media Lab; Casey Reas/ Ben Fry; Processing; Prototyping tools; Jurg Lehni; Jonathon Puckey; Scriptographer; the Blender Foundation; Patent wars; Douglas Rushkoff *Programme or Be Programmed*

1. Creative Commons (CC) as a non-profit organization devoted to expanding the range of creative works available for others to build upon legally and to share.

2–4. Some images from the Scriptographer community. Scriptographer is an open source project initiated by Jurg Lehni and Jonathon Puckey that creates a "scripting environment" for Adobe Illustrator.

2. *Sketchy Structures* by Acemi Caylak

3. *After Now* by Jurg Lehni

4. *Liquid 2 solid* by Jan Abellan

3

4

org proclaims that Scriptographer puts the tool "back into the hand of the user and confronts a closed product with the open source philosophy." In doing so, it defines a new relationship between designers and the software that is developed for their use.

Open source culture has infected a wide variety of fields, and typing "open source" into a Ted Talk search will reveal how this culture is benefitting product design, architecture, science, cancer research, economics, and even government. One great example of the benefits of open source culture in action is the Blender Foundation, based in the Netherlands. Blender is a not-for-profit organization that, according to Blender.org, provides "a free and open source 3D animation suite." Blender uses a GNU General Public License and is developed "by hundreds of volunteers from all around the world. These volunteers include artists, [visual effects] experts, hobbyists, scientists, and many more. All of them are united by an interest to further a completely free and open source 3D creation pipeline. The Blender Foundation supports and facilitates these goals—and employs a small staff for that—but depends fully on the global online community." As Karsten Schmidt points out, "They publish short films, Pixar-style animations, and they make every asset of the film open source so that other people can learn from the expertise they are developing. If you want to get into film production, it's the best resource there is. So you can really learn from professionals how to do a feature film. All the sound design, the character design, the timeline, the key framing, the motion graphics, 3D modeling—EVERYTHING—all accessible."

This is an idealistic world, seemingly full of world-changing possibilities, but there are powerful economic vested interests that seek to oppose it. In our recent conversation (see pp. 117–119), Karsten Schmidt highlights how corporations use patents to disable or interfere with the development of competitor technologies. The high-profile legal battles between technology giants such as Apple and Samsung are evidence of this phenomenon. Unfortunately, our obsession with ownership does not appear to be disappearing anytime soon. This economic momentum leads to the creation of technology that acts as a tool of consumption rather than encourages the utilization of its unforeseen potential. Open source development communities have the power to change our lives for the better, but our education systems need to feed these communities with young minds that have the confidence to examine what is behind an interface. It is widely recognized that code will be the defining tool of the new century, and its use will define the world we will create. The open source movement believes in placing these tools in the hands of the people so that they have control over what this world will look like. As advocate and writer, Douglas Rushkoff points out, either we program or be programmed!

There is no such thing as information overload, just bad design. If something is cluttered and/or confusing, fix your design.
Edward Tufte

Navigation

Navigation systems are a cornerstone of communication design. Maps, signage, pictograms, information graphics—even pagination or the humble contents page— are all design features that help people navigate space and information. Indeed, some of the world's most famous and recognizable pieces of graphic design were produced as navigation aids: Harry Beck's London Underground map; Massimo Vignelli's New York subway signage; Otto Neurath's Isotype pictograms. These projects all share the apparently straightforward objectives of practical communication and clarification, but navigation systems can have deeper implications. Design choices about how to present information actively shape the user's understanding, through selection, omission, and restructuring the data.

The need for navigation tools has only increased in a digital era. Not only do new digital spaces now exist, with people spending more and more time in virtual environments (computer desktops, Internet browsers, smartphone interfaces, social networks), but digital mapping tools allow users to navigate their physical world digitally. An equally momentous change is the massively increased access to information. This data explosion has two sources: more data is collected than ever before, and that information is shared more freely.

As people perform consumer and social transactions online, that information is being gathered and used to inform commercial and governmental decisions. Global trading takes place, and is recorded, online. Key texts and images of important artwork are being uploaded and shared with the world. And government, scientific, social, and consumer data is increasingly available to anyone who wants to engage with it. Even hidden information is gaining its freedom through channels like Wikileaks.

These changes present huge opportunities for designers because people need routes through the complex mass of information and ways to better understand it. Data visualizations are becoming a mainstream tool in news reporting, with flat graphics, video, and interactive interfaces all used to communicate ideas and statistics. This new way of thinking about information has also seen designers find thought-provoking ways to use data as a raw material, creating interesting or beautiful design work with it.

Designers are helping to map digital spaces and build interfaces that users can navigate with ease. Whereas in a physical space such as a town, communication designers will create signage or maps based on the existing reality, in the digital realm they can design a navigable environment simultaneously with its signposts. And as well as helping other organizations create usable digital interfaces, designers are building peer networks and channels for their own content.

Information Overload

As data creation increases exponentially, modes of communication are being shaped by new technologies and behaviors.

1

Data is always, relatively speaking, big. . . . It's the variety and interconnectedness of data that gives us new, predictive powers.
Martin Weigel, head of planning at
Weiden + Kennedy Amsterdam

SEARCH: Anna Richardson Taylor "Big Data and Creativity: Kill or Cure?"; big data/ IBM Big Data; Cisco Visualizations; data protection; Facebook; Google; Global Positioning System (GPS); interface design; Internet of Things/ industrial Internet; Nate Silver *The Signal and the Noise*; Smart Things; search engine optimization (SEO); social networks; TED playlist "The Dark Side of Data"; Twitter

Information is being gathered more rapidly than ever before: IBM estimates that 2.5 quintillion bytes of data are generated every day, and that 90 percent of the world's data has been created in the last two years. This data is gathered, processed, and shared electronically and online. And although the exponential growth rates of data creation and web usage means that any statistics rapidly fall out of date, it is worth noting just how rapidly computing has become a part of human culture. The first version of the Internet was created in 1969, and Tim Berners-Lee invented the World Wide Web in 1989. In 2013, the world population reached 7 billion, Facebook had 1.11 billion users, and Google was processing 100 billion searches a month. These changes have happened too fast for anyone to fully understand their potential implications, but industries across the world are looking for ways to respond to and capitalize on the changing landscape.

A lot of this book considers the repercussions of new digital environments on communication design. Design intended to help organizations or users navigate the world is likewise deeply affected, as even physical wayfinding takes on a digital dimension. Indeed, designers working on navigation systems, whether for spaces or information, are required to engage with underlying spatial and psychological shifts in order to create effective design outcomes. Undoubtedly some of these shifts will be unforeseen, but the last two decades have seen a number of technologies and behaviors develop, some that have already created new kinds of design practice, others that are being explored in myriad different ways, but all of which are shaping modes of communication.

Search Engines
Almost all users access the Internet through search engines, so when Simon Manchipp says, "It's not who you are, it's who Google thinks you are," he is not talking metaphorically: this is the reality of how consumers view brands on their screens. A search might lead to millions of pages of results, but most people are not going to look past the first few, hence the demand for search engine optimisation (SEO) experts who can bump a website or image up the rankings. The requirements of SEO mean that companies are describing, designing, and promoting themselves differently, to look good in the eyes of Google's ranking systems as well as attracting customers. Ranking algorithms are as interested in online traffic and the links around any given site as they are in the information contained within a site, which means that a brand has to think about building a whole network, not just one beautiful homepage.

Networks
The World Wide Web was built on a system of hyperlinks, and its very fabric has changed the way people think about connectivity and relationships. There is now an expectation that all content can be shared, commented on, and responded to. Social networks like Facebook and Twitter are driven by these expectations and have become extremely powerful platforms. They have created new hubs for social engagement and in the process not only

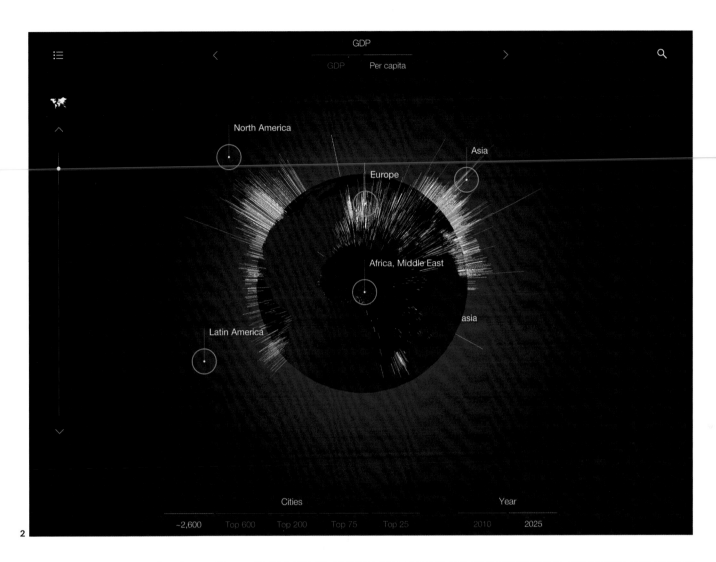

2

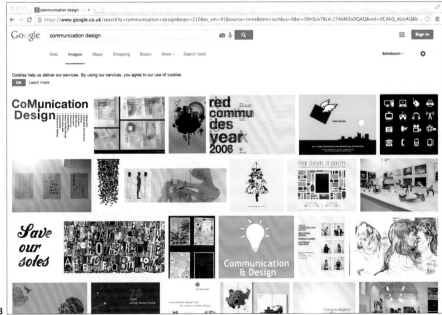

1. Search engines like Google impact how people access information online—and what is considered important.

2. The Urban World app, designed by Sennep for MGI, takes around 50,000 data points for more than 250 global cities and visualizes them in a way that is engaging and informative.

3. Image search is helping move the web away from a text-dominated environment.

have access to huge numbers of potential consumers, but are able to aggregate and analyze information about those people, tailoring advertising to an audience and providing companies with valuable insights about their consumers. These networks have taken the importance of peer recommendation to a completely new level, requiring brands to be "liked" by their audience and privileging share-ability over almost any other design outcome. If it is liked and shared across social media, an ad campaign could now have more exposure online than on any other media channel, and may even spread into new geographic regions without financial risk.

Big Data
The term "big data" describes data sets so large that they present challenges to standard modes of processing, but it is also increasingly used as an umbrella term for the enormous amounts of information gathered daily. This data is coming from everywhere: online activity of every kind, GPS tracking, sensors built into cars, international weather centers, financial transactions, political polls, scientific research, medical surveys. . . . The list may not be endless, but it would certainly present its own processing problems.

Organizations want to access this data because, with the right tools, data can aid understanding and prediction in order to make things better, make money, or both. In the commercial sector, data might provide consumer insights that inform an advertising campaign or even suggest new product innovations. For governments, integrated datasets could help provide awareness of and solutions to social changes, economic patterns, and public health issues. Or if a scientific researcher finds a way to process huge amounts of data on a specific bacterium, it may help develop a vaccine. On the one hand, designers are helping to build interfaces that allow these varied organizations to navigate datasets, and on the other, they are finding that decisions about branding, marketing, and product design are being driven by insights gleaned from that data.

Internet of Things
The Internet of Things, sometimes called the Industrial Internet, refers to the assumption that ever more day-to-day objects will be responsive, data-gathering, and connected to the Internet and each other. Of course, some objects are already online: Cisco estimates that the number of things connected to the Internet first exceeded the number of people in the world in

4

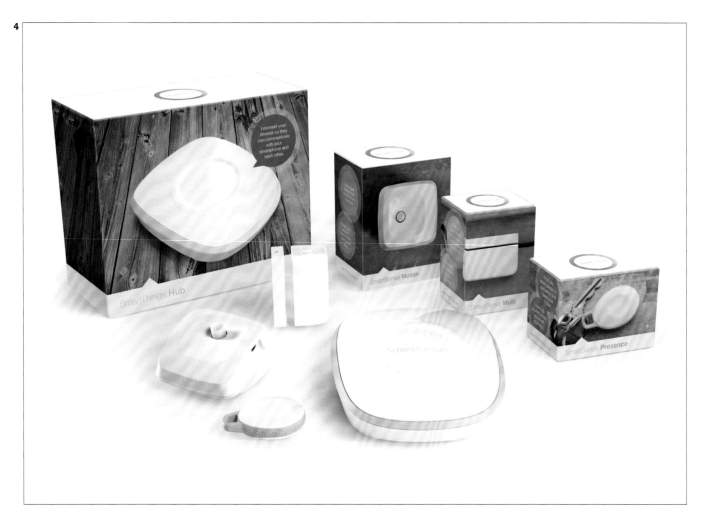

We face danger whenever information
growth outpaces our understanding of
how to process it.
Nate Silver

Most of the data sets published right
now cannot be read by machines—
they require a lot of manual processing
to actually extract meaning. The future
is linked data, data that is dynamically
linked to other data.
Karsten Schmidt

2008. Most smartphones, for example, have built-in
sensors monitoring sound, light, and movement, and
modern cars are similarly equipped. SmartThings, a
company that offers digitally aware products, already
sells devices to tell people when their children and
pets are home, or to help detect possible leaks. In a
wider vision of this technology, products from coffee
cups to curtains to cattle would be integrated with
some kind of monitoring and feedback capability.

As computer chips have become smaller and cheaper,
this is becoming a real possibility, and many design and
innovation companies are looking at ways the technology
could help make the world more efficient and responsive.
Coffee cups could tell the waitress when you need a refill;
curtains could close when it gets dark; cattle could alert
the farmer when they're becoming unwell. Linking objects
to the Internet is currently happening faster than getting
them to speak to each other, partly because of issues
around shared programming languages and the right
to access information. The possibility of such widespread
monitoring also raises the same privacy issues that have
surrounded smartphone GPS data and raises the question:
who will have access to these new data streams?

With ever more minute information coming
online every year, the Internet of Things will help make
big data even bigger, as well as further blurring the
relationship between physical and digital, which itself
presents new navigation issues. Creating interfaces and
products that help orient people and organizations in
this new landscape is going to be a design challenge.

Physical / Digital

There was a time when the "real world" was differentiated
from "cyberspace" both psychologically and semantically,
but it's hard to argue anymore that what happens online
isn't real. The Internet, and the devices through which
it can be accessed, are woven into the fabric of people's
lives, and a huge percentage of society's economic,
social, and political transactions now take place online.

However, there are meaningful differences
between these environments—not least, the nature of
physical and spatial engagement, both of which have
repercussions for navigation designers. Online, time
functions differently as information is accessed and people
communicate instantly. Spatially, digital interfaces are
primarily accessed through two-dimensional screens,
which require different navigation cues to a three-
dimensional environment. The assumption of instant,
linked information is feeding back into physical spaces,
while online environments are only slowly working out
how "flat" they can appear without losing usability.

5

4. SmartThings devices
instantly connect
to different sensors,
locks, light switches,
outlets, thermostats,
and other compatible
devices in the home,
allowing home-owners
to monitor them in
their absence.

5. Mobile devices are
growing more complex
and connected,
and are constantly
gathering data.

Curation

There has always been a role for
designers in selecting and showcasing
content, but now this role is far more
complex and significant.

One product of the expanding mass of information
available online is an acute need for filters. Perhaps the
most omnipresent mediators of content are search engines,
which automatically aggregate relevant websites based on
search terms. However, blogs, forums, news sites, online
shops, and guides are all offering users aggregated, curated,
or edited content to read, look at, or buy. When these
platforms gain large audiences, and their users' trust, they
can become powerful opinion formers and advertisers.

Designers can help organizations build new, and
better, platforms through which to filter content online.
That might be improving an existing model, for example
making an online magazine more appealing or enjoyable
to look through, or it could be finding new ways to
showcase content as a promotional tool. Intel's Museum
of Me did this by taking the user's Facebook information
and creating a virtual exhibition space, allowing the
viewer to see their social activity in a different light.
"Wilderness Downtown" is a music video for Arcade
Fire and a showcase for Google Chrome's functionality.
It also reconfigured user information, asking for a
postcode and then linking information from Google maps
with video and interactive elements to create a more
immersive experience than a standard music video.

This is not just an online phenomenon. There
has always been a role for selecting and showcasing

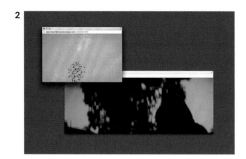

1 & 2. "The Wilderness
Downtown" is an
interactive music
video featuring "We
Used to Wait" by
Arcade Fire. Chris

Milk, Aaron Koblin and
B-Reel collaborated
to showcase the
capabilities of the
new Google Chrome
and create a new
user experience.

SEARCH: Aaron Koblin; Bing; Boing Boing; Boooooom;
Cool Hunting; Designboom; Dezeen; Facebook; Google; Intel
Museum of Me; It's Nice That; news channels/ newspapers/
magazines/ blogs; Pitchfork "Glitter in the Dark"; Snaps
App; TED (Technology, Entertainment, Design); The
Wilderness Downtown; Under Consideration; Yahoo

I think one of the biggest things we're going to see in the next few years is curation.
Vivian Rosenthal, Snaps founder and CEO

content through exhibitions and events, and print and broadcast media. These channels continue to evolve, and as with their online equivalents make money by selling access to their content, or indirectly through advertising revenue or brand exposure. With the growth of online communication and commerce, there is a general trend toward making physical channels more specialized, and talking directly to a niche audience through small retail and exhibition spaces, specialized conferences, and idiosyncratic publishing ventures. Often channels have an online and offline life: the *Guardian* and the *New York Times* have primarily national physical circulations but huge international followings online. And TED Talks (Technology, Entertainment, Design) began as a one-off conference and has become both a worldwide conference network and a hugely successful online resource.

As well as helping clients build audiences through well-designed identities, interfaces, and physical spaces, communication designers are creating their own platforms. Design is a field in need of filtering as much as any other, and plenty of designers are showcasing interesting work on blogs, sharing information relevant to design, or bringing speakers together at events (see Designer Publishers on pp. 180–181). Designers who can build an audience reap the rewards through selling products directly, advertising revenue, and increasing exposure.

3–8. Intel's Museum of Me created a virtual exhibition from visitors' Facebook data, allowing them to see their information in a new way.

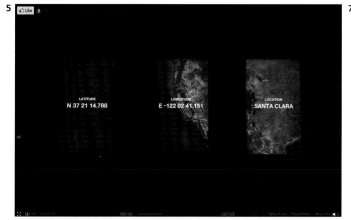

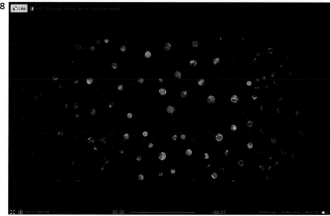

You can't just click your fingers and get an audience. You've got to crack on and keep going and show your commitment.

In Conversation

with Will Hudson,
founder, It's Nice That

In 2007, Will Hudson founded It's Nice That, a publishing platform that encompasses several different online, print, and events offerings as part of its mission of championing creativity across the art-and-design world. It's Nice That is made up of the main website, which showcases creative talent across a wide range of disciplines and attracts a monthly readership of around 350,000 unique users; the quarterly magazine *Printed Pages*; an audiovisual site First Broadcast; an events program, including the annual creative symposium Here; the Company of Parrots shop; a jobs board; and This at There, a dedicated arts-and-design exhibition listings guide to London.

Hudson first formed a design studio with Alex Bec in 2008. As well as collaborating on It's Nice That and If You Could, in 2011 Hudson and Bec launched INT Works, a London-based creative agency whose clients include Nike, COS, Unilever, ASOS, and Picador.

itsnicethat.com
intworks.com

Will Hudson, along with colleague Alex Bec, has built two companies and a host of editorial platforms from his interests in collaboration and celebrating creative work. Across those businesses, Hudson is finding ways to harness people's desire to connect, discover, and collaborate.

Will started It's Nice That as a response to a student brief while studying at Brighton. It was partly set up as a directory to keep track of work he was interested in and began as a simpler version of its current form: "image, title, to begin with, maybe two lines and link, and that was it. We were posting a couple of things a day." Also at Brighton, Hudson worked with fellow student Alex Bec on If I Could, a fundraising project where they collaborated with illustrators and designers, again building networks and showcasing work.

After graduating, as well as starting design jobs, the two maintained It's Nice That and If I Could, and found that they were beginning to be offered work as a result of them—"It basically got to a crunch point where I thought I could be doing my own thing." Hudson and Bec started doing freelance work together, "taking advantage of some of the opportunities people were offering," continuing the blog, and bringing their wide-ranging knowledge and creative network into play on commercial briefs.

Hudson says, "As Alex and I started working more closely together, we'd go and have new business meetings and talk about It's Nice That right at the end. And we learned that the thing people were really interested in was It's Nice That. The idea that we had this big network of creatives that we were in conversation with, or aware of, was very attractive." It's Nice That soon became "the main tool for going and talking to people," as well as providing a network of peers Hudson and Bec could collaborate with.

Thinking about why It's Nice That has become such a trusted platform for readers and clients, Hudson identifies a couple of features. The first is that, although it started up "when blogging became more accessible, there weren't a huge

number of people talking about the design realm." Hudson, as a student and young graduate, was well placed to explore this new way of curating and sharing content as he was "totally immersed in all sorts of design work anyway." Another thing is the company's attitude: "[we] try to be very humble and egoless. Something we luckily got right was calling it It's Nice That. Essentially, it's always going to be positive—because if we're not going to be positive about it why are we talking about it?"

Finally, there is reliability: It's Nice That has earned client trust and showed professionalism from the start. "Very early on, we established consistency—consistency both in terms of the tone and how much is posted. We now post about nine articles a day, but even right when we started there were four articles going up every day, which allows you to build a momentum. So people know if they go to the site, there's going to be new stuff."

Building and maintaining an audience is the center of It's Nice That's success, allowing them to generate revenue from editorial content that is largely free to access. Hudson points out that there's no magic formula to achieving this: "People will sometimes come to us and say they want a publishing platform, and they want a certain audience in a certain timeframe. But you can't just click your fingers and get an audience. You've got to crack on and keep going and show your commitment. We've been very lucky to build the audience that we have." Now that they're firmly established, It's Nice That steers clear of chasing the audience, instead "it's more about maintaining quality, working with interesting brands, and doing interesting things. I think the editing in what we do is really important. It's not just aggregating lots of stuff, everything has original writing, our own tone of voice."

The relationship between It's Nice That and INT Works is interesting. As Hudson says, "INT Works gets paid to do the work, whereas It's Nice That does the work to try and get paid." They are now separate, self-sustaining entities, as Hudson and Bec felt it was important that the publishing side was not funded by commercial agency work: "It doesn't sit well with either of us that you might pump money into something [like] a flashy business card to get commercial work. We want to run a sustainable publishing company." Through a mix of collaborative content and ads, and event, magazine, and shop sales, It's Nice That is now fully accountable and self-supporting.

While INT Works and It's Nice That have become more distinct, they are still driven by a shared belief in collaboration and continue to inform and support each other creatively, if not financially. "Alex and my mind-set was always about collaboration—collaboration with the right person for the right project. And that's what we maintain through to today. INT Works are still working with the people we feature on the site. It's Nice That is a great tool to start a conversation with people."

The thrill is still the commissioning and working and creating new stuff." Hudson also sees the relationship between the businesses as something that makes them stand out: "That cross-pollination of ideas, reference, conversation is really important, and it's one of the big things that sets us apart from other agencies."

Hudson refers to luck a lot in describing his and Alex's journey from university to company directors, but it's clear that he's driven by a desire to find new ways to connect and collaborate, both so valuable in today's design world: "My excitement comes from new projects, new things." And he can keep doing this because he is happy to trust and celebrate the talent that surrounds him: "We've been joined by really talented individuals. It's about making sure that when my attention comes off something there are the right people in place to look after it." It will be fascinating to see where they go next.

**Case Study:
INT Works and It's Nice That
Selfridges Windows:
Words, Words, Words**

In 2012, INT Works and It's Nice That worked together to art direct and produce four of British department store Selfridges' famous window displays. The displays coincided with the store's "Words Words Words" season. For the showpiece corner window on Oxford Street in London, they collaborated with interactive designer Stewdio to create The Word-A-Coaster, a playful fortune-telling machine. The 14-foot-high wooden rollercoaster (constructed by model makers Atom) was surrounded by a sea of 30,000 brightly colored balls, each filled with a unique fortune. The fortunes took the shape of a small, editioned card emblazoned with an adjective, generated by a computer script. The balls were available for free in-store and left each shopper with their own prediction for 2012. To complement the corner window, the It's Nice That team worked with three designers—Ben Long, Chrissie Macdonald, and Giles Miller—to create a physical interpretation of the word "words."

Will Hudson says "It was fantastic to have our name on those windows. It was really interesting to see the feedback and the people who discovered It's Nice That through that collaboration."

intworks.com/work/selfridges-words-words-words

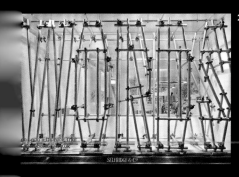

1. Ben Long window.

2. Giles Miller Studio window.

3. Chrissie Macdonald window.

4 & 5. The Word-a-Coaster at Selfridges.

Visualizing Data

Communication and data designers, along with programmers, analysts, and journalists, have a vital role in providing the structure or filter that will help us make sense of raw data.

1. Moritz Stefaner's visualisation of global trade flows helps Citibank investigate and demonstrate insights about economic trends.

2. *New York Magazine*'s "Approval Matrix" makes humorous use of information graphics.

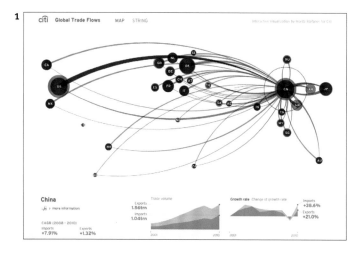

A data visualization needs to visualize things for humans, but also transform data so that it can be consumed by other machine processes or by other humans to do more with it. Then it becomes a language, no longer owned by institutions but owned by the public.
Karsten Schmidt

It is clear that individuals and organizations have access to unprecedented amounts of information, but much of it exists in vast and unwieldy raw data sets. However data is captured—numbers, words, or images—it tends to require some kind of structure or filter to make sense of it, which is where communication and data designers, along with programmers, analysts, and journalists, have a vital role. Data visualizations can take many different forms: a static chart, video, interactive datasets, live and evolving interfaces, even physical objects. As the public's infographics literacy has improved, using information design as part of a communication strategy is very appealing. The general understanding of charts, graphs, and maps is fairly good, which means that statistics can be conveyed quickly and easily, highlighting data that organizations want to share.

Most infographics, or data visualizations, are made in the service of one of three objectives, which could be broadly defined as reportage, research, and aesthetics. Reportage uses the data to tell a story; research needs models that help negotiate and interpret data, often as it evolves; and aesthetic design uses data to create visually appealing graphics or illustrations (see Beautiful Data on p. 142). Although in reality all visualizations sit at some cross-section of these three purposes, they provide a useful way to differentiate between different types of data design.

Reportage

News is a rich information environment, and infographics are increasingly used alongside headlines, pull quotes, and imagery to add an extra layer of narrative. Infographics can provide an immediate snapshot of a story before someone even starts reading, as well as presenting dense or complex statistical material more succinctly than a wordy explanation. Public familiarity with infographics means that journalists can also use the forms to create what are essentially humor or comment pieces, like *New York Magazine*'s "Approval Matrix."

While infographics help people process statistics visually, the old phrase "lies, damned lies, and statistics" exists for a reason. Data can be manipulated into showing a certain picture, and people are much more likely to read a statistic or a graph as true than they would an opinion piece, even if the graph has been chosen, contextualized, and visualized in such a way as to support a certain viewpoint. Designers must be aware that their choices will influence not only the way a statistic appears, but also how much contextual information is given regarding the reliability of the data source.

Journalism is not the only arena in which infographics are employed to help tell a story. Organizations often use them to highlight key parts of press releases and annual reports, adding visual interest while pulling out headline points. And television documentaries and museums use graphics to help explain and explore a wide range of subjects.

Research

Historically, a lot of large data sets have arisen from scientific research, and with them the need to

2

THE APPROVAL MATRIX
Our deliberately oversimplified guide to who falls where on our taste hierarchies.

HIGHBROW

Putin's Game of Thrones. (If only **Ukraine had dragons**.)

Jordan Wolfson's **animatronic dancing doll** at Zwirner: sublimely silly ...

... Or the sublimated **robo-sublime**?

Jonas Kaufmann's **worthy Werther** at the Met Opera.

Artist Fernando Botero insists he's **"not obsessed with fat women."**

Catherine Opie, Barbara Kruger, and John Baldessari **return to the MoCA board.**

FIVE CAME BACK

Ken Langone: *First they came for the billionaires,* and *I did not speak out—because I was not a billionaire?*

Branden Jacobs-Jenkins's *Appropriate*: undercooked and **overexplained** ...

... But that hoarder set is **clutterrific!**

Mark Harris's *Five Came Back*: **Frank Capra goes to war.**

Nate Silver's hot new website accused of peddling **uncool** global-warming science.

NASA-funded study predicts that the rich getting richer will cause society to collapse. It's **what happened on Caprica!**

Puppet fornication in "Hand to God": the most **poignant** sex onstage.

The **"Degenerate Art"** show at the Neue Galerie: Those Nazis hated some excellent art.

Remind us why NYC needs a pricey, so-far-tenantless **performing-arts center** at the WTC?

Or a super-subsidized "vanity project," **Tower 3**?

Lady Gaga gets puked on at a Doritos-sponsored SXSW event by a performance artist.

The **Twitter jokester** behind @GSElevator—who didn't work at Goldman—loses one big book deal, but jams his blood-funnel into another.

Tiles that **make you smile!** Museum of the City of New York's Guastavino show.

DESPICABLE   **BRILLIANT**

The truth is out there: weeks of fantastical **X-Files-style** flight MH370 coverage.

Tyler, the Creator is arrested for **inciting a riot** at SXSW. But Doritos told him to "Be Bold!"

Rx for Obamacare: President gets **My Drunk Kitchen** YouTube star to vouch for it.

The mordant joy of **Justin Vivian Bond**'s *The Drift* at Joe's Pub.

Bye-bye, **pink Observer.**

Chelsea Handler **manhandles** Piers Morgan.

Patti Smith and Iggy Pop at Carnegie Hall for Tibet.

That domed old Williamsburgh Savings Bank is now a catering hall named after a made-up person, **"Weylin B. Seymour."**

Locker-room pecking order! According to a study by the University of Brighton, jocks choose leaders **based on penis size.**

Mike Albo's *The Junket* moves Off Broadway. Take that, **Times ethics policies!**

FX's upcoming *Fargo* TV show. **Oh, for Chrissake here!**

Kylie Minogue's **"Sexercise"** makes gay men doubt they're gay.

Airbnb user returns to find **an orgy in his apartment.** Why doesn't this happen more often?

The Tumblr **My Husband's Stupid Record Collection.**

Earthquake face! KTLA anchor Chris Schauble tried to keep it cool.

Onetime Ridgewood, N.J., public-works inspector stole **$460,000 worth of parking-meter quarters.**

James Dolan **seduces Phil Jackson** with the help of the Eagles. *You can check out anytime you like ...*

Eva Green's **human-hair outfit** in *300*. (Hersuit?)

Eelslap.com.

LOWBROW

identify useful patterns within the data. This requires exploratory data visualization tools: interfaces that do not assume a certain result but rather allow researchers to model the data in different ways, possibly link it to other datasets, and identify patterns in order to make predictions. These highly specialized tools have been indispensable to modern research, allowing scientists to glean understanding from otherwise impenetrable datasets. In general they have been the domain of specialists because designing and using this kind of interface requires highly specialized knowledge.

However, using complex data for modelling and prediction is now common practice for big businesses, and a desire to sift through statistics has passed onto all kinds of engaged amateurs, from avid sports fans to political pollsters. This necessitates new kinds of data visualization that serves a range of knowledge levels and is visually appealing and accessible. Unlike infographic reportage, these visualizations may require their users to spend some time learning how the interface works in order to use it effectively. The *New York Times* Project Cascade, the OECD Better Life index, or the UEFA statistics area are all examples of exploratory tools for a more general audience.

Although producing tools for research and analysis may seem to have less scope for visual bias than journalistic graphics, they still act as a framing device controlled by the vision of the organization commissioning them and the designer building them. As Peter Hall puts it, "Rather than simply describe a pre-existing world, these technologies, in their methods of framing, selecting, and predicting, make up a world."

A Visualized World

Designers working with data face big moral questions about ownership and use, as information is fast becoming a highly valuable commodity. Indeed, data is widely referred to as a "raw material" hence phrases like "data mining," and big business has tended to exploit such resources, not always to the benefit of society. As such, many people working with data are passionate about the need to make statistical data free and linkable, among them Hans Rosling, founder of Gapminder, and Karsten Schmidt, founder of Thi.ng.

As datasets grow, there is enormous potential for people to create powerful visualization tools that can help people understand patterns in all sorts of areas and create solutions where there are problems. For this to happen as effectively as possible, data must be available in shared programming languages to anyone who wants to create tools with it and for it. If businesses are able to claim proprietary rights to data, the number of people working with it—and their aims—will be limited. Rosling says, "The data is hidden, down in the databases" but he and other data enthusiasts are working on ways to bring it out into the world.

Mapping

Mapping, or cartography, is another way to show information visually, but it is very much its own field. When designing a road map or a train network, cartographers work to privilege the information that users will need, while omitting unnecessary "noise." But like infographics, maps can be functional or idiosyncratic, sometimes telling stories while sharing information. Mapping apps are currently adding layers of information to traditional cartography, allowing users to access up-to-the-minute information about local events or bus arrival times. At the same time, projects like Legible London place physical maps in situ, so that tourists and residents have almost as instant access to local information as they would online, helping the city feel contemporary and accessible.

3

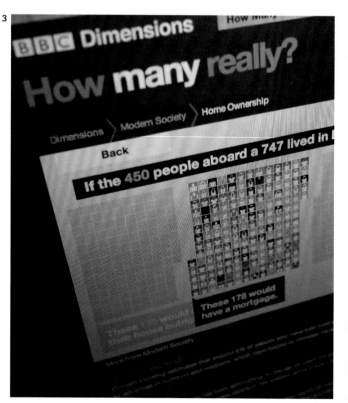

3. The BBC site "How many really?" developed by BERG allows users to map statistics onto their own group of Facebook friends.

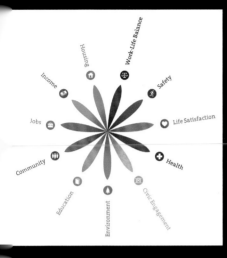

2

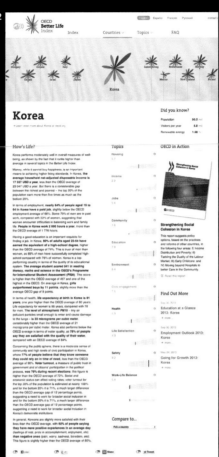

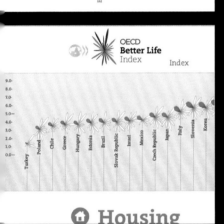

Case Study: Moritz Stefaner: Better Life Index

Launched on the occasion of the 50th anniversary of the Organization for Economic Cooperation and Development (OECD), the Better Life Index aims at comparing the world's well-being beyond traditional, material measures like GDP. Your Better Life Index is designed to let users visualize and compare some of the key factors—like education, housing, environment—that contribute to well-being in OECD countries.

The interactive tool allows users to see how countries perform according to the importance they give to each factor. Each country is represented by one flower, each factor by one of its petals. The length of a petal indicates the score of the respective country in that area (e.g., income in Germany), and the higher the total score, the higher the flower will rise. Users can interact by putting different weights on the indicators, for instance, making life satisfaction more important.

The resulting personal indexes and rankings can be shared and discussed on the Internet. For the OECD, this can provide an important back channel to get in touch with people and learn about the topics they are really interested in.

oecdbetterlifeindex.org
moritz.stefaner.eu/projects/oecd-better-life-index

1. The better life "flower," with each indicator represented as a petal.

2. Detailed breakdown of statistics for one country.

3. Looking at how countries compare on a single indicator.

4. Users can adjust the personal importance of key indicators, changing countries' overall ranking.

If you can't find what's interesting in the data, then you won't be able to design something interesting.

In Conversation

with Max Gadney, founder
and design director, After
the Flood

Max Gadney is founder and design director of After the Flood, a data experience design company. They make apps, interfaces, and videos that help clients communicate information internally or to their customers. Clients include Union of European Football Associations, UK Prime Minister David Cameron, the World Chess Championships, and BBC News. Gadney was previously responsible for the BBC website. He also hosts the yearly conference Design of Understanding and writes on information design.

maxgadney.com
aftertheflood.co

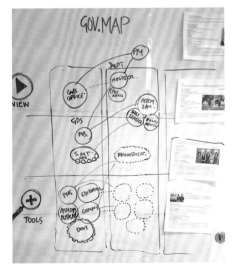

Max Gadney founded After the Flood to make digital products that create "the entire data experience," making not just the data visualizations, but the context for those visualizations— "the apps, websites, and experiences that people access the data in." His agency's principles are to:

1. Make digital products that show visual data.
2. Look to uncover the hidden truth in data.
3. Design for users and not other designers.

Starting from the premise that the data is out there, and it is better for businesses—and their consumers— to understand it, Gadney "is all about connecting users with data." More information is being gathered than ever before, whether about consumer preferences or sports stats: businesses both see more and record more. Gadney says, "People are interested in that data, but they'll probably need it mediated somehow, especially if you're making a website for someone's consumers."

To make effective digital products, Gadney explains that you need to understand the business, the data, and what the business wants from the data. If its creative team is making an interface for investment bankers, After the Flood has to understand those specific professional needs in order to create a product with a successful interface and useful information hierarchy. If they're designing for a company's consumers, there are further considerations, like "how users talk to each other—the information people want to access and how the company wants them to use it. You have to think about how it works across media, because it's not just about one person by themselves looking at the data: people are sharing things, talking to each other—so how do you plan for that?" When they have worked with sports statistics, it's important that fans can share them, so After the Flood helps build online discussions.

In this kind of work, the data really does rule. "Essentially, the client can say what they would like, but it comes down to the data. If you've

just got one row of numbers, you can't really do much with it," Gadney explains. Using the raw data, they will experiment with its possibilities. "We'll start by structuring it, we'll clean it, we'll find different ways to bring it all together. . . . You have to be up front about managing the data. Most of the time the issue is that you don't have enough. Sometimes you have too much. And you just have to work it out." Although After the Flood is learning to predict issues with client data, Gadney still says, "When you're working on projects that involve data, it's the data that will kill you. The data will kill the project management, the budget, the timings."

Because this is a relatively new area of business, Gadney finds that clients come to them with varied expectations and varied data sets. At the start of a project, After the Flood will work with the client to find out what the product should do and what it needs to function. "One of the ways we help them figure it out is we say why are you hiring us to do this? And we'll look at where they are, and what they've got in terms of data." Then they will suggest what to create and test initial ideas. "We have a concept stage at the beginning of each project, and that's really useful because we'll sketch out design ideas and present them to the clients, and they'll either say yes, that's good, crack on and make the thing, or they'll realize it's not right."

Gadney is passionate about making products that work and that do something unique. "We want the products to have integrity as well as utility. You find the difference by spending time understanding the data and who you're designing for." For him, the key to this is interested, engaged designers. "If you can't find what's interesting in the data, then you won't be able to design something interesting. If you're not interested in what you can do with that data, then you won't be a good designer."

Something that Gadney referred to frequently was his concern that designers are overly specialized, and insufficiently engaged with the wider world. He feels that many creatives are insufficiently interested in the industry they're designing for, whether that's chess or science. He compares design to journalism, or other "professions [that] teach you to be good at understanding the world around us—and I don't think design does that. I think design teaches you to understand what's in *Creative Review*." That is not to say you shouldn't understand the design world, but "if you're a designer and you need to design something like a new heart monitor, how are you going to have a conversation with your client if you only read about design?"

As designers are working increasingly with data, their materials shift—to information flows, coding, the understanding of how people use products rather than respond to messages—and as such they need to understand those new materials. Gadney says, "I think designers need to learn to write code. Even if you're not an engineer, you can understand your material. We need to be working across disciplines, be interested in the wider picture." He also points out that "if roles are just I/O or UX or visual design, if things are broken down as much as that, there's a danger that they'll outsource it." The Design of Understanding conference that Gadney runs every year aims to showcase a more expansive view of what information design could, and should, be.

Despite these concerns, Gadney sees huge opportunities for designers in the new digital era. He quotes new media commentator Lev Manovich, who has said that "the culture of the 21st century will be defined by the interface." Increasingly people spend their time, and money, interacting with digital interfaces, and Gadney points out that "at the heart of all digital products is data—and the many ways it can be collected, stored, processed, and presented. Designers who can work with data and marry the needs of engagement and utility, of science and art, will prosper in this new age."

Case Study: GDS Screens

Here, Max Gadney tells the story of how After the Flood came to work with GDS: "Richard Sargeant, director of performance & delivery at GDS (Government Digital Service), asked us to create a prototype for how we might use data to improve public services. His number one goal was to show how GOV.UK usage data could represent success or failure in a way that prompted people to take action.

"We based the main structure of pages on the different levels in the organization and their differing needs of detail. It became very apparent to us that senior people in the team need clear, concise insights that need little explanation, and it was only the analytics team or product owners that regularly needed the extra layers of detail and functionality.

"The design approach was loosely based on the optician eye-test chart—where everyone can read the letters at the top but the information becomes more complex and requires more time to decipher as you move lower down. Simple headline messages were presented at the top of the page, which could also be used on large screen displays, with more detail revealed as the user scrolls down the page."

gds.blog.gov.uk; gov.uk
aftertheflood.co/projects

1–3. Pages from the finished GDS Screens show how the information is split into levels of complexity, allowing users to interact with headline statements or more involved data.

4. Close-up analysis of specific statistics and explanation of unusual activity.

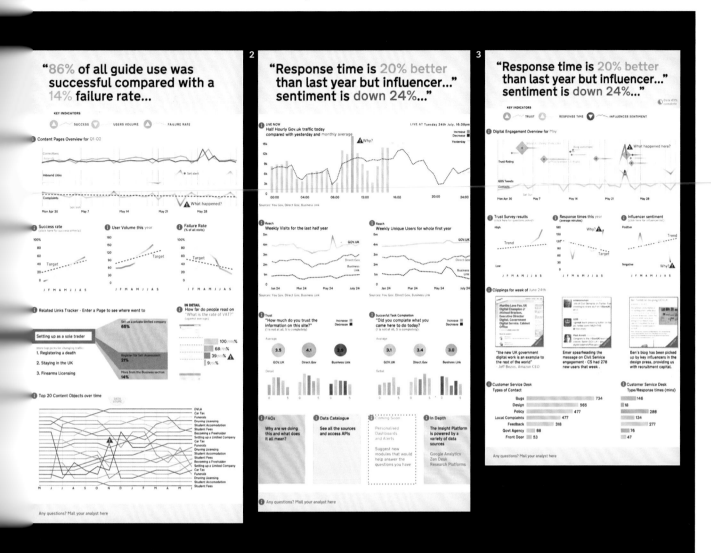

"86% of all guide use was successful compared with a 14% failure rate..."

"Response time is 20% better than last year but influencer..." sentiment is down 24%..."

"Response time is 20% better than last year but influencer..." sentiment is down 24%..."

How many people are visiting this site every month?

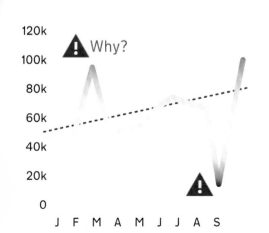

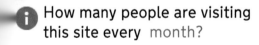

Explained

Public holiday on Mon 24th Feb resulted in a spike of hits to trade union pages
Lana Gibson

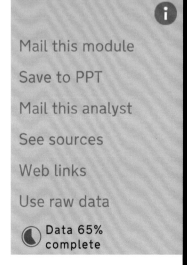

Mail this module

Save to PPT

Mail this analyst

See sources

Web links

Use raw data

Data 65% complete

Beautiful Data

The tools of information design are being used to do more than clarify statistics: they are now telling more personal, illustrative, or humorous stories.

"I'm interested in how designed information can help us understand the world. . . . Or, failing that, it can just look cool!" So says David McCandless, founder of Information Is Beautiful, and this idea that data can look great in and of itself, without necessarily helping viewers better understand a meaningful dataset, has led to some exploratory, visually led data design work. Instead of using the tools of information design to clarify statistics, designers are telling different kinds of stories that are more personal, illustrative, or humorous.

That is not to say this kind of work doesn't expand viewers' understanding or deepen their interaction; it just might be in the service of more diverse aims than reportage or research. Sarah Illenberger's humorous photographic visualizations for *Neon* magazine's sex survey do not help viewers read the raw stats—those

1
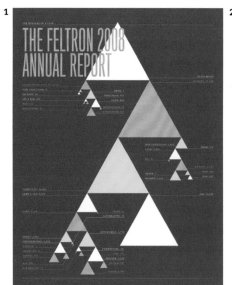

2

3

1 & 2. In the Feltron annual reports, Nicholas Felton applies his infographic expertise to data gathered from his own life.

3. The album artwork for OK GO's *Of the Blue Colour of the Sky* uses data gathered from the music itself to create graphics.

SEARCH: Ben Fry; Chris Jordan; data art; David McCandless/ Information Is Beautiful; Daytum; Eric Fischer; Fathom; Information Experience Design RCA; Martin Wattenberg; Nicholas Felton/ Feltron; Processing; Sarah Illenberger; Stanford Kindred Britain; Stefanie Posavec; TED playlist "6 Beautiful Talks by Data Artists"; visual storytelling

have to be shown typographically—but they give a visual approximation of relative values while setting a fun tone for the piece that will encourage readers to engage with it. Chris Jordan's images in his online gallery "Running the Numbers: An American Self-Portrait" communicate powerful statistics on waste and society but initially engage as photographic images, with the layers of meaning only becoming clear as the viewer zooms in and out and reads the accompanying explanations.

Another area designers are exploring is idiosyncratic datasets. In the Feltron annual report, data designer Nicholas Felton uses infographics to showcase the minutiae of his own life. A self-initiated project, it functions as an interesting piece of aesthetic design and brilliant self-promotion, as it has been featured on blogs and websites around the world. Felton, along

with Ryan Case, has also built Daytum, a website and app that allows users to gather their own life data and create simple infographics from it. Other designers find datasets in new places such as literary texts or music: data designers Stefanie Posavec and Ben Fry both created visualizations of Darwin's *On the Origin of Species* out of an interest in how they might visualize the story of its many revisions.

Often this work is about provoking the viewer to look at something differently, finding a new aspect of a subject people assume they know and then representing it visually. These personal data explorations are feeding back into the data design community, suggesting new visual aesthetics and different types of information exploration that could be applied in journalistic and research settings.

4

► 34

Wie oft im Monat schaust du pornografische Seiten im Internet an? (49% aller Befragten tun dies, 71% der Männer und 26% der Frauen.)

1 bis 3 Mal	4 bis 5 Mal	6 bis 10 Mal	11 bis 20 Mal	21 bis 30 Mal	über 30 Mal
37%	17%	15%	9%	6%	2%
Männer 28%	Männer 17%	Männer 19%	Männer 12%	Männer 7%	Männer 2%
Frauen 63%	Frauen 17%	Frauen 3%	Frauen 3%	Frauen 2%	Frauen 0%

4. Humorous physical infographics from Sarah Illenberger.

I want my data projects to appeal visually to someone who's passing by, but when they learn they are created from data they start to look closer.

In Conversation

with Stefanie Posavec, designer

Stefanie Posavec is a U.S. designer who moved to London after completing her MA at Central Saint Martins College of Art and Design. After a period working as a cover designer for Penguin Books, she now works freelance on information design, data visualization, book cover design, and book design. Projects include the MyFry app, OK GO album artwork, Left vs. Right poster (with David McCandless), and a recent Facebook residency as a data artist.

Posavec's personal work explores data illustration and has been featured in numerous design books and exhibited internationally at sites including the Museum of Modern Art in New York and the Victoria & Albert in London. She regularly speaks about information design at conferences.

stefanieposavec.co.uk

Stefanie Posavec started exploring data visualization while studying at St. Martins, inspired by another student's work and an interest in "John Maeda and things that are algorithmic, where you create a set of rules that are used to generate a visual." She explains that "I wanted to transform something I loved, which was literature, into something visual, which would let people see it from a different angle. I focused on *On The Road*, because that was a book that I really loved and gathered data from the text in order to visualize it."

In the end, it was Posavec's interest in literature, rather than information, that led to her next job, working as a cover designer for Penguin. But when her *On The Road* project was exhibited a couple of years later and then blogged about, clients started approaching her about data visualizations, opening up a different career path. "It was on Boing Boing, and 50 people in a day emailed me. Digital transmission is helping these small ideas kick around in a way that they couldn't before."

When she worked with David McCandless on the Left vs. Right website, Stefanie's online exposure increased again. She says that McCandless and other data journalists have helped make the field "really populist. People have been doing information design and data representation forever, but I think there was a very particular point where the entire world became interested in it."

Posavec's data work tends to be split between "traditional information design, which is more serious, that's my day job and I don't necessarily put it in a portfolio" and "the weirder stuff, which feels more illustrative and is often half self-initiated." Although the illustrative projects tend to be less commercial, she says it's still the work that clients are interested in. "I think people are buying a way of thinking, so if they hire me for a commercial project they might not get something so arty but they'll have that sense of ability applied to something very serious."

Posavec doesn't code, although she thinks she "needs to learn some basics." Instead, she works by hand

on self-initiated projects, spending "lots of time reading and rereading text and counting words or numbers or just going through subject matter repeatedly until I have all the data in a notebook, and then I use that data to create my graphics." She says, "I think I need to learn how to access larger datasets, but for me it's important to go through that marking process, because when I do, the ideas form in my head." When working with programmers, or data experts, Posavec still needs "to have my hands and my head around the data at some point. Even if I'm not analyzing the data, I need the person doing that to tell me the highs and the lows and the ranges, so I can start sketching, and thinking about what something will look like."

For client work, Posavec is more likely to work with data experts, often working in tandem with a data researcher who "crafts stories, finds the datasets and content for a client, and makes sure everything is truthful and accurate, and then I'm the one [who] shapes that visually." This kind of data journalism, or statistical storytelling, has a growing market because, as Posavec points out, "that's the way people understand stories now."

Talking about her working process, Posavec explains she is guided by her subject matter, both the raw data and the larger concepts: "I'm using the data to create form, so I try to find meaningful data in the subject matter—data that creates interesting patterns and where the pattern has meaning. So even if the main intention of the design work isn't to show insight but just to be decorative, or communicative, you can still see that there's a harmony, or something interesting."

The data shapes the work in numerous, sometimes unexpected, ways. "There's this process of discovery—you don't know what shape the data is going to take so there's always this unexpectedness, this experimentation. . . . It can be really frustrating because data can only take certain forms dictated by the numbers and relationships within the datasets, and clients will ask why something can't look a particular way, and I have to say because the data is not shaped like that, you just can't do it."

Despite those limitations, Posavec still tries "to find ways of communicating with a more intangible feeling about the data, shaping it metaphorically." For example, "For the OK GO artwork, the album was called *Of the Blue Colour of the Sky*, and it was based on an old pseudo-scientific text that talked about how blue lights could heal people and mentioned prisms and rainbows and ice and diamonds. So those were the colors and shapes we were trying to use when we made it."

It's important to Posavec that her work connects on this more emotional level, as well as to the viewer's understanding that the pieces are based on meaningful data. "It's a balancing act. I want the work to appeal to someone [who's] passing by, but when they learn about what

made it, it connects with them on another level, they see that it's a pattern, data made visual. And if I can, I'll have an explanation so that if they want to understand what it means they can access that to some degree. Those are three levels that I'm always trying to reconcile."

Posavec's diverse portfolio is all about finding new ways for people to experience information, and in the future she is interested in working more with "things that are dynamic. I'd like to design for something that is changing and shifting, rather than flat graphics. Or think about how data can be physical." She admires projects like Stanford's Kindred Britain "where there's a lot of data, and you're not going to get it instantly," but the visualization helps bring the complex connections to life and can tell stories. She says, "I'm interested in how you can communicate information in a way that's creative or new."

THE DIGITAL
RELATIONSHIP
DANCE

A DANCEABLE DIAGRAM
OF A COUPLE'S FACEBOOK
INTERACTIONS DURING
AUGUST 2013

DANCING THE DATA:

1 Put on some music (100 bpm is recommended) and stand in the start position.

2 The steps are arranged into groups of eight, and are danced in ⁴⁄₄ time.

Following the arrows, dance by cycling through repeated counts of 1-8 using the notation system below:

— If the count is shown in a circle, move your foot to this position.

— If the count is not circled, rest your foot or step in place in this position.

3 GREEN arrows indicate steps where both partners move at the same time.

UNDERSTANDING
THE DATA:

All individual posts from each partner (statuses, photos, etc.) and their interactions with each other are visualized in the dance.

Movement left and right represents movement across timelines, as per the layout below:

| LEFT | CENTER | RIGHT |
| Partner One's timeline | Shared posts (one is tagged by the other) | Partner Two's timeline |

A partner dances left or right to the other's timeline to post content, like, or comment on the other partner's posts.

When both partners are linked in a shared post, they dance together in the center.

Specially made for you by
Stefanie Posavec

Case Study: The Digital Relationship Dance

Stefanie Posavec spent a seven-week data artist residency at Facebook's Analog Research Lab in the summer of 2013 at Facebook's headquarters in Menlo Park, California. Her task was to create artwork for the campus, so she chose to create two interactive pieces on the floor, where she converted a month of a couple's Facebook interaction data into dance steps, referencing how couples often "perform" an orchestrated, public version of their relationship on social media.

The dance steps are timed to an eight-step count: by following the notation, passersby can move through an accurate representation of a couple's digital movements and interactions in the real world.

stefanieposavec.co.uk/data/#/facebook-art-residency-relationship-dance-steps

COUPLES' FACEBOOK INTERACTIONS, AUGUST 2013

LEGEND

All of PARTNER ONE's activity is indicated in blue

All of PARTNER TWO's activity is indicated in green.

● SHARED POSTS
Posts where the partners are joined together (they are tagged in same check-in, tagged in same photo, tagged in status update, and so on). The colour indicates which partner made the shared post.

● PERSONAL POSTS
These posts include all posts on a user's timeline that they have made themselves (status updates, link/photo postings, check-ins, and so on; no posts by other users or any posts that are automated by an external source are included).

● LIKE AND COMMENT

○ COMMENT

· LIKE

UNDERSTANDING THE DATA

All personal posts from each partner (statuses, photos, etc.) and their interactions with each other from the month of August 2013 are visualized in the dance.

All posts are in chronological order, starting from the top and moving downward.

Posts where one partner has responded to the other's post are in a bolder color, while posts where no mutual interaction has taken place is indicated by a pale colour.

Movement left and right represents movement across timelines, as per the layout below:

LEFT	CENTER	RIGHT
Partner One's timeline	Shared posts (one is tagged by the other)	Partner Two's timeline

A partner's path moves left or right to the other's timeline to post content, like, or comment on the other partner's posts.

When both partners are linked in a shared post, they both move towards the center of the diagram.

E THREE   COUPLE FOUR

1 & 2. Posavec's graphics in situ at Facebook HQ—two people can follow the steps to do the Digital Relationship Dance.

3 & 4. Posters showing Posavec's graphics include explanations of how she has used the data to shape her graphics.

I'm interested in using our communication skills to change the way things are.
Tibor Kalman

Advocacy

The tools of communication design have been used in the service of many causes, from political propaganda and charity fundraising to grassroots movements and fringe activism. Just as brands employ design to help win consumers, so campaigning organizations use it to win supporters, contributors, or fellow activists. Indeed, action groups, charities, and political parties are increasingly "branded" as they work to gain traction in a media-saturated world.

Throughout the 20th century, design has played a role in political and cultural change. Arguably at its most extreme, Soviet and Nazi propaganda made skilful use of graphic power in their large-scale branding and information campaigns, while the UK used poster campaigns throughout World War II to encourage army enrollment and home-front support. Over the decades, a wealth of campaigns have been supported by design work—for civil rights, gender equality, nuclear disarmament, wildlife protection, and sustainability among many others.

Sometimes this work can seem at odds with the commercial realities of communication design, but the same skills are at play, just turned to a different message. Ken Garland's 1963 "First Things First" manifesto was a call for designers to realize that, by designing for a company, they become an advocate for it, and that how designers choose to employ their skills has implications. Among the "high-pitched scream of consumer selling," the manifesto proposed "a reversal of priorities in favor of the more useful and more lasting forms of communication." It explicitly did not "advocate the abolition of consumer advertising," rather it encouraged designers to see that their skills had other applications, some of which might just improve the world.

Now that media platforms are omnipresent, with smartphones, tablets, and computers feeding people information throughout the day, communication can be even more insidious and designers' choices more complex. However, the awareness that design and as such designers' choices have an impact is now widely accepted, with many designers interrogating their clients' practices in order to decide what work they are comfortable taking on. Campaigning groups are increasingly developing long-term relationships with designers and agencies as they realize the importance of communication specialists. And social media has given interest groups new platforms, opening up opportunities for design activism at a grassroots level.

Activism

Designers lobby, raise awareness, and actively make change happen.

Sometimes, the key to political change isn't designing a logo or poster. It's simply having the courage to show up and make your voice heard, no matter what the cause—and no matter what the risk.
Michael Bierut

1. Shepard Fairey's *Progress, Hope* and *Change* posters became key visual symbols of Barack Obama's 2008 election campaign.

SEARCH: Adbusters; AIGA Design Business and Ethics; Barbara Kruger; Beautiful Trouble; Citizen Designer (ed. Heller); First Things First/ First Things First 2000; Johan Kugelberg & Philippe Vermes *Beauty Is In The Street: A Visual Record of the May '68 Paris Uprising*; Jonathan Barnbrook; Ken Garland; Lucienne Roberts "A Is for Activism"; Metahaven; Michael Bierut "The Poster that Launched a Movement (Or Not)"; Obey Giant; Occupy Design

Activism is normally defined as action aiming to bring about political or cultural change. For some people this is characterized by the visible manifestations of protests and picketing, but activism is wider and more complex than this. Three key ways that campaigners try to accomplish change are raising awareness, lobbying, and actively making a change happen: design can have a role in all of these. Giving campaigns a strong visual identity, creating thought-provoking or emotional graphics to highlight an issue, building communication platforms, and illustrating problem-solving behaviors are just some of the ways that design can help a cause.

There can also be a misconception about who "activists" are. Although campaigners are attempting to change the status quo, they are not always fringe or countercultural groups; for example, political parties are attempting to accomplish change through mainstream channels. It is also worth noting that there tend to be activists on both sides of a debate, as with the argument over abortion laws, where pro-choice and pro-life campaigners are equally passionate about their views.

These complexities mean that attempting to use design as a campaign tool can be fraught. Not all designers want to change the world, but many designers and agencies do put their creative skills to work for a variety of causes. One straightforward way this happens is by agencies establishing a client/designer relationship with a campaign group, whether pro bono or on a more commercial footing. Other designers create their own activist interventions, or work within campaigning groups on their graphic output.

Harry Pearce, a partner at Pentagram, has worked with Witness for nearly two decades. Witness "uses video to open the eyes of the world to human rights violations," so communication is absolutely central to its cause. Pearce has built a very strong relationship with the charity, explaining, "I feel my work for Witness has become part of the DNA of my creative life. Though I've never been able to donate funds of any consequence, I have given my creativity and literally months of my own and my team's time."

Their poster for the Witness Burma campaign became a visual symbol for protests in Burma and across the world, which was a significant moment for Pearce: "I always felt like even if I don't do anything else in my life again, at least I've done this." It is a testament to the power of design that an image can have such graphic resonance it becomes a symbol beyond the designer's original intention. A recent example: Shepard Fairey's *Hope* poster, a self-initiated piece that became a key visual symbol for Barack Obama's election campaign and which has been described by Michael Bierut as "one of the most ubiquitous and effective pieces of political graphic design of the decade, if not the century."

Ceding Control
One of the challenges for designers working on behalf of campaigns is that they may have to relinquish control of the final designs. Campaign groups often want their supporters to have ownership over the group's identity, so

design rules can be quickly broken. Lucienne Roberts talks about this in the context of designing a trade union logo, "Little did we know, as we painstakingly spaced and drew its letterforms, that the new UCU logo would be hand-rendered on signs, sewn on banners, stenciled on placards, even baked into cakes!" Despite her instinctive desire for design rules, she says it is "in the spirit of the cause. . . . We've been gathering images, and it's lovely really, because people have been taking the logo on as theirs."

There can also be an actively anti-design feeling among campaigning groups, due to concerns that anything too "designed" will look corporate—and expensive. This discomfort is wearing off as access to design tools increases and the amateur or grassroots aesthetic is less strongly differentiated from commercial design. Campaigning groups now more often use graphic language that will appeal to a broad audience of potential supporters.

2. The LucienneRoberts+ logo for UCU has been sewn onto flags, baked onto cakes, and hand-lettered onto placards.

3. Charity branding, such as Wolff Olins's work for Macmillan, helps the public recognize charities and their services.

4. Harry Pearce's *Burma* poster for Witness was used to raise awareness worldwide—and by Burmese citizens when protesting.

2

3

4

#Occupy

The Occupy movement that began on Wall Street and spread worldwide was started by the "global network of culturejammers and creatives" Adbusters. Adbusters is a media foundation, an activist network, and a magazine. It challenges consumerism head-on, often through the subversion and utilization of commercial communication tools. They undermine mainstream advertising messages with spoof ads and run annual marketing campaigns for Buy Nothing Day and Digital Detox Week.

From its inception the Occupy movement employed contemporary communication techniques. The initial call to action was presented as a hashtag, #OccupyWallStreet, launching it as a conversation on Twitter from day one. Adbusters also designed a striking poster with a ballerina atop the Charging Bull and a date for action. While Occupy has never tried to have a consistent graphic language, both graphics and copy were vital to its launch and ongoing resonance. Slogans such as "We Are the 99%", the Guy Fawkes mask popularized by hacktivist group Anonymous, and infographics relating to the financial inequalities being protested were all keystones for the movement.

Occupy Design and Occupy Design UK were both launched to shepherd the enormous graphic outpouring that the movement inspired. They encouraged designers to create posters, infographics, and marks that communicated the aims of the movement and the injustices it hoped to correct, stating that "this is one of the first social movements in history able to produce high-quality imagery using digital graphic design tools and distribute them instantaneously anywhere in the world using file-sharing and social media. It's also one of the first social movements with broad access to open data—which, if communicated correctly, makes it much more difficult for those who should be held accountable to hide from facts."

In the UK, designer Jonathan Barnbrook became heavily involved with Occupy, designing a logo, letting his typeface Bastard be used across the *Occupied Times*, and helping to coordinate a series of design events around the movement. At the time he said, "As a designer it gives me hope because we have been complicit in the feeding frenzy of the money-making; now as part of the Occupy movement, there are designers working without ego, just with a belief in what the movement is doing."

5

5. *The Occupied Times*, designed collaboratively as a part of #OccupyLondon, has continued as an online news site and publication.

6. The Adbusters poster that launched #OccupyWallStreet, which went on to become a global movement.

Design as a practice doesn't have much of a conscience, even if individual designers do.
Mr. Keedy

6

I think we try to
have it both ways
as graphic designers;
we like to think
that what we do is
important, but we
don't actually want to
be held accountable
for anything.

In Conversation

with Lucienne Roberts,
founder, LucienneRoberts+

Lucienne Roberts is the founder of LucienneRoberts+, a London-based studio "committed to making accessible, engaging graphic design with a socially aware agenda." Clients include the Wellcome Collection, British Council, Design Museum, UCU, and The Women's Library.

Alongside studio-based work, Roberts writes, lectures, and publishes on her subject. A signatory of the "First Things First" 2000 manifesto, her books include *The Designer and the Grid* (2002, Rotovision) and *Good: An Introduction to Ethics in Graphic Design* (2006, AVA Academia). Roberts also teaches and lectures internationally.

With design educator and writer Rebecca Wright, Roberts is principal founder of GraphicDesign&, a pioneering publishing house dedicated to creating intelligent, vivid books that explore how graphic design connects with all other things and the value that it brings to different subjects.

lucienneroberts plus.com
graphicdesignand.com

Lucienne Roberts has thought extensively about the ethics of graphic design, and her work and writing reveal a deeply considered view of the moral complexities in communication practice. She started our conversation by talking about how she approaches ethics within her own work, explaining that she has "always been quite political, so I'm interested in how you unite that with design." One of the ways that Lucienne has kept to personal principles is by being selective about who she works for, but she notes "there are different ways of coming at it. You could say that as long as you're making people's lives better, that's okay, and you could argue you're doing that as much by working for Nike as for someone else. . . . Of course how you define 'making people's lives better' is another thing."

An important conclusion Roberts has come to is that ethics must ultimately exist on a personal level. She says that committing to absolutes "became more and more difficult the more I thought about it. I could say what was right or wrong for me, but not commit to any hard and fast rules." And while you can make the "very simple and very profound" argument that a belief in free speech means that "everybody has the right for their message to be heard," individual designers and agencies must work out where their own beliefs lead them. She says, "You don't want things to be so gray that you can't make any decisions. You have to be true to yourself and you have to think through the things you're prepared to support."

When asked to present a talk on activism, Roberts "came up with the idea of lowercase a/capital A activism" to differentiate between her activist projects. "All challenge the status quo but some [A] don't shy from more overt protest while others [a] inform in order to persuade."

An example of an [A] project is the leadership campaign for David Miliband, as it was not only "very high profile" but also "potentially leading towards the next government." Miliband's campaign team chose to approach their communications design quite differently from the other candidates. "[Miliband] got criticized for spending a lot of money on his campaign, and although we didn't get paid a lot of money for it, when you looked at the other leaflets and design, they all looked very amateur. Which obviously they weren't, but that was the aesthetic they had chosen."

This attention to the campaign design carried on past Miliband's defeat. "When he didn't win, his team had a meeting to think about why not, and one of the things that they talked about were the graphics. And the idea that they could say it was partly your fault, when it was something that we personally were so committed to, was hard. They decided that it wasn't anything to do with the graphics, but even thinking about that really pulled me up short. In a way it was quite a good and shocking awakening, because I think we often try to have it both ways as graphic designers, we like to think that what we do is important but we don't actually want to be held accountable for anything."

By comparison, examples of [a] projects would be "the exhibitions we've done for the Women's Library, or the most recent example, which is probably a borderline A/a thing, was 'On Solid Ground'—a touring exhibition that we've done with the International Rescue Committee about refugees. It's raising awareness about immigration really, and trying to explain why there are immigrants. And that's an incredibly worthwhile and really wonderful project. It's lowercase a, according to my definition, in that it's not overtly political, but for me, it's very significant."

Roberts also talked about the changing landscape for government-funded and charity design. "Things have changed a lot. . . . When I was first a designer I did a lot of work for charities—Breakthrough, Cancer Research, Save the Children—partly because there were [fewer] designers and most of them didn't want to do it." Whether this kind of work has become fashionable, or there is simply an expanded design industry, charities now have a much more commercial relationship with design agencies.

"Charities have got wiser about design, but they've also moved towards working with people who have a commercial background. They've stopped using people who have only worked with the charity or voluntary sectors." For Roberts, "It's changed the landscape enough that we'd be unlikely to do that work, which is a shame. But they are commercial outfits, and we have to accept that they're trying to appeal to the widest possible market, which inevitably leads to something a bit tame. Because they can't afford to put anyone off."

As Roberts's practice has developed, education and engagement have become even more important in her work. Her studio has designed exhibitions for numerous clients, including the Wellcome Collection and Design Museum, and she says, "The great thing about exhibition design is that it always has educative content, and it's about entertaining and engaging people, so it ticks lots of boxes in terms of access."

GraphicDesign&, a joint publishing venture with Rebecca Wright, has grown out of this passion to involve and enthuse people. "We were writing a book together about the design process, and we thought it's all the other things that make graphic design exciting, it's not really the graphics." GD& links graphic design with other disciplines; for GD&Mathematics they teamed up with mathematician Alex Bellos and asked designers to visualize the Golden Section. Their hope is always to communicate beyond design. "We don't just want graphic designers to buy the book—we want to get people out there to understand what we do." Communicating a complex idea so that you will remember it is "absolutely what a graphic designer can do that a mathematician can't. And that's what Alex was saying is great."

Ethics are a thorny subject, and Roberts doesn't shy away from the difficulties in establishing a moral framework as a designer. But she is clear that designers can be rewarded for thinking about their personal principles. "It's stimulating. It's hard. But I learned such a lot."

Case Study: On Solid Ground

On Solid Ground is a touring exhibition, launched at St. Martin's in the Field on World Refugee Day and moving on to France, Croatia, Germany, and Belgium. It is a collaboration of photo agency Panos Pictures, the International Rescue Committee, and the European Commission's Humanitarian Aid and Civil Protection Department.

The exhibition aims to raise awareness about immigration and helps explain how people become immigrants. "Several photographers went out to meet people who had been refugees and talked about what has happened to them and why, and then their stories are told in pictures.

We needed something that would be easy and cheap to transport, so we worked with Michael Marriott, the product designer, on it. He came up with a very clever system using fabric, which means it folds down very easily, and then the structures are weighted with water, so it can all pack up and fit into a van very easily and then be reassembled elsewhere.

"We wanted to be very respectful to the images—they needed space and restrained design. The subject's stories are very strong narratives, and we wanted the images to have the same impact, to get across what life has been like for these people."

onsolidground.eu

3

4

1. The temporary structures for the exhibition can be easily set up in different locations, creating a large canvas to showcase the photographs and stories.

2. Extra display surfaces inside the canvas structures.

3 & 4. Newspaper designed to accompany the exhibition.

Social Responsibility

Communications agencies
are engaging with the idea that
organizations and individuals
have a responsibility toward
the larger community.

1 & 3. Candy Chang's
Before I Die project
captures the personal
hopes and aspirations
in a community.
Starting in Candy's
own neighborhood,
"Before I die" walls
have spread worldwide.

2. OgilvyChange used
artists to transform
metal shutters for their
Babies of the Borough
project.

Social responsibility is an ethical theory that organizations
and individuals have a responsibility toward the larger
community they operate in. In this context, society could
mean the whole of humankind, a particular country or
interest group, or a local community. Increasingly more
companies and communications agencies are engaging
with this idea by using their reach and skills to benefit
society, and these projects have proven to work beyond
their social impact: they are also a fantastic marketing
tool. Paco Conde, creative director at Ogilvy & Mather
Brasil, points to a shift toward human- and social-
centered projects across design disciplines and links it
to changes in the brand/consumer relationship brought
about by social media. He says, "You have a continuous
conversation with your audience or your consumers
or your users. . . . People can share our message, they
can like our message." In this environment, it helps
if you can give your audience something to like.

Companies are buying into this internationally, with
many high-profile brands linking themselves to social
issues. This can be for a single campaign, or alternatively
a social stance can become an entrenched brand value,
as with Dove's Campaign for Real Beauty. The creative
team has carried out extensive research into female
body image and are trying to challenge the "limiting
and unattainable" current perceptions of beauty across
all their marketing activity. As well as creating award-
winning ad campaigns like Real Beauty Sketches, Dove
runs online forums to support debate around the issue
and offer practical advice on female-centered issues.

The public and charity sectors have also embraced
the value of working more closely with designers, and
decision-makers' realization that communications
professionals can do more than just sell things has led
to some incredible creative partnerships. For example,
the Colombian Ministry of Defense has built a long-
term partnership with LOWE/SSP3 working to reach
guerrilla fighters in remote locations and encourage
them to demobilize. The campaign Operation Christmas
saw soldiers decorate trees in areas of guerrilla activity
with movement-sensitive Christmas lights. When people
passed the trees, they would light up and illuminate
a message urging guerrillas to go home. During
the period the campaign ran, 331 guerrilla fighters
demobilized, a 30 percent uplift on the previous year,
and the project was voted the most effective campaign
in the world in 2011. Iveth Carmen, communications
advisor for the National Ministry of Defense, said,
"Creativity is what has allowed the demobilization
message to reach the guerrillas where they are."

Charities can likewise provide designers the
opportunity to create imaginative work in the service
of issues they feel inspired by, not to mention the huge
professional caché to working with respected charity brands.
Large design agencies are, of course, themselves commercial
businesses with their own brand image. Not only do good
news stories get great media coverage and attract new
clients, employees enjoy working on projects with a positive
social outcome. Paco Conde again: "I think we're all aware
of the dark side of advertising, so we need to be able to feel

The ability to focus on local or targeted issues is no doubt part of the appeal of socially orientated communications work; while large-scale campaigns around profound issues like race inequality or deforestation may appear to face insurmountable barriers, locally targeted campaigns can see immediate engagement and impact. From large-scale corporate projects such as Dulux's Let's Colour campaign, which donates paint to transform run-down communities, to smaller projects initiated by individuals like Walk [Your City], which creates simple signage to communicate the walkability of an area, designers and other creatives are finding inventive ways to improve communities.

Co-Design

Now that "design thinking" has been recognized as a process that sits beyond any specific discipline, designers from a graphics or communication background have new opportunities to utilize their creative skills. Emerging models co-design and service design use design concepts such as iteration, rapid prototyping, and user testing in new environments, for example to improve public engagement or education models. In co-design, design professionals work with a user group to help them create products and services that work for them. This has particular resonance in the public sector, who are increasingly employing designers to find creative solutions to social problems.

In 2010, Project H Design undertook an immersive residence in Bertie County, one of the poorest parts of North Carolina: one in three children are living below the poverty line. Project H were invited to see what design thinking could do to help the education system, and while they started by effectively redesigning the school space, they ended up embedding a design program in the school's curriculum. The program worked with students to identify community problems and create design solutions; in 2011 their high school juniors designed and built a farmers market pavilion, the Windsor Super Market. As well as stimulating community engagement and providing a group of students with invaluable skills, the market has led to two new businesses and 15 jobs. Although this kind of project might look very different from a traditional piece of communication design, it is deeply rooted in design practice and draws on the practical creative thinking that designers are trained in.

As these diverse interventions coming from creative insights or passions are beginning to make a difference to communities, there is a growing appreciation for what design can do for society. And designers now have the choice to apply their skills in identifying and solving problems outside the communications industry.

What if we looked at the world like a design project—how might we begin to make it better?
Bruce Mau

I don't care about the reasons why brands are doing this kind of project; I just love that this is the way we are working, and it's good for society.

In Conversation

with Tara Austin and
Paco Conde, Ogilvy &
Mather

Ogilvy & Mather is a global advertising agency with more than 450 offices in 169 cities. Tara Austin is a senior brand planner at Ogilvy & Mather UK. As well as being brand guardian for a number of key clients, she created the Babies of the Borough/The Power of Cute project as an OgilvyChange experiment.

Paco Conde is creative director at Ogilvy & Mather Rio. He was the driving force behind the Immortal Fans project and is passionately optimistic about the contribution advertising might make to creating social change.

ogilvy.com.br
ogilvychange.com

International advertising, marketing, and public relations agency Ogilvy & Mather has embraced current research into psychology and behavioral economics and have a company-wide interest in how these ideas can help commercial enterprises make a positive impact on the world. Two of Ogilvy's 2013 Cannes Lions winners—The Power of Cute and Immortal Fans—draw on these ideas. Both projects were born from the creative and socially minded imaginations of Ogilvy staff and supported directly by the agency.

Tara Austin came up with the idea for The Power of Cute in the aftermath of the 2011 London riots —the reaction to a police shooting of a Tottenham man, which saw youths looting and setting fire to shops and businesses within the poorer boroughs of the city. She comments on how disturbing it was to watch people destroying their own communities. "Woolwich was a really sad example; people actually burned down the pub that they drank in." The obvious reaction of local businesses was to improve security, but the local council was reluctant to grant planning permission to add shutters.

As a planner, Austin has a background in research that she drew on when developing this project, looking first at the "broken windows" theory, which states that signs of neglect encourage further vandalism. Austin felt that "shutters did the same thing. . . . They're saying you're not welcome and are also very inhuman, as they're typically steel and completely blank." Secondly she considered the "baby schema," which shows that certain facial proportions such as "round cheeks, round heads, big eyes" promote caring behavior by activating a part of the brain associated with nurturing.

Using these pieces of insight, Tara wanted to "humanize the shutters," and inspired by street artists such as Ben Eine she used graffiti artists to paint the faces of local babies onto them. She wanted "to see if we could bring down antisocial behavior in the area and increase feelings of love and community and social cohesion.

It was really important that they were local babies so that it didn't feel like an advertising message."

Despite its small scale, the project generated global media coverage, and the local area saw a drop in crime. Now Austin is talking to clients about how they could expand this idea and is enthusiastic about what the right company could achieve. "As far as I'm concerned, this is a media opportunity. There's massive potential here for someone to do a corporate responsibility campaign, where someone pays to paint shutters and do something nice with them, rather than just do adverts or signage."

Like Austin, Paco Conde is passionate about the opportunities Ogilvy has to initiate positive social change. The Immortal Fans project came from an agency idea: to create a club-specific organ donor card. The creative team were so excited by this scheme that they directly approached Sport Club Recife, one of Brazil's most passionately supported teams. Conde explains that organ donation is a sensitive subject in Brazil, both because people choose not to donate beyond the family and because "when someone dies, there's no record of whether they want to donate organs, so the family mainly don't authorize the donation." Their idea was to "give a lot of people a reason to think about donating organs beyond their family— their love of their team—and then the organ donor card meant the family knew it was what they wanted."

While "the main idea was to create the organ donor card," the project team also "needed to tell fans about the card, which required a more 'normal' campaign." Conde's team worked with the Recife transplant center to find patients waiting for organs and featured them in a TV commercial. Along with spots donated by TV channels, they launched the campaign online, on the given team's fan page, in the match programs, and at a big game.

The campaign has been incredibly successful, both in fans signing up for cards and actual organ donations. "If we compare 2011 with 2012, there was an increase of 54 percent in organ donations in Recife.

Another amazing statistic was that the year before the campaign, there had been 1,047 people waiting for cornea donations. And after the campaign, it was zero. And in heart donations the same. The waiting list went down to zero." For Conde the most moving elements of the campaign were the stories from patients featured in the commercial. In fact he says that "only two or three months ago, one of the guys in the campaign, who had been blind for years, called us and said, 'thank you, you saved my life, I can see again, I just wanted to let you know'. . . . When I got that call, for me that was the best thing; it made me want to cry. It was amazing." Everyone who participated in the campaign now has the organ they were waiting for.

Immortal Fans was a pro bono campaign, but Ogilvy has no specific pro bono team. Instead, Conde explains, "We love to help people, so if we have a big client and we can help them to do something good for society, we try to help." He comments on the enormous enthusiasm for the Recife project within the agency and from external collaborators, many of whom helped for free, and puts it down to "the power of a good idea."

Conde links this success to a wider trend in advertising and branding, pointing out that a lot of the winning campaigns at Cannes had a social angle. Now that companies are selling "brands not products. . . . You have a continuous conversation with your audience or your consumers or your users, so you have to build a strong projection of your brand." In the age of social media, a good news story becomes a powerful communications tool: "People are waiting to share this kind of work. I don't know if it's an obligation, but I don't care about the reasons why brands are doing this kind of project. I just love that this is the way we are working, and it's good for society. I don't care if the final aim is to increase sales of the product. If the brands can help people, that's welcome."

They are now working to take the Recife donor card to other countries and other clubs. "We are taking a universal feeling—the passion a person has for their team— so it works all around the world. If all the teams around the world had their own donor cards, just imagine how many lives we could save."

Case Study: Immortal Fans— Sport Club Recife

Ogilvy and Sport Club Recife wanted to engage fans, tapping into their passion for the team to broach a subject that remains a taboo in Brazil—organ donation. They gave people a reason to donate organs to people beyond their immediate families.

Ogilvy created an integrated campaign with print, online activity, and a video showing real patients on transplant lists speaking to camera: "I promise your heart will keep beating for Sport Club Recife," "Your lungs will keep breathing for Sport Club Recife."

More than 51,000 fans signed up for cards, organ donations in Recife increased 54 percent, and the waiting lists for both hearts and corneas dropped to zero.

ogilvy.com.br/#!/cases/fas-imortais
ogilvy.co.uk/blog/the-work/the-babies-of-woolwich/

3

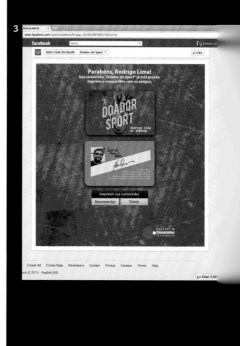

1. Fans used the huge flag promoting the campaign during football matches.

2. The Doador Sport donation card.

3. Fans could request a card through social media networks.

4 & 5. People waiting for an organ were enthusiastic about the campaign and starred in the television commercial and print ads.

6. The campaign had a dedicated website.

Sustainability

Designers are addressing the world's diminishing resources by communicating sustainable behaviors to the wider population and advocating sustainable products and services.

I think what many people in the post-industrial world are looking for and hoping to see is sustainable growth. We want to support companies that create growth without draining the world's resources.
Andreas Dahlquist, vice chairman / executive creative director, McCann Erickson, New York

The growing awareness of the world's diminishing resources, the environmental impact of industrial manufacturing, and the pressures of an expanding global population means that sustainability is on the commercial agenda—and it's there to stay. While sustainability has been discussed in design circles for decades, it often focuses on product and building design, and it can be hard for communication designers to work out how best to practice "sustainably." The main strategies by which designers can contribute to global sustainability are through their own work processes, by communicating sustainable behaviors to the wider population, and as advocates for sustainable products and services.

Sustainable Design and Production

There are many different levels at which designers engage with sustainable design, from choosing recycled paper to rethinking whole projects based on their life cycles. Practical guidance for sustainable design practice tends to focus on printed and built design and asks designers to consider the environmental impact of materials, production, and transport used throughout the design process. As digital outputs proliferate and screen resolution increases, issues around server space and digital energy consumption are also being considered. Websites such as lovelyasatree.com and re-nourish.com provide helpful resources and advice for designers trying to negotiate these decisions.

1 & 2. Puma's Clever Little Bag, designed with fuseproject, uses 75 percent less cardboard than a standard shoe box, reduces material and shipping costs, and removes the need for a plastic bag.

3. A Care Tag for Our Planet from Levi Strauss & Co. and Goodwill encourages consumers to put unwanted clothes to good use—not send them to landfill.

1

2

Research suggests that around 80 percent of a product's environmental impact is determined at the design stage—hence the phrase "waste is a design flaw." This means designers have the opportunity to more fundamentally change models for product manufacture and consumer use by considering a product's full life cycle, and rejecting the traditional linear take-make-dispose manufacturing model. In the UK, the RSA's Design Directors have launched The Great Recovery, a practical research project investigating alternative manufacturing and consumer models.

A key industrial alternative is the circular economy model, where technical and biological nutrients are recovered and safely fed back into production or the biosphere. Sometimes called "closed-loop" thinking, it aims for technical "nutrients" (such as plastics or computer chips) to retain their quality for reuse in manufacture, and biological nutrients (such as water or vegetable matter) to re-enter the biosphere without added pollutants. The circular economy is informed by natural systems, where one plant or animal's waste becomes food or fuel for another, and can increase efficiency while limiting environmental damage.

This cyclical way of thinking requires the integrated development of product, service, and communication design because to become truly closed-loop, not just the manufacturing process but

consumer use and disposal must be fully thought out. So designers may find themselves working as much with anthropologists and behavioral psychologists as with manufacturing and recycling experts.

Communicate

Sometimes designing for sustainability can just mean getting the message out there. Do The Green Thing and Green Patriot Posters are both initiatives using great graphic design to communicate environmental messages. Do The Green Thing identifies changes people can make at an individual level, like eating less meat, reducing water use, or switching appliances off, and then asks designers and illustrators to visualise them online. Green Patriot Posters is a website and book using the power of the poster to communicate issues and solutions related to climate change, again using celebrated illustrators and designers to create compelling visuals.

Design can also help communicate best practice directly to consumers. Clear labeling may not be what designers get most excited about, but a well-placed mark can make the difference between a product being recycled or going to landfill. Similar design interventions include energy efficiency ratings for appliances, marking on detergent that it will wash as well at 30°C, or showing that a product was made using renewable energy. Levi's A Care Tag For Our Planet states, "Wash in cold water.

3

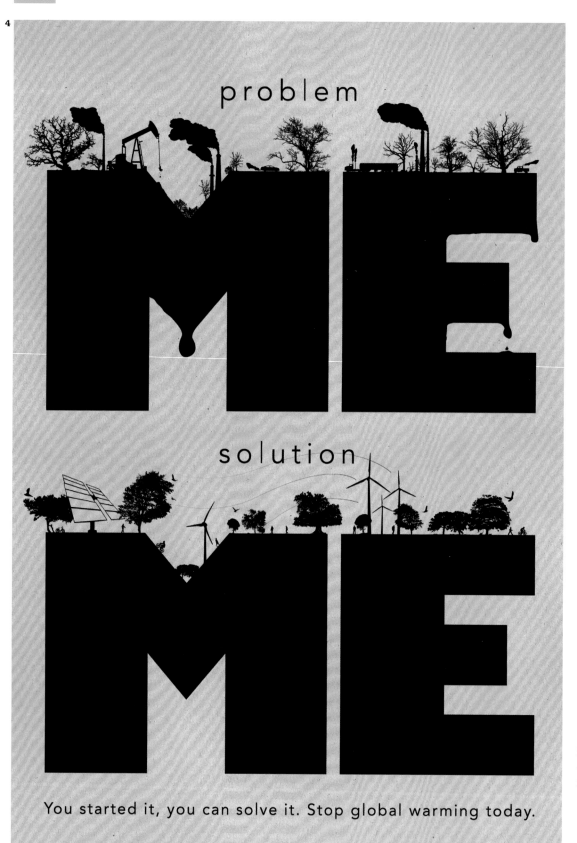

4

problem

ME

solution

ME

You started it, you can solve it. Stop global warming today.

It's people who are driving the environmental megatrends, and we know that people can change, and the people who are best at getting people to change are creatives.
Lucy Shea, Futerra

4. A book, a website and an exhibition, Green Patriot Posters harnesses the power of the poster in the fight against climate change.

5 & 6. Futerra's Change-maker Cards are designed to show some of the ways brands can encourage behavior change in their consumers.

Wash less. Line dry. Donate to Goodwill when no longer needed." Consumers will see these four simple instructions throughout their clothing's lifetime, encouraging Levi's wearers to adopt ecologically sound behavior.

Promotion

When products and services are sustainably designed, or promote sustainable behavior, then good communication design can help maximize their audience. Increasingly, agencies and companies promoting sustainable behavior are employing research from behavioral psychology to try to fundamentally change the way people consume, and often this is not about selling the sustainable credentials of a product. Sustainability communications agency Futerra works with international companies such as Unilever and Kingfisher to "maximize the good they do and minimize the harm," and their research shows that knowing a product or behavior is good for the environment is not enough to make consumers buy into it. Ecological messaging is doubly problematic because it inspires guilt in many consumers, and in the early days of sustainability "green" products were often seen as a lifestyle compromise—worthy but inferior.

As such, agencies are changing how they sell sustainability. In this new model, dry shampoo is sold on its convenience and how it makes your hair look rather than the fact that it saves energy; clothes swapping is not pitched as a way to save waste but a way to save money and have fun; and car-sharing services are not saving CO_2 but a healthier, cheaper mode of driving for contemporary urbanites. Large companies are increasingly realizing that as the global middle class expands, sustainable practices are crucial not just to protect the environment, but also to create business models with genuine longevity.

An example of a game-changing behavioral shift driven by technological advancements, and being successfully sold as a new consumer model, is the movement from ownership to access. Increasingly, rather than owning a physical product, consumers just want access to the experience it provides. This can range from accessing music, films, and words online, rather than owning CDs, DVDs, and magazines or books, to swapping existing goods via services like Freecycle and Swapz, to signing up to car-sharing services such as Zipcar. Sometimes called "collaborative consumption" this was one of *Time*'s "10 Ideas That Will Change the World" in 2011. Rachel Botsman, a leading authority in this area, is passionate about the changes that a shared approach to commercial transactions might bring, making the point in a recent TED Talk that "these systems are allowing people to share resources without sacrificing their lifestyles or their cherished personal freedoms." In short, they are seductively positioned and communicated, with the ecological benefits a by-product of consumption.

There is a growing sense that to achieve genuinely sustainable behavior patterns, we need to fundamentally alter our ideas of ownership and consumption. For communication designers, this is an exciting opportunity. While maximizing the ecological credentials of a single piece of design work may seem worthwhile but insignificant, helping to sell radically new ways of approaching consumption could actually reshape the world.

5

6

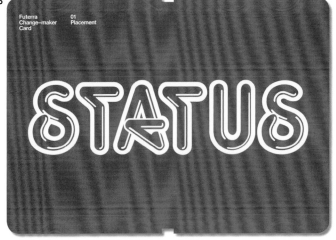

I've come to the conclusion that when you apply design skills to real world problems it becomes really interesting.

In Conversation

with Nat Hunter, founder,
Airside, co-director, RSA

Following early forays into psychology, graphic design, and programming, Nat Hunter became one of the first interaction designers in the mid-1990s, creating interfaces for spaceships in Hollywood movies and then founding Airside, one of London's most influential and idiosyncratic digital design agencies in 1998.

During the 14 years she ran Airside, Hunter began to realize the power that design has to change the world and started to use this power for positive social and environmental change.

As a result, she now utilizes her social, digital, and communication design skills to influence, educate, and innovate. She is currently co-director of design at the Royal Society for the Arts (RSA).

greatrecovery.org.uk

Nat Hunter did not initially train as a designer. During her first degree, she found herself excited by psychology and the emerging field of computing and as a graduate worked as a programmer in a bank before deciding she disliked the culture and needed to find a different work environment. Design was a chance discovery. "I got into graphic design on the job purely because I knew someone who needed an administrator." The studio she worked in adopted Macs, and Hunter was trained on the job as a junior designer, primarily for the music industry.

She found a way to marry her diverse areas of expertise in the very first MA in Interactive Multimedia at the Royal College of Art. "It was fantastic because the course [was] looking for people with either a psychology, programming, or graphic design background, so I just thought I had to do it." This new, multidisciplinary type of design work was also the inspiration behind Airside, which "was founded to create a cross-disciplinary design setting when most jobs required you to be either a programmer or a designer or a producer."

As Hunter's career has progressed, her understanding of the scope of design has developed to encompass the full breadth of design behaviors, "style, form, and function, problem solving, and framing." She says, "At the beginning of my career, I only really understood design as style, but now I see that the real power comes when we broaden out the definition along this scale. You need all four of these elements for truly great projects. I find myself gravitating towards the problem-solving and framing end. However, I'm definitely not saying that style isn't crucial—if you do some serious work up the framing and problem-solving end and it isn't beautifully realized, then you won't communicate what you need to."

While working at Airside, Hunter became increasingly interested in sustainability and social design, and in 2007 she formed Three Trees Don't Make a Forest with Sophie Thomas, a partner at sustainable design agency Thomas Matthews, and Caroline

Clarke, founder of lovelyasatree.com. Hunter says, "We started running workshops and events and consultancy to help people understand issues around sustainability. That was going really well, people were really interested and engaged, and then in late 2008 when the crash happened it was like a light bulb had been switched off. Sustainability suddenly went off the agenda." They observed a shift in priorities as finances contracted. "Emerging from that crash is an interest in social design and social enterprise."

It seemed like a good moment to take "the thinking a step forward. In a way we ran out of steam trying to have the same conversation with people again and again, where we were trying to explain that you if you wanted to make a brochure, if you've designed your brochure and got a cost from the printer and then suddenly look at printing it on recycled paper, they're going to quote you a lot of money and it'll seem like a difficult thing to do. But that's such a bad way to approach sustainability. You have to ask questions in the first place: why are you making a brochure, who are you making the brochure for, how can you make a brochure that is as sustainable as it can be within your budget? And then there are all sorts of creative innovations that you can make."

Hunter and Thomas are now co-directors for design at the RSA, and have "ended up with a much more ambitious project in a way— The Great Recovery." The Great Recovery has shifted their thinking to a much bigger scale: "from paper into enormous electrical products, and from thinking about lifecycles for one tiny thing into global supply chains." The RSA's "aim is to close the gap between our lives and the future to which we aspire, and we're putting design right at the heart of how we're going to get there."

Work on The Great Recovery is reiterating the importance of multidisciplinary teams. Hunter notes, "When you're thinking about the life cycle of a product, if you're a product designer making a toaster, you need to engage with a service designer to understand how someone is going to deal with that toaster when it breaks, how they're going to get it repaired, or what they're going to do with it when they throw it away completely. When I asked people what they would do with a broken toaster, everyone without fail said they'd put it into the black bin. No one knows about small electrical goods recycling. And you need anthropologists to ask why people have all these old mobile phones in their bottom drawer, rather than recycling them, and how we get them out of there."

The design landscape has fundamentally shifted, creating opportunities for designers to work in a new way. "Problems are becoming more complex, which is why we need multidisciplinary teams to face them. We need to have a top-level understanding of as many of those disciplines as possible. And we are moving from projects that had a beginning and an end to an iterative ongoing process."

Another part of Hunter's role at the RSA is managing the Student Design Awards, which provide students with the opportunity

"to apply design skills to social problems." Every year, Hunter is overwhelmed by the response from students, who "realize what they can do in the world." There is still an issue around how passionate designers can find relevant jobs, but "that's something we're trying to join up at the moment. We're trying to connect all the people in the industry who are more interested in design for problems, social design."

Hunter makes a passionate and convincing case for the possibilities inherent in the design role. "I believe design is changing and our roles as designers are changing for the better—it's a really strong and powerful thing that we all do. We need to embrace the enormous changes that are currently happening, take our valuable skills developed over years of traditional design work, and collaborate gracefully with experts in other disciplines. Then I believe that we do have the power to change the world for the better like Bruce Mau says. To get there we need systems thinkers and people who care about the world."

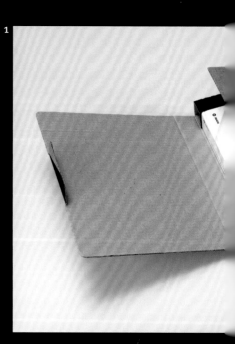

1. The Annual was shipped to members in a recyclable cardboard book wrap, limiting damage and potential wastage.

2. Harry Pearce's cover design pays homage to Fletcher Forbes Gill's iconic D&AD logo.

3. The strong design ensured the Annual would be a beautiful object, kept by owners for many years to come.

4. This infographic was designed to highlight how sustainability was built into every stage of the design and manufacture process.

5. Using light paper stock saved almost a kilo in weight from the 2010 Annual, reducing shipping costs and the paper's carbon footprint.

6. Using just three section dividers and marking categories with thumbcuts saved further weight.

3

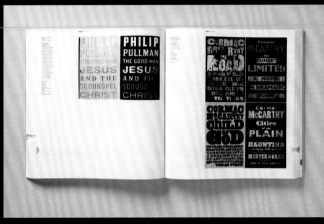

Case Study:
D&AD Sustainable Annual

In 2011, D&AD President Sanky collaborated with Pentagram partner Harry Pearce and Airside founder Nat Hunter to create the most sustainable Annual ever made.

Hunter started by questioning whether a book was the right format, considering whether the Annual could instead be published digitally. However, the Annual is not a disposable item; it is a treasured publication that is kept for years by individuals and agencies. So when the energy costs of keeping a digital artifact last for decades, the issues with digital longevity and the risk that people would print case studies out on inefficient printers were all taken into account, it was clear that a physical book remained the best solution.

The team interrogated every stage of manufacture to see where energy savings could be made. They considered materials, how production was fueled, the overall weight of the finished book, and the distance and methods of transportation. The layout was designed so that if a project won in more than one category, it was not replicated, saving even more paper. And finally, the inks and finishes were chosen so that if the book ever did end up in landfill it would be fully biodegradable.

At the end of the process Hunter commissioned Julie's Bicycle to analyze the energy savings. The analysis concluded that the 2011 Annual saved 82 percent of the carbon used in 2010.

dandad.org/dandad/news/latest/the-d-ad-annual-2011

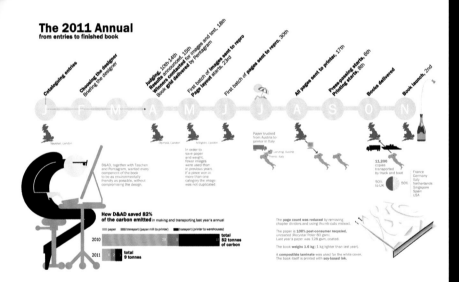

6

Case Study: Zipcar

Zipcar is a fantastic example of a service designed to promote sustainable behavior by building it into the consumers' way of life. Zipcar maintains a network of cars and vans across the United States and Europe that members can rent short term—for a couple of hours or for the day. By targeting urban markets where people's car needs are sporadic, and the costs of car ownership are high, Zipcar's creative team has built a loyal international customer base.

Two key ways that Zipcar stands out from its competitors are strong, easily recognizable graphics and a user-friendly booking interface. Zipcar's creative team has worked to make their service as seamless as possible, removing any possible frustrations to the user, and making use of smartphone technology to allow booking on the move. They have also worked to build a strong brand community, with an active social media presence across Facebook and Twitter, and their blog Ziptopia. As co-director of design at the RSA, Nat Hunter, points out, "If you think about something like Zipcar, you've got to make the whole experience appealing. You need really brilliant graphics all the way through."

By partnering with colleges and universities and creating the Zipcar U-pass in the United States, Zipcar is now preparing a new generation of drivers to have a completely different relationship with car ownership. Indeed, a 2013 survey commissioned by Zipcar showed that, more than any other age group, Millennials make a conscious effort to "reduce how much they drive, and take public transportation, bike, walk, or carpool when possible."

As of July 2013, the company had more than 810,000 members and offers nearly 10,000 vehicles throughout the United States, Canada, the United Kingdom, Spain, and Austria, making Zipcar the world's leading car-sharing network. The company also consistently wins awards for branding, innovation, and sustainability, a powerful trio in today's marketplace.

zipcar.co.uk/ zipcar.com

2

3

1

4

1. Strong graphics in situ.

2–4. A clear user interface makes using Zipcar easy for customers.

5. Zipcar U targets young people going to college, determining consumer behavior before they become car owners.

6. Zipcar's website makes use of mapping platforms to connect people with cars.

5

6

7. All cars are clearly branded as Zipcars.

8. The Ziptopia blog.

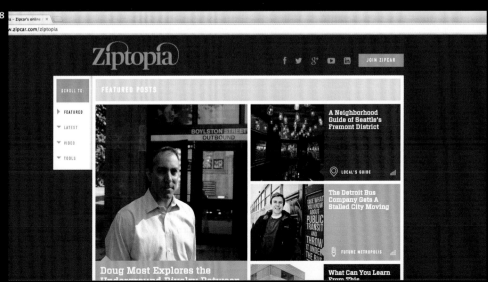

critique

Design criticism is everywhere, underpinning all institutional activity—design education, history, publishing, and professional associations. "What Is This Thing Called Graphic Design Criticism?" *Eye 16*, Spring, 1995

Communication design, especially in a commercial setting, is often characterized as reactive rather than proactive. The designer's role is to give shape to someone else's message or concept by responding to a brief, to client specifications, to a target audience, and to budget restrictions. From this comes the idea that good design should be "invisible" or transparent—in Beatrice Warde's famous phrase, a "crystalline goblet, which is worthy to hold the vintage of the human mind."

However, set against this is a long and growing tradition of designers using their own specialized tools—type, imagery, printing, publishing—to discuss issues and ideas about design and beyond. In the early 20th century, when graphic design first emerged as a profession, typographers Jan Tschichold and Eric Gill began to use self-authored and designed publications as a way to explain their theories in both word and form. This desire to share ideas—practical or ideological—can be seen throughout 20th-century design culture, from protest posters and zines to books on the typographic grid, via monographs, books, and design magazines.

The introduction of the first Apple Macs to studios in the mid-1980s saw the more rapid growth of designer-led publications, which in turn opened up debate about the designer's role. The *Emigre* magazine, art-directed by Rudy VanderLans, was in the vanguard, utilizing desktop publishing to critique, question, and showcase contemporary design work. Out of this growing design discourse came a new awareness of the designer as author, with designer-writers such as Michael Rock, Anne Burdick, and Ellen Lupton all tackling the thorny issue of whether, when, and how designers should create their own content.

Today there are numerous forums online, in print, and in person for writing, dialogue, and debate around communication design. Alongside the development of this critical discourse around design, there has been a growing commercial interest in the thinking and expertise designers can bring to their projects. A new range of skills—from content and product creation to exploratory thinking and public speaking—are helping agencies and individuals to differentiate themselves and their work. With this comes a new range of creative opportunities for contemporary designers to showcase the value of their own minds.

Design Discourse

There are new opportunities for designers and critics to build a meaningful discourse around the subject.

1

More people than ever are engaged with design, and designers, when given a chance, can be articulate, inspiring advocates for the power of design.
Michael Bierut, "Graphic Design Criticism as a Spectator Sport," Design Observer, 2013

Communication design is a relatively young discipline, normally tracing its history back to the emergence of graphic art in the early 20th century. Design academia is equally youthful, with practice and theory still strongly linked; unlike creative subjects such as literature and art, communication design does not have a long tradition of independent criticism. As such, the majority of design critics are also practicing designers, although some exceptions have helped define the field, notably Rick Poyner, founding editor of *Eye* and co-founder of Design Observer.

This makes for an interesting, and sometimes frustrating, critical landscape, with multiple platforms for discourse around contemporary communication design but few that reach far beyond the design community. The scarcity of dedicated critics can also result in little formal differentiation between showcasing work, commenting on it, offering more detailed critique, or actually challenging the ways design and designers function.

Showcasing individual designers, design projects, and working methods no doubt has an important role to play in the conversation about communication design. Magazines, blogs, monographs and many conference presentations focus on sharing great work or exciting practice, providing inspiration and encouraging comment. Alongside this lively commentary on contemporary work, writing about design history and emerging design trends has helped to establish a more complete picture

2

3

1. *Emigre* magazine (1984–2005), published by Emigre Graphics, became an important platform for design writing.

2 & 3. Websites such as Brand New and Design Observer create a space for conversation around design.

4. Adrian Shaughnessy's 2013 book *Scratching the Surface* collects his writing on various aspects of design.

of communication design as a discipline. The extensive design conference circuit is another space for exchanging ideas, with events taking place all over the world and covering subjects from typography to coding, via education and even the state of design criticism. Online forums have given designers even more platforms for debate, whether it's Design Observer's wide-ranging essays or Brand New, Armin Vit's popular site discussing branding.

Arguably the most important role for design criticism is to provide a deep critique of the purpose and possibilities of design. Ken Garland's "First Things First" manifesto is probably the most famous attempt to reframe the role of graphic design through writing, but many of the strongest design voices over the past decades have tried to tackle the thorny issue of how their skills could best be deployed. In the 1980s and '90s, designers like Tibor Kalman and Bruce Mau challenged fellow practitioners to take more responsibility for the impact of their work, a conversation that continues both in critical forums and in more practical collaborative efforts to make tangible change (see Advocacy, pp. 148–175).

When it comes to rigorous intellectual critique, communication design is still in its infancy. Although there has been a steady increase in writing and debate around communication design since the 1990s, the sense that there is not yet a fully-fledged critical discourse remains a disappointment to many commentators. Mainstream art critics rarely consider design part of their remit, and

Adrian Shaughnessy (interview pp. 182–185) reflects that despite the growing interest in design writing, critique remains "fragmentary, dissipated, and parochial." It is possible that the fledgling world of design criticism has suffered from a more general movement away from long-form writing. In his 2011 Design Observer article, "Another Designer Falls Silent," Rick Poyner observes, "Graphic designers were always, it can hardly be denied, a group with little commitment to serious reading," and the digital age has seen print publications suffer across disciplines. Despite this, design writing is better establishing itself in the academic sphere, with a number of new masters courses focusing on critique, so there may be a new breed of critical voice in design's future.

As Michael Bierut points out in his essay "Graphic Design Criticism as Spectator Sport," in the January 2013 issue of Design Observer, graphic design is now of interest to people outside the world of design. While this might seem to primarily manifest itself in cries of "my four-year old could have designed that," Bierut rightly points out that this wider interest is also an opportunity for designers to become "articulate, inspiring advocates for the power of design." It remains to be seen exactly how the discourse around communication design will play out in the coming years, but there's certainly an opportunity for designers—and critics—to build a more meaningful critique of the discipline.

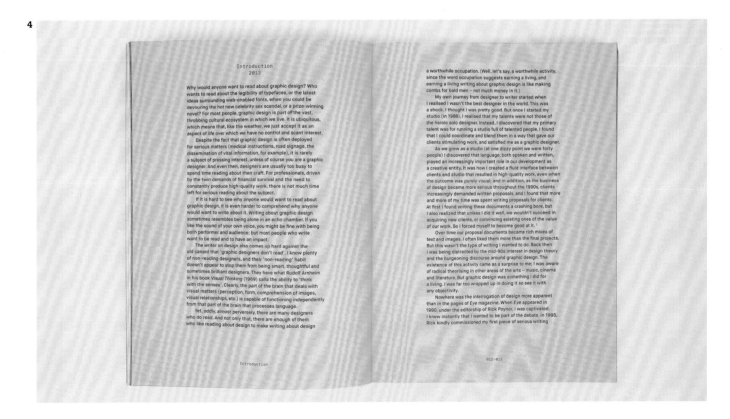

4

Designer Publishers

Recent years have seen an increasing number of independent, design-led publishing ventures.

1

In our day and age, what are books for? What do they do? Books serve not just to be read but also to be displayed, exchanged, reviewed, collected, shelved, archived, reproduced online, and circulated in libraries. Designers today use books, blogs, and zines as outlets for so-called "personal work."
Ellen Lupton in "Reading and Writing," in *Graphic Design: Now in Production*, Walker Art Museum, 2011

Publishing and graphic design are closely linked: developments in printing and typography, from the invention of the printing press and moveable type to desktop computing and offset lithography, chart the evolution of both fields. Designers have always been an integral part of the publishing process, through typesetting, page layouts, and cover design, but recent years have seen an increasing number of independent, design-led publishing ventures.

A number of factors have allowed designers to initiate their own publishing endeavors. The growth of communication design as an industry means that there are many more designers out there, and more general interest in graphics, which has created a much bigger market for design-focused writing and beautifully designed books. Alongside this, digital products have transformed the publishing landscape. While traditional publishing is no longer as remunerative as it once was, the Internet provides a platform to post text, video, and graphics online, find a niche audience, self-publish, promote print-on-demand products, and crowd-source funding before any initial outlay. With financial expectations and barriers to entry both lowered, there are many creative people willing to enter the publishing industry to create experimental or personal works they feel passionate about.

Stuart Bailey of Dexter Sinister also makes the point that with the advent of desktop publishing, designers found themselves increasingly dealing with proofreading and editing by default, which, for designers who were interested in the content they were working with anyway provoked a desire "to actually claim the responsibility for that and work with it and model it." This ambition to take ownership of the production process and bring a personal vision to life has motivated wonderfully diverse publishing projects. To mention just a few, Unit Editions publishes beautifully executed books about design; Visual Editions brings visual writing into the mainstream; Four Corners Familiars explores new ways of using illustration; and Dexter Sinister is merging publishing with live performance.

One of the most interesting things about these projects is they often bring disciplines together; after all it is not just designers but authors, artists, photographers, and illustrators who want to control and shape their publications both visually and linguistically. And as these groups demand more, traditional publishers are also thinking creatively about design, as in Maira Kalman's fully illustrated books for Penguin or Leanne Shapton's *Swimming Studies*, which weaves text, photography, and illustration into an integrated whole.

SEARCH: Chip Kidd; Dexter Sinister; Emigre; Four Corners Books; FUEL publishing; Graham Rawle; GraphicDesign&; Hyphen Press; Inventory Books; Irma Boom; Leanne Shapton; McSweeneys; Occasional Papers; Rollo Press; Roma Publications; Unit Editions; Visual Editions

1. *Bulletins of the Serving Library #4* from Dexter Sinister.

2. Poster for *The Electric Information Age Book* by Inventory Books, "a platform for the synthesis of textual and visual research on transformations in urban spaces and culture."

2

3

What we're trying to do is make books with wonderful visual writing, beautiful production; books that are lovingly designed, designed to be read, and that those books are read by many not just by a few.
Visual Editions

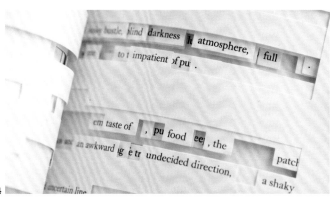

4

5

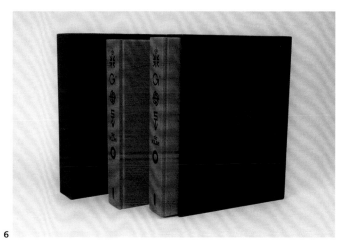

6

3 & 4. In *Book of Codes* (Visual Editions) Jonathan Safran Foer makes a new story from an existing book by physically removing parts of the page.

5. *Kapow!* (Visual Editions), written by Adam Thirlwell and designed by Studio Frith, uses its typographical layout as part of the storytelling.

7

6. *FHK Henrion: The Complete Designer* (Unit Editions) is a comprehensive monograph of this influential designer.

7. *SVK* is a collaboration between writer Warren Ellis, artist Matt Brooker, and design studio BERG. SVK uses an invisible ink that can only be seen with the SVK object included with the comic novella.

I slowly realized that I had many of the skills needed to write, design, and edit the books I actually wanted to produce.

In Conversation

with Adrian Shaughnessy,
co-founder, Intro and
Unit Editions, runs
ShaughnessyWorks

Adrian Shaughnessy is a graphic designer and writer based in London. In 1989, he co-founded the design company Intro and now runs ShaughnessyWorks. Along with Tony Brook (Spin), he founded Unit Editions in 2009, a publishing company that produces "high-quality, affordable books on graphic design and visual culture." Shaughnessy writes regularly for *Eye*, *Creative Review*, **Design Observer, and** *Design Week* **and has written and art directed numerous books on design. In 2013, he was one of the organizers of AGI Open in London.**

uniteditions.com

Adrian Shaughnessy starts by talking about why he decided to set up Unit Editions with Tony Brook. "I had extensive experience of working with commercial publishers before co-founding Unit Editions. I'd written and designed five or six books with a successful publisher who was very supportive and highly professional. There were, of course, benefits—professional editorial support, a super efficient production department, and funding. But there were frustrations—for example, we always had arguments about cover designs and layouts—even subject matter had to be manipulated in the hope of meeting with mass approval and existing parameters. The production cycle was cumbersome and attenuated, and production techniques were limited to a narrow repertoire of standardized options.

"But I slowly realized that I had many of the skills needed to write, design, and edit the books I actually wanted to produce. And when I hooked up with Tony Brook and Trish Finegan, my Unit Editions partners at Spin, who already had experience of self-publishing, I saw how it was possible to form a publishing company that was independent of the traditional publishing structures."

Unit Editions sets out to produce "books by designers for designers," something that has become economically viable due to a growing design community and new ways to reach it. "Unit Editions is, at the moment at least, a niche publisher. It is one of the ways—perhaps the only way—that we can survive independently," Shaughnessy says. "We have found an audience for our books, but this has only been made possible thanks to the Internet. With the Internet—and especially social media—we are now able to find the 2,000 people in the world who are interested in Total Design in the 1960s and invite them to visit our website, join our database, study our book on Total Design, and hope that they are impressed enough to buy it. In other words, we have built a "community" (a much abused word in the context of the Internet); in truth, it is really an audience of like-minded designers

who are happy to be kept informed about our publications and who, from time to time, will buy books from us."

Shaughnessy sees various reasons behind the growth in design-led publishing ventures—"freedom; the desire to share personal obsessions and interests; distaste for mainstream publishing"—and sees it as positive trend. "It is a growing area with huge potential. I often tell people who approach us with ideas for books to publish it themselves—it's possible!"

Shaughnessy and Brook chose their own publishing program through "endless discussions, debates, arguments, and personal convictions." The impetus to make books they are personally passionate about remains strong: "We will never produce a book that we don't both agree needs to exist. It is important that we share a vision for each book so that it can be given total commitment by both of us." Although taking on different roles, they are both thoroughly involved in the production of every book. "Roughly speaking, Tony does visuals and I do words, although we comment, critique, and contribute to both aspects."

As well their books, all of which use carefully chosen finishes and production techniques, Unit Editions has published work in less formal formats. The Unit Research Papers were printed on low-cost newsprint and aimed to "take specialist subjects that perhaps didn't merit a full book, but which would fit into the more modest format of a tabloid newspaper and which would constitute some sort of research or investigation." One project published in this way was ThreeSix, which showcases the thinking and process behind a typeface design.

"Tony and I are longstanding admirers of Hamish Muir and his work with 8vo, and latterly with Paul McNeil. They talked to us about their typeface and said they were keen on producing some sort of publication. The ThreeSix project was perfect [as a research paper], mainly because Hamish and Paul had an ideological viewpoint on their typeface—it wasn't just another font to add to the millions that already exist. Plus, they were willing to share their thinking and explain their process."

As Unit Editions has developed a reputation as a publisher, more of their projects are externally motivated. "Increasingly we are being approached by interesting design world figures about publishing material that they own and by authors and designers with ideas for books. Most of these we turn down (we can only cope with five to six books per year), but we are keen to produce more books from external sources."

Although most Unit Editions publications are highly visual, their success is no doubt partly due to a growing appetite for design writing. This is a trend that Shaughnessey recognizes—"I meet lots of design students who are determined to combine writing as a part of their practice"—but he still feels that the critical discourse around communication design is "fragmentary, dissipated, and parochial."

A key issue is the lack of engagement from cultural or art critics outside the design world. "Until communication design is critiqued by some strong independent voices, there will be no really effective critical discourse. I don't, for instance, think of myself as a critic; I'm too close to the coalface to be effective. I am a commentator and observer, and increasingly a writer of design history. To be a critic you need to be above the daily grind." One of the challenges is that "no one is paying to include design criticism in their newspapers, magazines, journals, or TV programs." Independent publishing is one way that designers can bring writing to the public.

While contemporary design writing might be "mostly preaching to the converted," it seems likely that as design criticism and design history become more established, they will begin to reach into a wider cultural sphere. And designer publishers such as Unit Editions, who bring academic and aesthetic rigor equally to bear on their publications, are an important part of that process.

Case Study: *Type Only*

Type Only is an image-led book celebrating the current design trend to use type and letterforms unsupported by illustration or photography. Through the work of designers from across the world, *Type Only* explores the communicative and emotive power of type when used in isolation.

In an introductory essay, Mark Sinclair, deputy editor of *Creative Review*, provides an overview of how typography has evolved from the early "type only" experiments of the Dadaists and Futurists, via Modernism and Post-Modernism, to today's radical typographic trends, digitally made and shared instantly on the Internet.

For the publication of *Type Only*, Unit Editions set up a blog to showcase further examples of this trend, giving the book a pre-publication platform.

uniteditions.com/shop/type-only
typeonly.tumblr.com

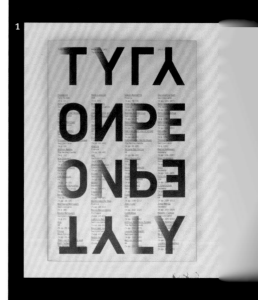

1

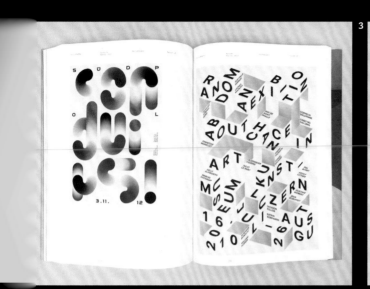

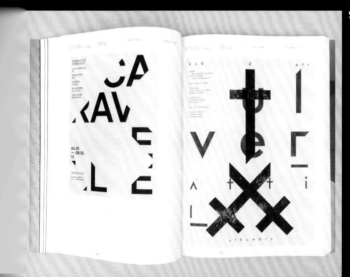

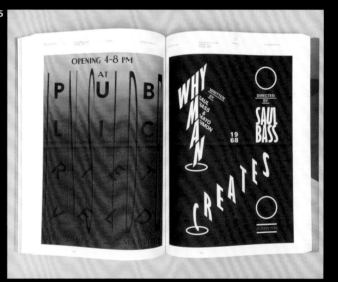

1. *Type Only* cover

2–6. Spreads from
Type Only

Speculative Design

Design can be used as a tool
to question the status quo and
visualize potential futures.

From furniture to transport, media channels to medical treatment, the human world is shaped by products, and, increasingly, interfaces, which have been conceived of, developed, and made to look good by designers. The degree to which design can mold the world is part of the thinking behind speculative design practice (sometimes called critical design or design fiction), which questions the status quo by creating products and visions of the future. Anthony Dunne, who first coined the term "critical design," sets it in opposition to "affirmative design," "design that reinforces the status quo."

Some of the models for speculative design are science fiction in literature and film and the fantastic, wide-scale thinking associated with architecture, in particular the "Italian Radicals" of the 1960s. Like these other explorations, critical design brings conceptual thinking to life, producing objects or imagery that stimulate viewers to imagine where current trends in science, culture, and technology might lead. By giving physical or visual shape to research and critical theory, designers can prompt wider engagement with difficult ideas. And as with its counterparts in other disciplines, critical design uses humor and disquiet to engage its audience.

Due to the questioning function of speculative design, it tends to break out from the client/designer relationship that shapes most communication design, and to shift fluidly between different design practices.

Underlying some of this is us questioning where the boundaries and borders of design as a practice are. Does it have to be linked to ideas of consumption and production for an industry? Can it ask questions?
Matt Ward DWFE

1

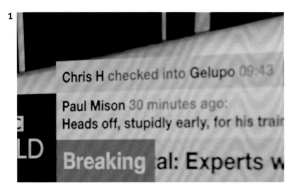

1. BERG's film *Media Surfaces* explores how existing screen technologies could have a more sophisticated mix of outputs. In collaboration with Dentsu London.

SEARCH: Anthony Dunne *Hertzian Tales*; Archizoom/ Archigram/ Superstudio; BERG; critical design; Dunne & Raby/ RCA Design Interactions/ Speculative Everything (vimeo); DWFE; IDEO Designs On–; Marti Guixé; Metahaven; Natalie Jeremijenko; Simon Bowen Critical Theory and Participatory Design; Stuart Candy/ the sceptical futuryst

2

2 & 3. DWFE's Recreational Bombs project provides an antidote to oversanitized everyday life and the saturation of screen-based entertainment.

4. Algae Digester from Dunne & Raby's *Designs for an Overpopulated Planet: Foragers.*

Critical designers are often linked to academic programs or institutions, such as Dunne & Raby at the RCA or DWFE at Goldsmiths, and commissioned work is often research or exhibition oriented.

Critical design has always drawn from product design, architecture, graphics, computer programming, and film to bring concepts to life, an adaptability that is becoming more common with the growth of design and innovation consultancies. Some of this new breed of design companies are utilizing critical design practices for more commercial purposes: by using speculative objects as a part of product development designers can challenge themselves, their clients, and their audiences to entirely reframe problems. BERG's *Media Surfaces* films imagined alternative futures for media, partly to showcase actual projects and partly as a speculative exercise. By seeing these potential products in action, clients and consumers respond to them as actual possibilities, even if they are not yet fully developed.

Digital design and innovation consultancies have also started to use speculative design as a way to showcase their internal research, raising their profile, and possibly winning new business (see Research / Content, pp. 194–195). For example, the IDEO Designs On– series aims to "advance global discussion in the creative community by presenting forward-thinking provocations" and has become a multiple award winner for the agency as well as sparking debate in the design community.

3

4

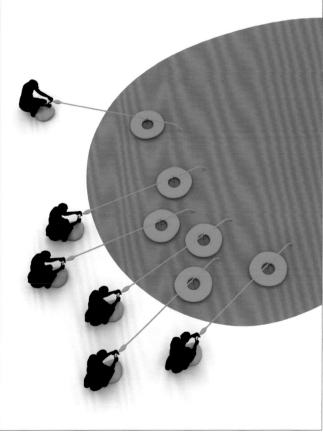

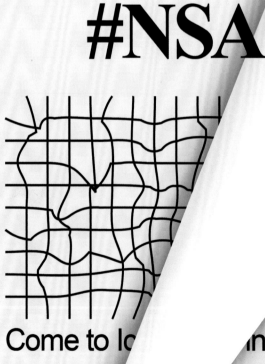

TINKER TAILOR SOLDIER SKYPE

#NSA

1. Metahaven graphics responding to issues around freedom of information.

Come to lo... ...ing Data.

2 & 3. Facestate, commissioned for exhibition *Graphic Design: Now in Production*, is a research project about social networks and the state.

4. Metahaven designed a series of scarves and T-shirts in support of Wikileaks.

Metahaven

Metahaven is an Amsterdam-based design and research studio founded by Vinca Kruk and Daniel van der Velden. Metahaven's website describes the studio's work as reflecting "political and social issues in provocative graphic design objects," and have used design to explore ideas of statehood, national borders, data havens, freedom of information, and government data. Their 2010 book *Uncorporate Identity* brought together their work up to that point, incorporating text and graphics with case studies to create a provocative investigation of design and power.

Two recent projects, Facestate and Nulpunt, imagine different possible futures modeled around social media. Facestate is a research project examining parallels between Facebook and the state, Facebook as possible channel for government surveillance, and then the visual translation of these ideas, drawing on the standardized graphic language of Facebook. As Metahaven notes in an interview with Andrea Hyde from 2011 for the Walker Art Museum's magazine: "There is often a bland acceptance of the terms of service given by the social network, just as we take it for granted that the state routinely infringes on civil liberties and privacy."

Conversely, Nulpunt is a web application that would allow users to access all documents produced by the Dutch government. It reimagines social media as "civic media, used to follow and control government rather than deployed as a surveillance dragnet and wholesale replacement for the public sector," as noted in an interview with Joshua Kopstein about the Nulpunt project from July of 2012 on The Verge website.

As with other speculative designers, Metahaven has a strong sense of the potential and limitations of design, as noted in this statement from Metahaven's interview with Kyle Chayka, "Graphic Design as Political Practice": "Graphic design can change things, but it also plays a very strong role in sustaining things as they are. . . . We are interested in finding collaborations, or alliances, or conversations, where graphic design can become a useful tool."

We believe that design can play a part in generating discussion around what kind of future we would like.

In Conversation

with Anthony Dunne
and Fiona Raby,
co-founders Dunne &
Raby

Anthony Dunne and Fiona Raby make up Dunne & Raby, a studio that uses design to explore "the social, cultural, and ethical implications of existing and emerging technologies." They employ research, writing, and making to create work that provokes discussion and debate around culture and technology, and their work has exhibited and published internationally. Dunne is professor and head of the design interactions program at the Royal College of Art in London. Raby is professor of industrial design (id2) at the University of Applied Arts in Vienna as well as reader in design interactions at the RCA. They see their teaching and practice as linked activities, always informing and interacting with each other.

dunneandraby.co.uk

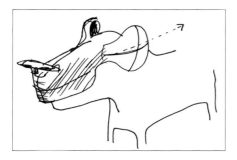

Anthony Dunne coined the term "critical design" in his book *Hertzian Tales* (1999), and it has since become a widely-used descriptor for speculative, provocative design work that aims to challenge both assumptions about our world and established modes of thought. Ideas that Dunne & Raby have explored in their work range from robots to overpopulation and from DNA to the transportation of the future.

In describing the rationale behind their work, Dunne and Raby talk about the desire to find a space between established design methods for shaping or challenging society. They say, "For many people, design is about problem-solving, from the day-to-day to massive global problems. There is an innate optimism in that viewpoint, but also massive barriers to achieving large-scale aims." Another model is commentary or critique, which while effective at provoking debate can become "disengaged" and "nihilistic." Critical design aims to make a space between these two models, harnessing the optimism of the former but opening people's minds to new ways of thinking and helping challenge and inform the values that will mold the future.

In the commercial world, future modeling is primarily used to design for probable futures, second-guessing society to create something valuable (and profitable) for the existing or near-future world. Dunne and Raby talk instead about Stuart Candy's model of potential futures, adjacent to and informed by reality. "We want to shift away from designing for how the world is now to designing for how it could be—and that's very different from how it should be. How it should be is someone telling us what the future is; how it could be is about generating many different possibilities for the future." From this comes the interesting idea of "preferable futures," opening up a discussion about how we would actually choose to live.

The self-imposed limit of Dunne and Raby's work is that of scientific reality; they work with experts from a range of fields (scientists, ethnographers, sociologists, engineers) in order to ensure that

the work stays within those limits and does not end up "just the personal vision of the designer." This is, they point out, "where a lot of science fiction happens." Ultimately it has to make sense if viewers are to engage. And getting people to engage with complex or esoteric problems is where they see the value of critical design. "Design is very good at taking abstract research and turning it into concrete and tangible examples that we can then discuss."

An example of this is their project Designs for an Overpopulated Planet: Foragers, commissioned by Design Indaba and "based on the UN predicting there will be 9 billion people in 2050, so food production will have to increase by 70 percent, and then a lack of faith in governments and big business to meet this challenge. The point that we wanted to make was, what if we stopped thinking about designing the world around us to meet our ever-expanding needs and instead redesigned ourselves to fit within the limits of the planet."

Dunne & Raby "dramatized" this idea by imagining "a group called the foragers, drawing on a variety of contemporary trends and technologies, including DIY hacking, countryside foragers, and synthetic biology" and then creating objects and images that suggested personal bio-manipulation to better source food from the environment. It does not aim to give answers, rather to provoke us to think widely around the issue: Is this a good solution? Would we want it to happen? Could we avoid it happening?

One of the challenges when creating speculative work is how close to "reality" it appears visually. Dunne and Raby feel that, however tempting it might be, to make things look too realistic can be problematic. Viewers might think the objects or scenarios are real, which as well as "bordering on trickery" is not the end-goal of Dunne and Raby's work. Instead, they say, "We're much more interested in inviting people to make believe, not making them believe, or fooling them into belief."

This desire to stimulate people's conscious imaginations is crucial to the way Dunne and Raby present their designs. Although products are central to their design work, the way that these are presented to viewers, either online or in an exhibition space, is as important as the products themselves. They are not designing a product, but a stimulus: "In everyday life, of course, we have to design things that are transparent—natural and easy to use—but in these projects the user isn't the person in these pictures using the product. Instead, the user is the person looking at these pictures and imagining as a result of the pictures. . . . And so to make that work the objects have to be more evocative, maybe very unnatural or a bit glitchy." It is a challenge to get the balance right, to provoke thought without looking "too phony"; humor can play its part in striking that balance by acknowledging the absurd within the speculative situation.

Exhibitions are an important framing device for Dunne and Raby, where objects are "unmediated by the commentary you get online." One of the key imaginative models they refer to is the museum, where visitors reconstruct whole worlds around the fragments that remain from a long-gone culture. With exhibitions, Dunne and Raby can encourage viewers to bring these "conceptual window-shopping skills" to bear on the objects they create, evoking an alternative future society. For the St. Etienne Design Bienniale 2010, they created an exhibition where everything was treated as an object, including text and image, equalizing the role of everything on show.

Dunne and Raby's work helps imagine the world of tomorrow, and through this, challenge and rethink the status quo. As technologies develop faster than we can assimilate them, this kind of work is arguably ever more important. "Increasingly we're finding ourselves working with organizations who want to use design as a way of having conversations about the impact of technology on everyday life, its implications, and the way it fits into day-to-day life." For the future, Dunne and Raby are interested in how designers can become part of scientific research, "exploring new methods, contexts and roles for design."

1 & 2. Communo-nuclearists: a no-growth, limited population experiment. Using nuclear power to deliver near limitless energy, they live on a continually moving, 3-kilometer mobile landscape.

3. Bioliberals: essentially farmers, cooks ,and gardeners. Gardens, kitchens, and farms replace factories and workshop.

4. UMK at the Design Museum, London.

SEARCH: Critical Design/ Dunne & Raby/ *Hertzian Tales*/ United Micro Kingdoms/ Stuart Candy / the sceptical futuryst/ Archizoom / No-Stop City/ Political Compass/ Speculative Everything vimeo

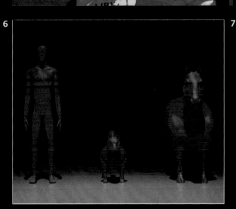

Case Study:
United Micro Kingdoms
United Micro Kingdoms imagines a future where England has devolved into four super counties. Dunne and Raby used the Political Compass as a starting point for defining the counties and gave each one "a combination of a technology and a political ideology. . . . All technologies in some way have ideologies embedded in them; we're just not always sure what they are."

"We wanted to do what Bruce Sterling, the sci-fi writer, has called 'tell worlds, rather than tell stories' and see if, dealing on the small scale of design objects, we could do this." Drawing from the tradition of transportation as a vision of the future, and the architectural culture of "mega-visions," they modeled different types of transport for each county.

unitedmicrokingdoms.org

6 & 7. Anarcho-evolutionists abandon most technologies, or at least stop developing them and concentrate on using science to maximize their own physical capabilities through training, DIY bio-hacking, and self-experimentation.

5. Digitarians depend on digital technology and all its implicit totalitarianism. Their society is organized entirely by market forces; citizen and consumer are the same.

7. "Very large bike," from the anarcho-evolutionists.

Research / Content

Theoretical expertise can be used as a springboard to attract media attention, gain new business, and establish a competitive advantage.

As communication design has become more developed as a discipline, with corporate identity followed by branding established as key business strategies, designers have become more accepted as industry partners (see Strategy, pp. 18–21). "Design thinking" is now a recognized phrase, and business schools are increasingly integrating it into their curriculum, with the result that the client/designer dynamic, while still in existence, is frequently being remodeled as a collaborative, integrated relationship, rather than one of unequal footing. With this has come a new set of roles for designers—strategy, research, innovation, content creation, service, and experience design—some of which are only tangentially related to more traditional design skills.

As the number of communication designers has grown, and the roles that they might go into have diversified, agencies have begun to find new ways to demonstrate their work, and their particular specializations. Wolff Olins was one of the first agencies to use their own theoretical expertise to promote their business, using Wally Olins's writing and talks on branding—from corporations to countries—as a springboard to attract media attention, gain new business, and establish a competitive advantage. Writing remains a core method of self-promotion, but because it has become much easier to broadcast your ideas in the age of the Internet, agencies have to find creative ways to differentiate their special qualities.

Wolff Olins continues to have a thought-driven blog that carries on the company's tradition of developing ideas around branding. But other designers have new takes on the format. Johnson Banks, a London agency who specialize in "unusual and interesting" problem solving, uses their *Thought for the Week* blog as a place to talk about a diverse range of subjects they find personally interesting, perfectly reflecting the agency mentality. Method set up the series *10x10* in order to publish essays from its employees, giving them space to discuss an idea they felt had wider implications and was important to share.

It is not just through writing that designers can share their ideas. Conference and video forums such as the TED talks or DO lectures give designers a way to vocalize their own ideas or explain how they're harnessing contemporary thinking in their practice. Again, due to the Internet these platforms have a far greater reach than speaking to a design conference audience, not least because they may be seen by potential clients and collaborators rather than primarily design peers. In this context, designers can become "thought leaders" and may find themselves commissioned for an area of expertise tangential to design.

It's important to note that not all design thinking is in the abstract. Sometimes designers make publications, products, or videos to give form to abstract ideas—or to share ideas that are about form rather than theory. This kind of work is often self-initiated design work, which has historically had a promotional purpose, as it allows designers to present the kind of work they would choose to be commissioned for. However, agencies are beginning to use these pieces to demonstrate their

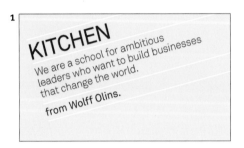

1. Kitchen is a school for ambitious leaders run by Wolff Olins. The agency uses it as a platform to share their creative team's experience and learning.

2. Synthetic Biology explored as part of IDEO Designs On-Packaging.

3. The Energy Flow app allows users to play a huge variety of short digital films that showcase Field's design innovations and expertise.

SEARCH: BERG Vimeo; Field Energy Flow; Ico Taste; IDEO Design Thinking; Johnson Banks Thought for the Week; Method 10x10; Ogilvy Red Papers; Saatchi & Saatchi Lovemarks; SomeOne Manifesto/ Brand Worlds; Stanford dschool; Wally Olins On Brand; Wieden + Kennedy blogs

more particular proficiencies. *Taste*, a self-initiated publication from ico Design, draws on two key areas of expertise—design for food brands and copywriting—and exhibits them in a content-led newspaper on the subject of taste. In this context, design becomes just one of a cluster of skill sets put on show.

For designers working with cutting-edge technology, self-initiated work is sometimes imperative, as actually demonstrating design possibilities can be the only way to explain them to others. Vera-Maria Glahn from Field has commented that at least part of the purpose of a project like Energy Flow was to help visualize some of the programming outputs they could offer to future clients. Although the output is an app available from the Apple App Store, the project was essentially a research project for Field.

Perhaps unsurprisingly, some of the most successful contemporary agencies harness multiple mediums for sharing their ideas and expertise. IDEO, for example, has published books, created Designs On– to address contemporary issues, regularly have their key thinkers speaking publicly, and keep an online archive of writing "authored by IDEO." This presence is part of what has established IDEO as a hugely successful, and highly respected, global design company.

Part personal perspective, part collective manifesto, Designs On— is, at its core, a flexible forum that drives exploration, iterative thinking, early prototyping, and sharing, minus boundaries or constraints.
IDEO

3

Case Study: *Taste*

Russell Holmes, strategy director, explains the idea behind *Taste*: "We have a lot of clients and contacts who work in food, and we wanted to create a promotional piece that demonstrated our interest in the industry. We had had some opinions of our own but hadn't found an appropriate platform. I suggested that if we approached people to contribute to a publication on the subject of 'taste,' we could combine their content with editorial that came from us.

"*Taste* was very much driven by the need to create engaging content; we wanted it to appeal to anyone with an interest in food, or even business, not just those who cooked for a living. My brief was always that if someone picked it up and read it, they might not at first realize it had been put together by a design agency, and if they enjoyed it they'd then look us up. This meant having a carefully considered balance to the content—roughly 70 percent comes from contributors and the remaining 30 percent is from us or our clients.

"In terms of distribution, my aim was always to look outside the design industry and to spread the net a little wider. Printing as a newspaper made it easy to distribute, with Foyles Bookstore taking a thousand copies and Mark Hix stocking it in his restaurants. We also produced a digital edit of the magazine formatted for viewing on phone, tablet or laptop."

Taste has worked for ico on multiple levels. Holmes says it was "a way to thank and promote some of the people we've worked with," a chance to "meet some interesting people," and "an opportunity to reach out to people whose work we liked." Relationships built off the back of *Taste*—both new clients and collaborators—have continued to be fruitful.

taste.icodesign.com

1

1. *Taste* is designed to be accessed across multiple platforms.

2 & 3. ico used *Taste* as an opportunity to collaborate with photographers and illustrators they wanted to try working with.

4. The publication gave ico a chance to showcase some of the knowledge they have gathered through working with clients in the food industry.

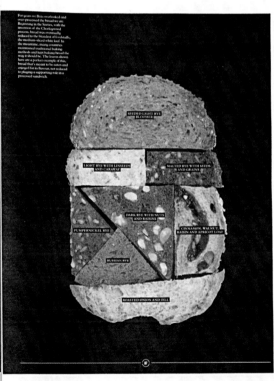

It's a way of saying this is what we stand for, this is what we believe in, this is what we think is the future.

In Conversation

with Lindsay Liu, editorial manager for 10x10 series, Method

Method is a consultancy specializing in experience design, with offices in New York, San Francisco, and London, that creates "integrated brand, service and product experiences" for a diverse range of clients. Its creative team works collaboratively and strategically, integrating clients and consumers into the design process.

_10x10_ is a series of ideas pieces written by Method's in-house experts and hosted on their website. Lindsay Liu was director of global marketing at Method and managed the editorial program for _10x10_.

method.com

Lindsay Liu explains how _10x10_ got started: "We launched our first piece in February 2010 and have been carrying it on since. At the time, it was 2010, so the idea was let's do 10 ideas in 2010, so _10x10_—that's where it came from, as a name." Although it was initially a marketing concept, the idea "was definitely really fully supported and driven by the leadership of the company." Liu considers this commitment to be crucial to the project's success. "It's not a marketing team writing about what we think is going on in the industry, it's actual design leaders writing about their observations— the buy-in had to come from the entire company, they had to say we're actually going to invest time in growing these ideas."

_10x10_ has been a very successful way of showcasing the thinking behind Method's practice and helping to promote the agency's focus on strategy. Liu comments that Method has always had "a content-led approach" and as such, "putting something out there that engages people, that is interesting, that is relevant for them, that would foster conversation" helps to "position us as a strategic partner." For Method, the creative team's ideas and their work are equally important to self-promotion, sharing equal billing on their website, and _10x10_ has been a key tool in spreading those ideas more widely.

Liu makes sure that the content in each _10x10_ piece gets as much coverage as possible by presenting it across multiple platforms. "That's actually one of the really interesting aspects of it, all the different channels that the content spans. There's obviously the PDF printable artifact and the website that it lives on. We syndicate with Fast Company, which helps get the content out there, and then in certain cases we'll also make sure that other publications with the right audience also get it. We aim to spread the thinking to the right distinct groups and audiences for each piece." The pieces have proven to have a long lifespan, which Liu puts down to the fact that "they're out there, they're living and breathing in the world" and as such, "people

stumble across them when they're looking for something in particular." It also helps their longevity that although the pieces help raise Method's profile, they are not directly promotional. Authors may refer to specific projects in the context of the idea they are discussing, but the pieces are not case-study led and never would be unless a piece of work offered direct lessons and enhanced the overall content.

In addition to the articles themselves, the idea behind each piece can gain its own traction. Each subject is launched with a forum in all of the Method studio locations in order to stimulate discussion around the subject. These intimate forums bring together an intimate group of "thought leaders and interesting, thought-provoking people," in order "to loosely discuss the topic in hand." The attendees are chosen depending on the theme to be discussed, always including a mix of Method staff and clients.

The forums have proved very successful, with many of Method's clients commenting on how valuable it is to meet with "a group of people who truly understand about a subject, who can have these discussions about it in a meaningful way." Giving people an intimate space to discuss ideas that aren't necessarily understood by their immediate colleagues strengthens bonds between Method and their clients and promotes their collaborative approach. It also gives the ideas energy beyond the initial publication, as Method tries "to connect everyone afterwards and keep the conversation going between individuals, or between people where there's a fit."

Liu says that when appropriate, they will also pitch for the authors to speak at relevant conferences, and if a topic really picks up they'll often find that the author is asked to speak as an expert in their subject. It's clear that the success of _10x10_ lies in the content; Liu can promote the pieces but she's aware that "one of the reasons that ideas transfer to all these forums is that the author has already spent so much time thinking about the idea and fleshing it out. . . . They're really subject matter experts."

Liu also talks about the general importance, as a design agency, of putting content out into the world. She remarks that "it's more important now than ever," especially because of the "ease of self-publishing" through multiple channels. Using blog platforms, photo sharing, and social media, "people are using all these different ways to put content out there that engages different audiences. And so in many ways, that makes it much more imperative for other agencies to get on board with that and find their niche and find the kind of content that people want to be engaging with them on."

One of the things that Liu comments on is that this content can be hugely varied; it doesn't "necessarily need to be words." She cites BERG's videos and products, and the R/GA and IDEO start-up residencies as examples of agency-generated content in different mediums. What links all these outputs is that they are "ways to communicate what your thinking is and what you believe in. It's a way of saying this is what we stand for, this is what we believe in, this is what we think is the future."

10x10 may also expand into new territory: "One of the things we're playing around with as well is changing the mediums, so we could have different artifacts coming out of it." Some possibilities Method is exploring are "video interviews with authors and subject matter experts" and "actually creating concepts or prototypes around things that we think are where the world should be heading." Liu points out that "because of the nature of designers as creators, writing doesn't always come as naturally as doing, and so there is the potential to find some really, really interesting ideas and convey them in a more effective manner than forcing people to write a thousand word essay." This is characteristic of the thinking around 10x10: it stays relevant because it shares research and thinking that the creatives at Method are passionate about and experts in. As such, it needs to continue working for those experts. As Liu says, "It's a case of being efficient with people's time and making sure that they stay inspired in whatever they are focusing on."

Case Study: *10x10*

10x10 is Method's thought leadership series, which highlights new approaches and ways of thinking about varying industry challenges, needs, and trends. It is published on the Method website, available as downloadable PDF, and syndicated to key news outlets.

Each *10x10* piece is launched with events in the Method offices.

method.com/ideas/10x10

_. Articles are
syndicated through
sites such as Fast
Company to increase
their reach.

2. All the _10x10_ ideas
are collected on a
dedicated page of the
Method website.

3–6. Each _10x10_ piece
is published as a fully
designed PDF.

Appendix

Further reading

Albinson, I. and Giampietro, R., *Graphic Design: Now in Production,* New York: Walker Art Center, 2011.

Davis, M., *Graphic Design Theory.* London: Thames & Hudson, 2012.

McLuhan M., *The Medium Is the Massage,* London: Penguin, 1967.

Potter, N., *What Is a Designer: Things, Places, Messages,* 4th edition, London: Hyphen Press, 2002.

Shaughnessy, A. and Brook, T., *Studio Culture: The Secret Life of the Graphic Design Studio,* London: Unit Editions, 2009.

Brand

Bos, B., *TD 63–73 Total Design and Its Pioneering Role in Graphic Design,* London: Unit Editions, 2011.

Bruinsma, M., "Learning to Read and Write Images," *Eye 25:* Summer 1997.

Janser, H. and Junod, B., *Corporate Diversity: Swiss Graphic Design and Advertising by Geigy, 1940–1970,* Zurich: Lars Muller Publishers, 2009.

Olins, W., *On Brand,* London: Thames & Hudson, 2004.

Rand, P., *Paul Rand: A Designer's Art.* New Haven: Yale University Press, 2001.

Van der Velden, D. and Kruk, V., *Uncorporate Identity: Metahaven,* Zurich: Lars Muller Publishers, 2010.

Experience

Crow, S., "Magic Box: Craft and the Computer," *Eye 70:* Winter 2008.

Hare, S., "Make it Real," *Eye 70:* Winter 2008.

Kahneman, D., *Thinking Fast and Slow,* London: Penguin, 2011.

Odling-Smee, A., *The New Handmade Graphics: Beyond Digital Design.* Brighton: Rotovision, 2003.

Soar, M. and Hall P., "Images over Time," *Eye 60:* Summer 2006.

Walter, S. and Hanson, M., *Motion Blur: onedotzero,* London: Laurence King, 2004.

Conversation

Brown, T., *Change by Design.* London: HarperCollins, 2009.

Owen W., "Messy Medium," *Eye 64:* Summer 2007.

Reas, C. and Fry, B., *Processing: A Programming Handbook for Visual Designers and Artists,* Cambridge, MA: MIT Press, 2007.

Roberts, L. and Wright, R., *Design Diaries: Creative Process in Graphic Design.* London: Laurence King, 2010.

Rushkoff, D., *Program or Be Programmed: Ten Commands for a Digital Age.* Berkeley: Soft Skull Press, 2011.

Participation

Thaler, R. H. and Sunstein, C. R., *Nudge: Improving Decisions about Health, Wealth, and Happiness,* London: Penguin, 2009.

Jenkins H., *Convergence Culture: Where Old and New Media Collide.* New York: New York University Press, 2008.

Dubberly H., "Design in the Age of Biology: Shifting from a Mechanical-Object Ethos to an Organic-Systems Ethos," www.dubberly.com/articles/design-in-the-age-of-biology.html, 2008.

Reas, C., *Form+Code in Design, Art, and Architecture.* New York: Princeton Architectural Press, 2010.

Armstrong, H. and Stojmirovic, Z., *Participate: Designing with User-Generated Content.* New York: Princeton Architectural Press, 2011.

Stallman, R. M., *Free Software Free Society: Selected Essays of Richard M. Stallman.* Boston. MA: GNU Press [Free Software Foundation], 2009.

Navigation

McCandless, D., *Information Is Beautiful,* London: HarperCollins, 2012.

Rendgen, S., *Information Graphics,* Cologne: Taschen, 2012.

Silver, N., *The Signal and the Noise: The Art and Science of Prediction,* London: Allen Lane/Penguin Books, 2013.

Tufte, E., *Envisioning Information,* Cheshire, CT: Graphics Press USA, 1990.

Advocacy

Braungart, M. and McDonough, W., *Cradle to Cradle: Remaking the Way We Make Things,* London: Vintage, 2009.

Heller, S. and Vienne, V., *Citizen Designer: Perspectives on Design Responsibility,* New York: Allworth Press, 2003.

Kolster, T., *Goodvertising: Creative Advertising that Cares,* London: Thames & Hudson, 2012.

Roberts, L., *Good: An Introduction to Ethics in Graphic Design,* Lausanne: AVA Publishing SA, 2006.

Critique

Bierut, M., *79 Short Essays on Design,* New York: Princeton Architectural Press, 2008.

Dunne, A. and Raby, F., *Speculative Everything: Design, Fiction, and Social Dreaming,* Cambridge, MA: MIT Press, 2014.

McCarthy, S., *The Designer as...: Author, Producer, Activist, Entrepreneur, Curator and Collaborator: New Models for Communicating.* Amsterdam: BIS Publishers, 2013.

Shaughnessy, A., *Essays: Scratching the Surface.* London: Unit Editions, 2013.

Picture credits

Every effort has been made to trace, clear, and credit the appropriate copyright holders of the images produced in this book. However, if any credits have been inadvertently omitted or are in error, the publisher will endeavor to incorporate amendments in future printings.

Courtesy **Accept + Proceed** (p. 68)/Courtesy ©**Adbusters Media Foundation**, Occupy Wall Street Poster, (p. 153) /courtesy **After the Flood** (pp. 139, 141)/courtesy © **AllofUs/ Science Museum**, "Who Am I?" Gallery interactive exhibits (p. 51)/courtesy © **AllofUs/Work Club/Carte Noire**, Carte Noire Instinct "Window of Intensity" (p. 50)/ courtesy © **BBDO West**, Advertiser: GOODWILL; Product/Service: GOODWILL & LEVI'S, Agency: BBDO WEST, San Francisco; Executive Creative Directors: Jim Lesser and Jon Soto (both BBDO West San Francisco); Senior Art Director: Heward Jue; Art Director: Melanie Barti; Media placement: Care Tag— On Care Tags for Levi's Jeans (10/21/2009), (p. 167) /courtesy **Bear**, Foxton's MINI, Photographer: Nick Veasey (pp. 20–21)/ courtesy © **BERG**, Little Printer (p. 80), Little Draw (p. 81), Remote Interface (p. 81), Daily Puzzle (p. 81), Run Publication (pp. 81, 85); How Many Really (p. 136); Media surfaces (p. 186)/courtesy **The Canary Project**, *Green Patriot Posters*, front cover image, Global Warming, 2009. Shepard Fairey/ObeyGiant. com; *Problem Me, Solution Me*, 2010 (p. 168) Steve Le for Green Patriot Posters /courtesy **Bibliothéque** (p. 15), (pp. 16–17)/courtesy **B-reel.com** (p. 128 (1&2))/courtesy **James Bridle**, (p. 69 (9))/courtesy **David Carson** (p. 92)/courtesy ©**Candy Chang**, Before I Die Wall Photos (p. 158 (1), 159)/courtesy **De-De** (pp. 110, 111)/All images courtesy **Kate Dawkins**, Olympic Games audience pixels, ©**Immersive**, (pp. 56–57)/courtesy © **The Designers Republic™**, Wipeout 2097/Client: Psygnosis/Sony, Design: Made In The Designers Republic™, © 1996 Ian Anderson/ Siân Thomas licensed to Return Power Shift Control Ltd T/A, The Designers Republic™ under exclusive license to Psygnosis (p. 58); Wip3out/Client: Psygnosis/Sony, Design: Made In The Designers Republic™, ©1999 Ian Anderson/Siân Thomas licensed to Return Power Shift Control Ltd T/A The Designers Republic™ under exclusive license to Psygnosis (p. 58); BOTnet/Client: *Wired Magazine*, Design: Made In The Designers Republic™, BOTnet version ©2006 Ian Anderson/Siân Thomas licensed to Return to Power Shift Control Ltd T/A The Designers Republic™ (p. 59)/courtesy **Droga5** (pp. 109, 113 (3–5)); Droga5 Jay Z/Bing Decode (pp. 114, 115)/courtesy **Dunne & Raby** (pp. 191, 192, 193)/courtesy ©**Shepard Fairey/ObeyGiant. com**, Obama Progress (p. 150) /courtesy © 2008 **Nicholas Felton**, Feltron 2008 Annual

Report (p. 142 (1&2))/courtesy © FIELD.io 2012 (p. 195) /courtesy ©**fuseproject**, Yves Behar, Puma, 1–3 (p. 166)/courtesy ©**Futerra Sustainability Communications Ltd**, Futerra Change-maker Cards (p. 159)/©**Eddie Gerald/ Alamy** (p. 89)/**Google** and the **Google logo** are registered trademarks of **Google Inc**, used with permission (pp. 26, 124, 125 (2))/courtesy **ico** (pp. 18–19, 196–197)/courtesy **IDEO** (p. 77)/© **Sarah Illenberger**, Sex Survey (p. 143)/© **International Business Machines Corporation**, used with permission (p. 11)/©**iStock** (p. 127)/courtesy **It's Nice That** (p. 131); **INT** and **It's Nice That** with Chrissie MacDonald (p. 133 (3)); with Ben Long (p. 133(1)), with Giles Miller Studio (p. 133 (2))/ courtesy **Leila Johnson** (p. 69)/courtesy © **Kin Associates Ltd** (pp. 63, 64–65, 83); Adidas Innovation Event, **Kin with Kate Dawkins** (p. 45) /courtesy **Labour and Wait/Andrew Moran** (p. 38)/courtesy ©**The Len Lye Foundation** with support from the Govett Brewster Art Gallery. From material preserved and made available by the New Zealand Film Archive Ngā Kaitiaki O Taonga Whitiāhua (p. 42)/courtesy of **Lowe-ssp3** (p. 160 (3–6))/ courtesy of LucienneRoberts+ (p. 155)/ courtesy ©**Bernard Lodge**, Title sequences *Doctor Who* (p. 43)/courtesy ©**Me Company** 1994, Bjork "Army of Me" 12" cover (p. 59)/ courtesy ©**Metahaven**, *Metahaven in Collaboration with IMMI: Data/Saga*, 2013 (p. 189 (4)); Metahaven. Facestate device, 2011 (p. 188, 189 (2&3))/courtesy **Method** 10x10 (p. 200)/ courtesy **Tim Milne** (p. 69)/courtesy © **Moving Brands** (pp. 10, 12, 13, 18, 23, 25, 39, 75, 82, 84 (1), 92 (1–3), 104–106, 117, 118, 119), Design: Kin for *Wallpaper** (107)/courtesy **MultiStorey** (p. 34 center right, 35, 112 (1&2)/©2014 **New York Media LLC**, approval matrix (p. 135)/ courtesy **Nike + FuelBand** with permission (p. 70)/© **Nintendo**, Kinect (p. 84)/courtesy **02** (p. 27)/courtesy of **onedotzero: New Live Show, Taipei**, Artist: United Visual Artists 2005/2006, commissioner: onedotzero, photographer: Shane Walter/onedotzero (p. 44 (5)); **House of Cards** [Radiohead], artists: James Frost & Aaron Koblin, 2009, commissioner: Radiohead, photographer: Tom Bland/onedotzero (p. 44 (6)); **Motion Graphics Title: Body Paint**, artists: Mehmet Akten, 2009, photographer: Tom Bland/onedotzero (p. 44 (7)); **Monolith**, artist: United Visual Artists, 2006, commissioner: onedotzero, photographer: Tom Bland/onedotzero (p. 47); **Case Study: onedotzero ID**, all images courtesy of onedotzero (pp. 48–49); **Interactive Festival Programme**, design: So Touch, Mindstorm, onedotzero, 2009, commissioner: onedotzero, photographer: onedotzero (p. 75)/ courtesy **Occupied Times of London**, ©**Tzortzis Rallis**, The Occupied Times Issue 18 (p. 152)/courtesy **Ogilvy and Mather** (pp. 163, 164–165)/courtesy **On Solid Ground** (p. 157)/©

Ortiz (p. 38)/courtesy ©**Peepshow Collective**, Edinburgh Fringe Festival/Series of poster and program images illustrating different themes showcased at the Edinburgh Fringe Festival/Design & Art Direction by Marque, Photography: John Short (p. 37); Overgrown/ Photography by John Short (p. 37); Orange Campaign/Selection of images from Orange mobile network poster and print campaign 2008–2011, Agency: Fallon London, Photography: John Short (pp. 36–37). Illustration by Chrissie Macdonald, Photography by John Short (p. 36)/cover of *NUDGE* by Cass R. Sunstein and Richard H. Thaler—reproduced with permission of **Penguin Books Ltd** (p. 98)/courtesy ©Pentagram Design (p. 151); client: D&AD with Nat Hunter (p. 173)/Courtesy ©**Pitchfork. com**/by Laura Snapes, Photos by Shawn Brackbill, Bat for Lashes Cover Story (p. 129)/ courtesy of Project H (p. 160)/courtesy Stefanie Posavic (pp. 145, 146–147)/Courtesy ©**Projector, Intel** (p. 129 (3–8))/Courtesy ©**Red Bull Content Pool**; photographer: Nika Kramer/Red Bull Content Pool (p. 28); Photos/Red Bull Content Pool (p. 29 (7)); photographer: Mike Blabac/Red Bull Content Pool (p. 29 (8))/courtesy **Scriptographer**: Sketchy Structures/Acema Caylak (p. 120); After Now/Jurg Lehni (p. 121(3)); Liquid 2 Solid/Jan Abellan (p. 121 (4)) /courtesy **SEA** for G F Smith (pp. 66–67)/courtesy **Sennep/Olo** (pp. 60–61, 74, 77); Sennep. for MGI (p. 124 (3))/ courtesy ©**The Serving Library**, Bulletins of the Serving Library No. 3 (p. 181)/courtesy **Adrian Shaughnessy** (p. 183, 184, 185)/ courtesy Smartthings.com (p. 126)/courtesy ©**SomeOne** (p. 31, 32), Big Eyes (p. 33)// courtesy **E. Tautz & Son** (p. 39 bottom)/ courtesy ©**Moritz Stefaner**, OECD Better Life Index (http://oecdbetterlifeindex.org)/Moritz Stefaner with Raureif Gmbh, 2011–2014 (p. 137); Global Trade Flows/Moritz Stefaner for citi, 2012 (p. 134)/courtesy ©**UCU** (p. 151)/ courtesy ©**urinalfly.com** (p. 99)/courtesy ©**ustwo ltd**, (pp. 86–87, 90–91), **ustwo ltd** with Chris Stephens (p. 95)/courtesy **Vital Arts**, Healing Space/Designed by architects Cottrell and Vermeulen and designer Morag Myerscough, The Anne Riches Healing Space—Activity Space 2013, 7th floor The Children's Hospital at The Royal London Hospital, credit: Gareth Gardner (p. 52 top. left & right); Journey Around my Pencil Case/ Peepshow Illustration Collective Journey Around my Pencil Case, Routes to Theatres, 6th and 7th floors, credit: Jess Bonham (p. 52 bottom); Bedside Views/Ella Doran Bedside Views, 2011, Royal London, 7th floor, credit: Jess Bonham (p. 53)/courtesy of **Tim Willshire** (p. 69)/courtesy of **Wolff Olins** (pp. 34 top, 151 (3), 194 (1))/courtesy **Zeus Jones**, (p. 101), with © Betty Crocker (pp. 102–103)/courtesy **Zipcars** (pp. 174–175).

Index

Acknowledgments

The authors would like to thank all the amazing practitioners who were interviewed and provided images for this publication. It wouldn't be the same book without your generous contributions.

Derek would especially like to thank: Adrian Ho for his insight into the American market and opening up connections with the likes of Droga5 and Hashem Bajwa; Carly Bennett at Droga5 for patiently tolerating my endless requests "for one more image of…"; Rory Sutherland for introducing me to Tara Austin, and Paco Conde and Simon Manchipp for introducing me to Rory, Mason, and the gang at Bibliothéque; Russell Holmes, for all of your guidance and connections, in many ways a ghost author! Shane and Sophie at onedotzero—working with you on Cascade provided the insight around which this book is based; Mat Heinl and Georgina Milne at Moving Brands—always supportive, always able to find time to help; Matt Rice and Matt Wade, it was great to find a reason to talk—you are always an inspiration; Denise Wilton for lots of conversations not featured in the book but intrinsic to its creation; Joe, Neil, Gyppsy, and the one and only Mills at ustwo (my second home for a while)—I won't forget your hospitality; and the elusive Karsten Schmidt, not easy to pin down but once you do, the conversation is always worth the wait.

Also massive gratitude goes out to all the staff at both Camberwell and Winchester who patiently worked around my distracted book days— you know who you are, but in case you don't—Darryl Clifton, Matthew Hawkins, Tracey Waller, Zoë Bather, Sam Blunden, and Luise Vormitagg— I owe you.

Finally and most importantly, I'd like to say a very special thanks to the amazing Lucy Porter for putting up with me. Also to my son, Olly, and my stepdaughter, Nelly— hopefully, now Daddy should be able to play a bit more.

Jessie would especially like to thank: Nat Hunter, Adrian Shaughnessy, and Dunne & Raby for making time in their extremely busy schedules to share so many thought-provoking ideas, which I hope will fire our readers' imaginations as they did mine; Will Hudson and his infectious optimism; Lindsay Liu and the team at Method; Max Gadney and Stefanie Posavec for guiding me around the new frontiers of data (next up: learn to code); Lucienne Roberts for being immensely generous with her time and a constant inspiration.

I also have to thank Derek, my co-writer, mentor, and general good egg: your enthusiasm for design, teaching, and life is truly extraordinary.